Aikido

O-Sensei's Sublime Synthesis

volume 1

An Anthology of Articles from the *Journal of Asian Martial Arts*

Compiled by Michael A. DeMarco, M.A.

Disclaimer
Please note that the authors and publisher of this book are not responsible in any manner whatsoever for any injury that may result from practicing the techniques and/or following the instructions given within. Since the physical activities described herein may be too strenuous in nature for some readers to engage in safely, it is essential that a physician be consulted prior to training.

All Rights Reserved
No part of this publication, including illustrations, may be reproduced or utilized in any form or by any means, electronic or mechanical, including photocopying, recording, or by any information storage and retrieval system (beyond that copying permitted by sections 107 and 108 of the US Copyright Law and except by reviewers for the public press), without written permission from Via Media Publishing Company.

Warning: Any unauthorized act in relation to a copyright work may result in both a civil claim for damages and criminal prosecution.

Copyright © 2016 by
Via Media Publishing Company
941 Calle Mejia #822
Santa Fe, NM 87501 USA
E-mail: md@goviamedia.com

All articles in this anthology were originally published in the *Journal of Asian Martial Arts*.
Listed according to the table of contents for this anthology:

Drengson, A. (1992)	Volume 1, Number 2	pages 58–69
Crawford, A. (1992)	Volume 1, Number 4	pages 28–43
Taylor, K. (1994)	Volume 3, Number 4	pages 64–103
Watson, C. (1996)	Volume 5, Number 1	pages 48–71
Grossman, E. (1998)	Volume 7, Number 2	pages 26–53
Suenaka, R. & Watson, C. (1998)	Volume 7, Number 4	pages 36–45
Ward, B. (1999)	Volume 8, Number 1	pages 50–55
Olson, G., Cook, M., & Brooks, L. (1999)	Volume 8, Number 2	pages 42–49
Dykhuizen, C.J. (2000)	Volume 9, Number 3	pages 8–31
Taylor, K. (2001)	Volume 10, Number 2	pages 60–75

Book and cover design by Via Media Publishing Company
Edited by Michael A. DeMarco, M.A.

Cover illustration
Artwork by Jon Parr
www.jonparr.com
Email: parrspen@hotmail.com

ISBN: 978-1893765252

w w w . v i a m e d i a p u b l i s h i n g . c o m

contents

iv **Preface**
by Michael DeMarco, M.A.

CHAPTERS

1 Aikido: Its Philosophy and Application
by Alan R. Drengson, Ph.D.

13 Spiritual v.s. Martial Aikido: Explanation and Reconcilation
by Christopher Watson, B.A.

35 The Martial Yen: American Participation in the Aikido Tradition
by Andrew Crawford, M.A.

53 Use of the Knife and Short Staff in Aikido Training
by Kimberley Taylor, M.Sc.

94 Toward a Semiosis of the Martial Arts:
Aikido as a Symbolic Form of Communication
by Eliot Lee Grossman, J.D.

121 Aikido Kokyunage: The Sublime & the Practical
by Roy Suenaka & Christopher Watson, B.A.

131 Energy Projection in Aikido Wrist Techniques
by Bob Ward, B.A.

136 Aikido's Armlock (ude-gatame) Technique: What Tissues are Affected?
by Gregory Olson, M.Sc., Morgan Cook, B.S., & Lisa Brooks, Ph.D.

143 Culture, Training, and Perception of the Martial Arts: Aikido's Example
by C. Jeffrey Dykhuizen, Ph.D.

167 Ukemiwaza: The Art of Attacking in Aikido
by Kimberley Taylor, M.Sc.

186 **Index**

preface

How can we fully understand aikido, or any other martial art for that matter, when we have only been exposed to part of it? While learning about the art, we can easily make assumptions and be tricked by false impressions. In most cases, even instructors do not have enough background to grasp the entirety of the art and are happy to work with part of it.

The content in this special two-volume anthology details the many facets of aikido as it was formulated by Morihei Ueshiba (1883–1969)—O-Sensei, the great teacher. Each chapter contributes to a piece of the aikido puzzle by providing historical details, insightful technical drills (bare handed and with weapons), and components that have flavored this art with a spiritual essence.

From the Ueshiba wellspring flows a number of streams—political splinter groups offering their own take on what aikido should be and how it should be practiced. Each branch may stand on its own, but a good number of scholars and practitioners prefer a more encompassing representation of what O-Sensei taught. So, chapters in these volumes help "put Humpty Dumpty back together again."

Volume I includes ten chapters and volume II another fourteen. The authors—twenty-three in all—present superb credentials as scholars and practitioners of aikido. On the academic side, you'll find chapters that detail aikido's philosophy, from ethical relationships and practical theory to the subtle spiritual dimension. A few authors highlight the circumstances regarding the transmission of aikido from teacher to student. Some authors show how culture influences the perception and understanding of aikido when it travels outside Japan.

Aikido is often practiced as a system of body movement encompassing a philosophy of peace and harmony. Others may focus on learning the art for its effective methods of self-defense. Composed of material previously published in the *Journal of Asian Martial Arts*, this two-volume anthology is heavy on the technical aspects of aikido that both teachers and students would benefit by reading. Training methods are discussed in detail, supported by hundreds of illustrations of attack and defense.

Whatever your primary interest is in aikido, *Aikido: O-Sensei's Sublime Synthesis* will prove to be a great reference for the scholar and practitioner. We hope this convenient collection of quality material dealing with Morihei Ueshiba's martial discipline will benefit your research and inspire the practice of this elegant art.

Michael A. DeMarco, Publisher
Santa Fe, New Mexico
February 2016

· 1 ·

Aikido: Its Philosophy and Application
by Alan R. Drengson, Ph.D.

Part I
HARMONY WITH NATURE AND THE UNIVERSE

Basic Concepts

My first interest in martial arts grew out of my study as a philosophy of Daoism and Zen Buddhism. In many respects one can fail to understand the concepts of these philosophies if one lacks the insights to be gained through an experience of their practice. The martial arts associated with these philosophies offer a Western student one of the most accessible routes to this deep understanding. After many years of study of martial arts and other meditative practices, what was once a scholarly interest has broadened into an enlarged way of life. From practice arises deepened experience which enables one to understand these philosophies in greater depth. One realizes that aikido is applicable to all aspects of one's life, not just in the *dojo* (place of practice of the Way).

Aikido is often characterized as the non-fighting martial art. Aikido, unlike most of the other arts, usually does not allow competition. Rarely does one find contests in which opponents are pitted against one another. Aikido is a martial art in which the primary focus is not defeating an opponent but overcoming the attachments within ourselves which kindle the conditions for aggression.

Ai:
- to combine; to unite; to gather; to collect
- to close; to shut

Ki:
- air; gas; vapor; atmosphere
- breath
- spirit; character
- bearing; manner
- influence

Do:
- road; path; street
- the "way" in a metaphysical sense
- way; method; principle

Aikido is a martial art in which the martial, or chivalrous, way is used to transcend the impulse to fight with others. Thus, aikido has important spiritual aspects that add significant dimensions to its highly purified, integrated and commanding arts of self-defense.

Aikido literally means "the way to spiritual harmony". The three words in aikido each have deep meaning in Japanese culture. *Ai* means not only "harmony", but is also a homonym for "love". The founder of aikido, Master Morihei Ueshiba (1883–1969), said that this art is "the spirit of loving protection for all beings." This spirit of loving protection that ai implies has affinities with Zen Buddhism and also with older traditions in Japanese Shintoism, which is a nature religion with great similarities to Daoism. *Ki* (*qi* in Chinese) means "spirit" or "energy". Ki has deep metaphysical, practical and experiential significance. The power of energy referred to here is considered in Japanese traditions as the natural universal energy that animates all that lives. Ancient Shintoism views nature as an animate, creative, organic, living unity, an ongoing process alive with consciousness and intelligence. Thus, ki refers to the creative force that is expressed not only in our actions, but also in our thoughts and feelings. Finally, *do* (*Dao* in Chinese) literally is a way or a road. It is most often used in the arts to mean a Way, as in a Way of life. Thus, aikido is said to be a Way to harmonize ourselves with the universal energy of nature. The various meditations, movements, evasions, submissions, exercises, postures and throws that form its practice have as their unifying principle the realization of our oneness in nature. In aikido the participants express through their movements the fundamental principles of the natural world. Aikido philosophy holds that by perfecting our capacities to move, stand, and sit properly, we can at the same time "correct" or purify ourselves in other ways. This means that aikido is a practical study in which its philosophy is expressed in the effective cultivation of the body and mind as a dynamic unity, integrated and unified by the cultivation of spiritual strength and the power of love and respect.

Value of Practice

The value of the martial arts in a balanced physical education program has become increasingly obvious to people in education. These arts have an important contribution to make to higher education, not only because of the backgrounds sketched above, but also because of the contribution they make to the cultivation of healthy, strong human beings. In aikido there is great stress on mutual respect and proper manners, which are integral to its broader philosophy of harmonious living. The cultivation of ourselves as spiritually developing beings should be seen as the center of education. Nothing is of greater importance to learning how to work effectively together than ethics. Our own cultural ideals, from the ancient Greeks onward, have stressed the importance of the harmonious development of the whole person: body, mind, and spirit. Realizing the good in our daily lives was stressed from Socrates on. Plato, in the *Republic* emphasized the importance of the rule of reason as involving the balanced development of the whole person. For him *The Good* must be realized through a long process of physical, mental, and spiritual discipline and training. The chivalrous tradition in the West also stressed the cultivation of not only strength and martial abilities, but also of spirit and manners.

The practice of aikido enables us to realize the extraordinary power of the human being when we are fully unified persons. Its movements and throws are effective because they develop and enhance the smooth flow of our naturally endowed inner power when this is used in harmony with universal energy.

Forms and Movement

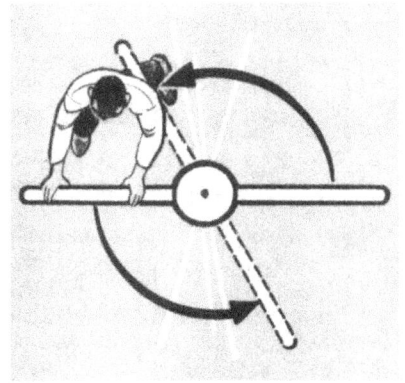

The aikidoist develops supple and graceful movements that issue from a center that is like a still point. Sensei Ishiyama, who teaches aikido in Victoria and Vancouver, compares this movement to that of a freely moving turnstile. Whoever pushes a turnstile with full force will be thrown away by his own force. In a similar fashion, aikido develops the capacity to remain stable and centered, like a gyroscope, while one is in dynamic motion. This produces a stability and solidness, as if one had three legs, at the same time as it enables one to move with dynamic nonresistance and flexibility. Its practice cultivates poise and balance in daily life which reflect the relaxed attention and concentration it enables us to develop.

Aikido founder O-Sensei Morihei Ueshiba (*O-Sensei* means great teacher) mastered all of the basic fighting arts, including the sword, spear, staff and hand-to-hand combat. These, together with his spiritual understanding, were combined and transcended to form the variety of movements basic to aikido. These basic movements allow for endless variations and improvisations. The patterns of movement in aikido begin with entering movements that move away from the line of attack, to place one in harmony with the partner's energy and also in the partner's most vulnerable spot. Other movements are circular, spherical, or describe a spiral or figure eight. The thrower (*nage*) guides the partner's (*uke*) body around his or her center of gravity. Nage and uke switch roles so that each takes the active and then the less active part. (The alternation of *in* and *yo* [*yin* and *yang* in Chinese] can be seen in this pattern of movement and practice. Here we see the complementary reconciliation of opposites and harmony resulting from their dynamic unity.) In this action the body moves as a unified whole, so that one's fingers, arms, shoulders, legs and toes all move together. A finger is not only a leading edge of movement, but points beyond itself as one projects one's energy (*ki*) beyond the finger tip. Students of aikido learn how to project or extend their power out from their center (*hara*) which is located about two inches below the navel. They are able to lead the partner's ki (and mind-body) in such a way that the throw happens almost by itself, as if the partner threw him/her self. Thus, one does not meet the partner's energy head on, but blends with, and directs this power away from oneself, so that it runs its course harmlessly and is resolved. This clearly requires the utmost of precise timing, balance, flexibility, breath power, and a very calm mind. Various exercises and mediations help to develop this concentration of great power, which expresses itself as gentle strength. From the standpoint of activities such as skiing, handball, tennis, and other sports, aikido can serve to improve one's abilities to concentrate, and move harmoniously with power. In other aspects of daily life, its applications are many and deep. We will turn to these in the second part of this essay.

Conclusion of Part I

Let us conclude this first part with words from founder O-Sensei Ueshiba:

> "Understand aikido first as a *budo* [martial art] and then as the ways of service to construct the human family... This is not mere theory. You practice it. Then you will accept the oneness of the power with nature."

Part II
AIKIDO AND DAILY LIFE

Coming to the Way

As was explained above, aikido is usually viewed as a noncompetitive martial art which stresses the development of the whole human being through working with others to realize the perfect forms of aikido in practice on the *tatami* (mats) in the *dojo* (place of practice of the Way). The various techniques and arts, the meditation, the ethics, the community sense, the emphasis by instructors and students on mutual respect, respect for the

Way, for teachers, for practice weapons, for the dojo, for flowers that have been placed on the shelf, for ourselves, for nature, these and many other things instruct us in the Way that is the heart of aikido. As we observed, "aikido" means a Way to realize harmony with the energy of the universe. That there are such Ways implies that the human person can become disharmonious.

We can feel a sense of separation and alienation from ourselves, from others, from the world, and from nature. Through unfortunate habits of living (which in part we inherit from our environment during a long period of total dependence and in part we originate) we find ourselves having difficulties. Perhaps we become aware of our disharmony because we have problems with fellow workers or we have conflicts within our family. There may be long standing feuds with relatives. Or, perhaps we feel sad or aggressive and we regret this. We might be afraid of dogs and do not want to be. There are a multitude of things that can lead us to feel that we are not at our best. Having realized there are problems, we may try to find ways to overcome what we think is the source of the problem. It is the other person who is at fault or the animal or nature. Then we try to change the other, but we fail to do so or maybe create even more difficulties. After struggling a while, we might give up. Out of this surrender may come an insight into our circumstances. We see our situation in a different way, as created by dynamic relationships. We realize that every situation is a result of relationships that we help in part to create. If this is so, each of us has the power to affect the quality of these relationships.

A fundamental change in the way we are in the world can alter their nature. The world is rich with creative possibilities and deep in meaning. We each have the creative spirit of the life force within us which can reconcile and harmonize these relationships.

By some such process as the above we might be led further to discover that there are ways of practice in certain disciplines that can release our creative powers. Seeing the world for its richness and realizing a sense of meaning in life involves, as Dr. Ishiyama observed in the Winter 1987 *Heartwood*, working with and being with others; it involves validating ourselves in a variety of ways. Seeking validation we are led by our own explorations to take up a discipline, a practice, a healing art, a Way.

As was mentioned above, I was drawn to aikido partly because I teach a course in Eastern philosophy. In my studies I had learned of the Japanese and Chinese conception of the Way (*Do, Dao*). The Way, as we have seen, is a lived philosophy of life, a practice, a spiritual discipline that cultivates persons so that they continuously evolve in *love* and *learning*. The ultimate realization of a Way is nothing less than enlightenment itself, which is a form of life or the Way of being that fully confirms life's intrinsic value and continuity. This is a confirmation of life that resolves our existential anxiety, our underlying fear of death.

DO

Ancient Script   "Grass" Script   Modern Script

Aikido and Zen

We have been reflecting upon the process of being drawn to a Way. Let us now reflect more on what a Way is by means of a story that Gary Snyder told in an interview in *East-West* 7/6 (June 1977) several years ago. It described how his perceptions changed when he saw the unity of practice of a Way in formal meditation (*zazen*) and in daily life. He had travelled to Japan to study Zen Buddhism. When he first entered the monastery, the *roshi* (teacher) told him just to observe life there for a while and he could gradually get involved in Zen practice. Snyder observed the monks during their formal meditation sessions in the *zendo* (place to practice meditation as the Way) and while they were at work. As he watched them, it occurred to him that many of their jobs could be made more productive by introducing certain changes. He made note of the various improvements he thought would be useful. When he got a chance, he talked with one of the monks. The monk listened politely, acknowledging the positive aspects of his ideas. Then he remarked that Snyder had overlooked one important thing.

From the Zen standpoint there is no difference between work, meditation and devotion to the Way. All of life is Zen (*zazen*). Snyder said that this came as a revelation to him, for in our traditions we tend to regard work as something to get through as fast as possible, so we can get on to things that are more important, and on to play. In the Way one does not make this kind of distinction between work and relaxation. The Way is both means and end. We purify ourselves, integrate, unify, validate, authenticate, harmonize and complete ourselves, as we live the Way. We are not, then, thinking of time running out. We are not in a hurry, trying to get to some grand, transcendental place or experience in the future. We try to live fully, completely and perfectly now. To paraphrase Zen Roshi Joshu Sasaki, realization of this perfection in daily life is the full realization of the meaning of religion; those who realize the perfection of this moment are fully religious and have no need for religion. The Way is to be realized in daily life.

The Way, then, is not restricted to the zendo or dojo, but is a practice that is in all that we do, whether working, meditating, doing martial arts, relaxing, being with others, working with animals, or just dwelling on the planet. Humans, perhaps unlike whales, must practice a Way. In aikido we learn of the Way through the practice of the martial art. What we learn in the dojo carries over to daily life. In aikido as a martial art we learn to match our *ki* (spiritual energy) with that of our partner in practice of the various forms (*kata*). We strive to harmonize our ki when practicing together with the *jo* (staff), *bokken* (wooden sword), *tanto* (wooden knife), or in the empty-handed techniques. Our ki is expressed in our whole vital force, which we project through full attention and in other ways involving full participation of the complete body/mind.

In aikido we practice exercises called *kokyuho* (breath) exercises. These help us to coordinate our breathing, harmonize the body-mind in focus of attention, and settle into the *hara* (which is our vital center of movement and energy just below the navel). With relaxed attentiveness and whole body movement, coordinated with the movements of others, matching our ki, we move together in a harmonious way. When done well there is a sense of completion together.

The aim of aikido is not to beat an opponent or to show that we are strong or to become enamored with technique, but to create beauty and harmony together. The purpose of practicing the martial art in the dojo is to purify our total self of all kinds of impurities, physiological, psychological, and spiritual. It increases our power, flexibility, capacity to relax, and ability to pay attention. It purges us of stress.

Aikido and Nature

By practicing aikido together we develop and purify ourselves and help one another to realize the Way. In this practice there is community spirit in our joint efforts. The purpose of aikido is realization of this harmony with each other and with nature. We can see this if we turn to an example of wilderness travel.

We climb a mountain together. If we climb in the spirit of aikido, we together appreciate and enjoy the activity. We help one another and are solicitous of each other's needs. We do not care who steps on the summit first or who leaves it last. If you are more secure on a certain type of pitch, you take the lead, but on other ground I might lead. We love the mountains together; we share enthusiasm. While climbing we set a pace that is comfortable for us both. Pace is important in climbing, for walking with the proper rhythm, where one's breathing and movement are coordinated, brings harmony to climbing the mountain; then it is not a struggle, but a joy. This allows us to draw on our full powers.

This form of climbing purifies the body/mind by the Way of Aiki. We become empty of small self and are filled with the Self of Nature. It is the total activity with its breathing meditation that pulls us out of the small mind of calculative thinking. In the dojo, aikido teaches us to learn pace, breathing, and harmony together; it enlivens the meditative mind. Only in aikido practice have I found the Way of Wilderness Travel in the city. In both activities, we can realize timelessness. In our climb together we realize love in the mountains, with the sky, with each other, with the animals, and with nature. We share mutual respect and affection. This is dwelling in a state of intrinsic value, which we can understand from the mental and physical practice of aikido and then in daily life.

Aikido and Work

We are sawing wood together. We live in the country and use wood for heat and cooking. We have no power tools and use handsaws. We take a well sharpened, two-person handsaw to the wooded lot. We prop up a log and we saw. First we are a little jerky; the saw gets pinched; our rhythm is not smooth or well coordinated. Then we begin to settle into the right pace. Our movements are synchronized. The saw begins to sing with an almost effortless movement, as we are each pulling the saw with just the right pressure and speed. We have settled into it. Our movements and breathing are one with the sawing.

The ringing whisper of the saw, resinous odors, the smell of mushrooms, the songs of birds, rustling leaves and wind in the fir boughs, these are all part of our sawing together. We saw in silence, then exchange a few words. We are together in the sun, doing good work. This harmonizing of ki (*aiki*) through community and communion of good work is the same as that realized when doing aikido together.

Aikido and Helping Others

Many years ago a friend went to work in a private psychiatric hospital. On his first day the supervisor took him aside and shared some of his knowledge. There were many people in this hospital who were suffering a great deal, and who often had little control. Some were potentially dangerous to themselves and to others. The supervisor did not want his young assistant to see this potential as threatening. He told my friend that he could not function effectively there without self control. He said that one must not let the patient control the situation by being out of control oneself. He said he would have to be alert so that he could be aware when a patient was becoming distressed. Be alert as well, he advised, to your own feelings. Do not conceal how you feel. Be authentic with the other person, but pay close attention so as not to let your feelings be pulled along with the other person's anger or fear. In aikido this would be described as maintaining one's own center. The thrower (*nage*) and the receiver (*uke*) match ki and the thrower becomes the center of movement; the partner's ki is redirected to create a beautiful nonviolent form.

My friend was then told that when he detected that the patient was becoming angry or distressed, he should not resist him, but first match his psychological energy with the patient's. When he had done this, he could then lower his own level of intensity. The other person would follow his energy (*ki*) and the situation would be resolved and balance restored. In aikido we meet the partner's attack by harmonizing and redirecting, rather than clashing with his or her ki. ("Loving attack" would be more accurate here, for we are referring to how the partner whole-heartedly grasps or strikes at *nage*, as he is invited to do.) My friend practiced what his supervisor had suggested, and after a time he was able to do what had been explained to him. His supervisor illustrated this art to him in actual situations, just as aikido instructors illustrate centering, matching, blending and redirecting. Honesty of practice and authenticity of self invite a like response from others.

A word of caution here. Some of the techniques just described could be misused as powerful ways to manipulate others, whether in clinical, martial or everyday settings. This is one of the reasons we must practice with an ethic of respect that aims for harmony with other persons. We must not be manipulative, but caring and respectful. In aikido philosophy we say that remaining centered, harmonizing ki, respecting other persons, and finally, realizing the love that *ai* implies is the Way in practice or daily life. When we say that we live the Way, we do not mean that we are perfect, but that we try to recognize and correct our errors, correct the flaws in our techniques and character, as we learn together. Seen from the standpoint of aikido as a Way, life is learning and loving. We do not deprive others of their efforts to learn or their own joy of discovery, but are helpful as friends are helpful, supportive but not meddling or judgmental.

Through practice in the dojo then, we increase our participation in life. Before taking up a Way our participation rate may have been low. Aikido increases our participation at every level, physiologically, psychologically, spiritually, in all our activities and relationships. We become more fully alive through it.

Aikido and Child Rearing

One can learn the essence of aikido as a Way of life from many fine teachers both in the dojo and out. Some of the most important lessons can be learned in daily life from children, other adults and animals. Playing with, learning from and loving one's children gives one unlimited opportunities to learn to live the Way more fully. I once asked an aikido friend about raising children, for I was newly a father, and he was a father of experience. Our first daughter was about two at the time. I was concerned that she needed to learn discipline and wondered whether it should start early. This was an expectation that came out of my parents' background. I asked him about discipline and children. He smiled and said, "Love them as much as you can, while you have a chance because, before you know it, they will not be around much, and their peers will be very important to them." For me his response expressed the spirit of aikido. As soon as he said this, I realized in what ways my thinking was in error.

If we want our children to realize the love that is at the heart of the Way, we can only help them to learn by being compassionate. Then we can share our knowledge and learn together. We must respect them, for how else can they learn self-respect and respect for others, unless we respect them? This does not mean that we do not show them right ways to do things, but we respect their unique nature, and we learn from them as well. In this way we draw out of our relationships with others that which is best for both of us. The Way is as simple and as difficult as this: simple in concept, but difficult to realize perfectly in each situation, whether it is doing a martial art, counselling, teaching, or washing dishes. We can approach a situation with indifference, with fear, with anger and with aggressiveness, or we can give each situation our full caring attention.

In aikido we do not overcome enemies, but work with partners in cooperation and friendship. The patience and kindness of aikido instructors exemplifies the spirit of aikido, and as its students we try to carry this attitude and approach into our relationships outside of the dojo. When we are able to give our daily life our fullest caring attention, we have learned what Socrates and Professor Morihei Ueshiba would have called the Art of living properly and well. Aikido practice attunes the entire self so that we can be our best in whatever we are doing. It is not for the dojo alone, but for the whole of life.

Aikido as Love: Words from the Founder

It is appropriate to end this essay with these words from the founder of aikido, O-Sensei Morihei Ueshiba:

> "True budo [chivalrous, martial Way] is a work of love. It is a work of giving life to all beings and not killing or struggling with each other. Love is the guardian deity of everything. Nothing can exist without it. Aikido is the realization of love . . . True budo is the loving protection of all beings with a spirit reconciliation. Reconciliation means to allow the completion of everyone's mission... I want considerate people to listen to the voice of aikido. It is not for correcting others; it is for correcting your own mind. This is aikido. This is the mission aikido and should be your mission."

Bibliography

Creel, H. (1958). *Chinese thought from Confucius to Mao.* New York: Mentor.

Drengson, A. (1980, January). Aikido: Its background and philosophy. *Rim Express 1* (1987, Winter).

Aikido: Harmony with the universe. *Heartwood* 5, 14 and 20.

Drengson, A. (1987, Spring). Aikido in daily life. *Heartwood* 6, 17–20.

Heckler, R. (Ed.) (1985). *Aikido and the new warrior.* Berkeley, CA: North Atlantic Books.

Ishiyama, F.I. (1987, Winter). Self-validation. *Heartwood* 5.

Kapleau, P. (1980). *Three pillars of Zen.* New York: Doubleday/Anchor.

Kauz, H. (1977). *The martial spirit.* Woodstock, NY: Overlook Press.

Klickstein, B. (1987). *Living aikido.* Berkeley, CA: North Atlantic Books.

Lao Tzu. (1963). *Tao te ching.* (D.C. Lau, Trans.). Baltimore: Penguin.

Leonard, G. (1975). *The ultimate athlete.* New York: Viking Press.

Ono, S. (1970). *Shinto: The kami way.* (W.P. Woodard, Trans.). Tokyo: Charles Tuttle Publishing Co.

Plato. (1977). *Plato's Republic.* (G. Grube, Trans.). Indianapolis: Hackett.

Ross, N. (1966). *Three ways of asian wisdom.* New York: Simon and Schuster.

Stevens, J. (1987). *Abundant peace.* Boston, MA: Shambhala.

Stiskin, N. (1972). *The looking glass god: Shinto, yin-yang, and a cosmology for today.* Tokyo and London: Weatherhill.

Suzuki, D.T. (1956). *Zen Buddhism: Selected writings.* (W. Barrett, Ed.). New York: Doubleday.

Suzuki, D.T. (1970). *Zen Buddhism and Japanese culture.* Princeton, NJ: Princeton University Press.

Ueshiba, K. (1986). *The spirit of aikido.* Tokyo: Kodansha.

Ueshiba, K. (1969). *Aikido.* Tokyo: Kodansha.

Victoria Aikikai. (no date). *Aikido forum: Journal of aikido education and training.* Victoria: Aikikai.

Watts, A. (1975). *Tao: The watercourse way.* New York: Pantheon Press.

Westbrook, A. and Ratti, O. (1970). *Aikido and the dynamic sphere.* Rutland, VT, and Tokyo: Charles Tuttle.

Yamada, Y. (1981). *The new aikido complete.* New York: Lyle Stuart.

Moriehei Ueshiba in his Iwama dojo. Aiki Festival, April, 1964.
All photos courtesy of R. Suenaka.

· 2 ·

Spiritual v.s. Martial Aikido: Explanation and Reconcilation
by Christopher Watson, B.A.

The word "aikido" is written with three characters: *ai*, for harmony; *ki*, meaning breath or life energy; and *do*, for the way. Thus, aikido lends itself to numerous, though similar, translations. The most common are "the way of spiritual harmony," "the way of universal harmony" or "the way of harmonizing one's spirit with the spirit of the Universe." Just as numerous are the ways the art is perceived and understood, both by its practitioners and the uninitiated. I was once told by an instructor at a jujutsu school that aikido was really just "watered down Daito-ryu," just as I once read a fervent published discourse by an aikido practitioner who insisted aikido was never meant to be a method of practical self-defense, but solely a spiritual pursuit. While both opinions contain elements of truth, neither is wholly accurate and both demonstrate a basic lack of understanding of the art, most notably its history. The prevailing opinion seems to be that aikido is either a wholly spiritual pursuit without practical self-defense value or a purely physical one, effective only if regressed to its more brutal Daito-ryu roots with spirituality relegated to off-mat contemplation.

Before one can reconcile these divergent perceptions, one must first understand their origins, to wit, by examining the life of Morihei Ueshiba, founder of aikido, and the more contemporary history of one of its most celebrated practitioners, Koichi Tohei, founder of the International Ki Society and Shin-Shin Toitsu Aikido.

Aikido founder Morihei Ueshiba was born December 14, 1883, in Tanabe City, Wakayama prefecture on the main island of Honshu, Japan. A rather sickly child given to frequent illness, O-Sensei ("Great Teacher," as he is known by aikido practitioners) was more inclined towards academic and spiritual pursuits than physical ones, studying Shingon Buddhism beginning at age seven, then later Zen Buddhism, as well as demonstrating an aptitude for mathematics. Even at this early age, Ueshiba's spiritual bent was evident. Because of his frail nature, his father, Yoroku, a respected local businessman and political leader, encouraged his young son to engage in more physical activities, such as swimming and sumo.

When Ueshiba was twelve years old, Yoroku Ueshiba was roughed up by some local toughs employed by one of his political opponents. Intent on avenging his father's beating, young Morihei vowed to develop himself to the peak of physical power and martial prowess. To this end he traveled Japan, learning as much as he could from the masters he encountered before moving on. As a result, by his early twenties Ueshiba had studied arts as varied as *kenjutsu* (particularly the Yagyu-ryu school of swordsmanship), *jodo*, *Aioi-ryu* and *Hozoin-ryu* spear and bayonet arts, and jujutsu.

Many features of these diverse arts would later help to shape aikido. Ueshiba also saw active combat duty as a soldier during the Russo-Japanese War. As his martial prowess increased, so did his physical strength until in his prime, five-foot one-inch Ueshiba weighed nearly two hundred pounds. Photographs of him from the 1930's and 1940's show a solid, squarely-built man with massive shoulders and wrists and forearms thick as two-by-fours.

The most significant stage in Ueshiba's martial development occurred in 1912, when twenty-nine-year old Ueshiba led an expedition of settlers to the frigid northern island of Hokkaido. It was here that he encountered Sokaku Takeda, acknowledged master of the unforgiving art of Daito-ryu jujutsu, whose fierce appearance and temperament were reflected in his martial technique. Ueshiba studied exclusively with Takeda, serving as the master's personal disciple and receiving his *menkyo-kaiden* teaching certificate some five years later. More than any other art, it is Daito-ryu that would most profoundly affect the development of aikido.

In late 1919, upon receiving news that his father was gravely ill, Ueshiba departed Hokkaido for home. This journey marks the beginning of the most significant phase of the founder's spiritual development. Along the way, he stopped in Ayabe to meet Onisaburo Deguchi, leader of the new Omoto-Kyo Shinto sect, known for its meditation techniques designed to unify one's spirit with the Divine. Though this visit lasted barely a month, Deguchi made a deep impression on Ueshiba and, upon his father's death the following January, Ueshiba returned to Ayabe and began a relationship with Deguchi and Omoto-Kyo that would last the rest of his life.

In order to understand the origin of aikido's spiritual aspect, it is essential to note that as Ueshiba's study of Daito-ryu profoundly affected his martial technique, his study of Omoto-Kyo equally affected his spiritual development. In 1922, Ueshiba formally incorporated the two, the brutally physical and the transcendently spiritual, into a system he called aiki-bujutsu, which may be translated as "the martial system of spiritual harmony." Despite its forgiving name, the Daito-ryu influence was readily apparent in Ueshiba-ryu aiki-bujutsu, which relied heavily on the former system's excruciating joint-immobilizing techniques and bone-shattering throws. Whereas the aikido of Ueshiba's later years relied much on evasive, indirect turning and blending techniques (*tenkan*) now widely identified with the art, this infant version of aikido relied more on forceful, direct entering techniques (*irimi*) (however, irimi techniques still constitute a substantial portion of the aikido repertoire). Yet, throughout it all, the physical and the spiritual were inextricably intertwined; rather than creating conflict, one served to illuminate and feed the other, like two flames burning atop a common candle.

Just as essential to the evolution of Ueshiba's technique was the inexorable changes in society during his life. Born less than twenty years after the start of Japan's Meiji

Restoration, Ueshiba witnessed the rapid, forced decline of the militant feudal samurai state and the political rise of the mercantile classes. Although the samurai code of bushido was still very much alive, ingrained as it was into the basal fabric of Japanese cultural consciousness, solving disputes and satisfying honor with the strike of the sword was no longer acceptable. The traditional techniques were forced to redefine themselves, evolving with and adapting to the changing times, or perishing. Thus, kenjutsu, the martial system of swordsmanship, became kendo, the way of the sword; the hoary roots of jujutsu bore the new fruit of judo, and so on.

Likewise, as he studied under the martial masters of his day, gaining in physical ability and wisdom, Ueshiba recognized the necessity of this change. Daily practice of martial systems, even when great care was taken, often resulted in serious, sometimes crippling injury. Ueshiba saw this as self-defeating. Rather than viewing the attacker (*uke*) and defender (*nage*) as separate entities, he viewed them as a whole, for without one there was no need for the other. "To injure an opponent is to injure yourself," wrote Ueshiba. "To control aggression without inflicting injury is the Art of Peace" (Ueshiba, 1992: 64). This should not be seen as an argument for complete passivity nor renunciation of the necessity for physical self-defense. More directly, Ueshiba recognized the need for physical technique to evolve in a way that accommodated his philosophy while remaining an effective martial system.

In 1925, the third most profound experience of Ueshiba's life took place. Challenged to a wooden-sword (*bokken*) duel by a visiting naval officer, Ueshiba declined, instead meeting the officer's challenge by merely moving out of the way of his increasingly more frantic strikes until the officer lay exhausted on the mat, defeated by his own aggression, while Ueshiba was victorious, having never once landed a blow or injuring his opponent. Afterwards, Ueshiba walked out into his garden and, in his words, experienced a "golden light" descending on him from heaven, accompanied by complete clarity of thought and a unification of mind, body and spirit. It was then Ueshiba realized that "the true nature of budo is in the loving protection of all things," a philosophy that, to this day, lies at the heart of aikido (Stevens, 1987: 32–33; Ueshiba, K., 1984: 98).

To this end, in 1936, Ueshiba changed the name of his system from aiki-bujutsu to aiki-budo, "the martial way of spiritual harmony (Ueshiba, 1991: 14). Around 1941, spurred in part by his profound despair at the increasing militarism of the Japanese government, Ueshiba began calling his system aikido (ibid, p. 18).

To see films for the first time of Ueshiba in action in his later years is a curious experience. Attackers come charging in, only to be dispatched with what appears to be an ineffectual wave of the hand or a light, guiding touch to the attacker's body. Many observers are skeptical, concluding that the attackers must be "faking it," merely pretending to be thrown and agreeably taking the fall, in deference to their teacher. Yet those fortunate enough to have had the opportunity to study under the founder will tell you that attacking Ueshiba was like being caught up in a whirlwind.

Many times they were hard-pressed to figure out how they'd been thrown. That Ueshiba was able to repel attackers without touching them, merely by leading their mind and their ki, is eloquent testimony to his extraordinary spiritual and martial development, attained only after a lifetime totally devoted to arduous, ceaseless study.

As students studied with Ueshiba, so too did they leave and open their own aikido schools. The technique they taught was not only flavored by individual skill, but by the state of Ueshiba's martial and spiritual evolution at the time of their study with him. One who studied with Ueshiba in his pre-war days will demonstrate a much more aggressive *irimi* (direct entering) style of technique, more akin to Daito-ryu, than one who studied with the founder in the 1960's. Similarly, what these students comprehended of the founder's technique and philosophy, regardless of when they studied with him, equally affected their teaching.

Often in his later years, Ueshiba was said to comment, "This old man is still learning." Aikido for him was never static, never meant to be a finite catalog of techniques of which one can take a mental snapshot at any given time, but rather a life-long spiritual journey along the path of Aiki, of harmony with the Universal spiritual force, the energy of Creation, with progress both aided by and manifested in competence in physical technique, not separate elements, but one and the same, continually evolving and born from a cultivated, fundamental connection with Aiki. "When the myriad variations in the universal breath can be sensed," Ueshiba wrote, "the individual techniques of the Art of Peace are born" (Ueshiba, 1992: 22). He expressed this philosophy as *takemusu aiki*, a spiritual state in which perfect physical techniques arise spontaneously out of this connection with the Universe. It is not an evolution of technique in the sense of modifying the mechanics of the techniques themselves or discounting their martial value, as is often mistakenly thought, but an evolution of skill and spirituality so that Ueshiba's techniques become so ingrained in one's being that they evolve from a rote, conscious, physical maneuver to a natural, unconstrained, pure expression of spirit (Stevens, 1987: 111–112). Again, in the words of Ueshiba, "In essence, the sword is the soul of the warrior and a manifestation of the true spirit of the universe; thus, when you draw a sword you are holding your soul in your hands" (Ueshiba, 1991: 31). This was aikido as envisioned and expressed by the founder: a fundamental blending of the physical and spiritual designed to bring mind, body and spirit into perfect harmony so that one may live perfectly and spontaneously.

Though it is the intent of all earnest aikido practitioners to truly embody the philosophy of *takemusu aiki*, it can be a daunting pursuit, a goal perhaps none but the most gifted can attain. It is inevitable that the primary students of Ueshiba, those most responsible for spreading aikido across the world, latched onto that which they best comprehended of the founder's philosophy and concentrated their energies there, sincerely espousing that this or that was the essence of the art, ignoring or perhaps discounting what they could not grasp or bring to their technique. This should not be taken as a criticism but viewed simply as human nature, and one of the reasons there are so many different aikido styles and philosophies today, as there are varying styles within other martial systems. However, there is another reason, born as much of political as philosophical differences, which can be traced to the first deliberate effort by Ueshiba to spread aikido beyond Japan.

Suenaka (r) and Tohei at a party honoring
Ueshiba's Hawaiian visit at Punalu. March 1961.

In February of 1961, Ueshiba was invited to Hawaii to preside over opening ceremonies of the first aikido dojo established there. At a farewell party held in his honor just before his departure from Japan, Ueshiba briefly addressed the assembled well-wishers, summarizing his feelings thusly:

> The reason I'm going to Hawaii is to build a Silver Bridge of understanding. I have been building a Golden Bridge, within Japan, but I also wanted to build bridges overseas and through aikido to cultivate mutual understanding between East and West. I want to build bridges everywhere and connect all people through harmony and love. This I believe to be the task of aikido.
> – Ueshiba, K., 1984: 121

Although Ueshiba's first and only visit to Hawaii did not occur until 1961, construction of his Silver Bridge, or "Shinbashi," began with Koichi Tohei's visit there in February of 1953, at the invitation of Dr. Katsuzo Nishi, owner of the Nishi Kai health club in Honolulu (Tohei, 1976: 89). Born January 17, 1920, Tohei, a former judo practitioner, had just turned thirty-three years old at the time of this historic first visit. Having begun his study of what was then known as *aiki-budo* in 1939, by 1953 Tohei was ranked eighth degree and was chief instructor (*shihan bucho*) at the Aikikai Hombu, all of which made him a natural choice to introduce this relatively new martial art to the Western world. Among those attending this first formal U.S. demonstration of aikido was Roy Yukio Suenaka.

Suenaka was born in Honolulu and began his martial education in 1944, at age four, under his father. He began his aikido study at age twelve upon Koichi Tohei's 1953 visit to Hawaii. As an Air Force serviceman in 1961, he traveled to Japan and Okinawa, studying for eight years directly under Tohei and Ueshiba at the Aikikai Hombu, where he was a live-in student (*uchideshi*), then later a personal disciple to Tohei. When Tohei formally separated from the Aikikai in 1974 to develop the International Ki Society, Suenaka went with him and was Southeastern U.S. Ki Society representative and a chief Ki Society lecturer before himself breaking away in 1976 to form his own organization, the American International Ki Development and Philosophical Society. During his life, his instructors have also included judo's Yukiso Yamamoto (who later himself concentrated his study on aikido), Kazuo Ito and Kyuzo Mifune, Kodenkan jujutsu's Henry Seishiro Okazaki, kendo's Shuji Mikami, Kosho-ryu kempo master James Masayoshi Mitose, and Hakutsuru Shorin-ryu karate founder Hohan Soken. He is ranked second degree in kendo, third degree in judo and jujutsu, and sixth degree in Hakutsuru Shorin-ryu karate, his rank awarded by Hohan Soken himself.

Left: Suenaka (l) with Koichi Tohei at Iwana. April, 1964. Center: Suenaka (r) and Koichi Tohei at the Ki Society Headquarters in Tokyo. Summer, 1971. Right: Suenaka (r) with tenth-dan judo master Kazuo Ito at the Kodokan in Tokyo. Winter, 1969.

Left, left to right: Mrs. Soken, Mrs. Kanako Suenaka, Valeries and John Suenaka, Hohan Soken. Photo taken at Soken's home. Right: Suenaka with Hakutsuru Shorin-ryu karate grandmaster Hohan Soken at his dojo in Okinawa. Summer, 1970.

He received an *okuden* certificate of advanced aikido proficiency from Koichi Tohei and a *menkyo kaiden* certificate of aikido mastery from Ueshiba. He is recognized as eighth degree in aikido by the International Black Belt Federation and was one of the first people to teach aikido in many parts of the world, including establishing one of the first U.S. aikido schools in Sacramento, California, in 1958 and opening the first successful aikido school in Okinawa in 1961. Today, he resides in Charleston, South Carolina, where he teaches Suenaka-Ha Tetsugaku-Ho Aikido and Hakutsuru Sohrin-Ryu Karate.

As a former senior apprentice of Koichi Tohei, Suenaka was directly involved in many of the events that led to the rift between Tohei and the Aikikai following Ueshiba's death and the subsequent formation of the Ki Society and development of Tohei's Shin-Shin Toitsu style of aikido. It is this rift which, perhaps more than any other single cause, gave rise to the "spiritual" versus "martial" schools of aikido thought and practice, particularly in the U.S. Very little has been published concerning Tohei's separation from the Aikikai, other than what Tohei himself wrote. The account which follows is based on Tohei's published record, augmented by Suenaka's observations and recollection as a participant in the events.

Suenaka with Ueshiba at Iwama, home of the Aiki Jina (shrine). April. 1964.

Suenaka (r) with Kissomaru Ueshiba at Iwama. April, 1964.

Although the well-documented split between Koichi Tohei and the Aikikai officially occurred in 1974 with Tohei's formal proclamation of Shin-Shin Toitsu Aikido, the underlying differences leading to the sundering of relations were apparent years earlier, even before Ueshiba's death in April of 1969. In the years following Tohei's initial Hawaiian visit, he grew in reputation and in skill. As chief Hombu instructor, he was charged with overseeing and in many ways shaping the technique that was taught there, in addition to continuing to make occasional visits to the U.S. and other countries, while Ueshiba's son and successor, Kisshomaru Ueshiba Doshu, although an active teaching presence, primarily concerned himself with administrative duties. Koichi Tohei was a popular figure, a superb technician whose powerful technique and undeniable command of ki were matched by his charismatic personality. As such, he was an extremely effective instructor and salesperson for aikido, as history attests.

Over the course of his martial and personal development, as he distilled Ueshiba's spiritual teachings into language the less-enlightened could comprehend and codified the founder's techniques, Tohei began also to expand on Ueshiba's teachings. Much of this change was a direct reflection of Tohei's studies, beginning in 1946, with Shin-Shin Toitsu-Do founder Tempu Nakamura (Tohei, 1976: 87; Pranin, 1991: 78), who taught meditative techniques designed to unify mind and body and develop ki awareness (Shin-Shin Toitsu Aikido, or "Aikido with Mind and Body Coordinated," is an obvious reflection of the strong influence Nakamura's teachings had on him). In many ways, Tohei's involvement with Nakamura mirrored Ueshiba's alliance with Onisaburo Deguchi, for just as Ueshiba's time with Deguchi further aroused and developed his spiritual nature, so too did Tohei's studies with Nakamura.

While at first Nakamura's teachings served to augment Tohei's lessons under Ueshiba, aiding him in his own journey towards spontaneously executing techniques (takemusu aiki), they also helped precipitate a fundamental change in Tohei's martial philosophy and teaching style. Ultimately, his Hombu classes stressed ki development more than physical aikido technique, contrary to Hombu doctrine. Although the quality of his physical technique remained undiminished, there appeared a deliberate separation of spirituality and martial application. Suenaka recalls Tohei often spent most of his class time teaching what he dubbed the "four basic principles" to unify mind and body (keep one point, relax completely, weight underside, extend ki) and his six ki training methods, which included the four basic principles plus *ibukino-ho* breathing techniques, *aiki taiso* (basic exercises which embody actual aikido physical technique, much like kata), *seizaeno-ho* seated meditation, *kiatsu-ho* pressure-point massage therapy, and *ki-no-kempo* weapons techniques, primarily with the *jo* (Tohei, 1976: 16–23; 1974a; 1974b; 1978).

Tohei has written that his reason for increasing emphasis on ki in his teaching was that he felt the Aikikai, in the years following the founder's death, was shifting its emphasis in the opposite direction, with no discussion of ki and no effort to incorporate it into aikido technique. In his *Book of Ki: Co-ordinating Mind and Body in Daily Life*, Tohei writes he was "shocked" at the state of aikido being taught at the Aikikai:

> Most people only practiced aikido techniques and forgot Ki development.... people not only became unable to understand Ki but also ceased using the word. Techniques became incorrect and if a strong man held most students, they could not move him. If it were left as it was, Master Ueshiba's aikido would become merely formal techniques.
> —Tohei, 1976: 90

Believing the state of techniques at the Aikikai, as he perceived it, was contrary to Ueshiba's teachings, Tohei felt compelled to stress ki and ki development in his own teachings to compensate. This shift in emphasis, combined with Tohei's powerful personality, quickly placed him at loggerheads with Kisshomaru Ueshiba, as the latter saw Tohei's growing insistence on teaching ki development techniques as a direct challenge to his authority as aikido *Doshu* (Leader of the Way).

Following Ueshiba's death, the philosophical and political tensions between Tohei and Doshu quickly bubbled to the surface. Barely six months passed before Tohei called Suenaka and the rest of his closest disciples together at his Tokyo apartment and asked them to declare allegiance to either him or the Aikikai, saying that changes were afoot but declining to give details; it could be that at the time Tohei was himself unsure of exactly what he intended to do. Suenaka recalls the prevailing mood as one not of betrayal of Ueshiba's principles, but rather an inevitable further alliance with who had been for him and his fellows their primary instructor before Ueshiba died, even more so now that Ueshiba was gone. Their understanding was that by allying themselves with Tohei they were making a political declaration only, while staying true to Ueshiba's memory and philosophies and continuing to practice the techniques he developed.

In the years between this first informal meeting of Tohei's disciples and his official separation from the Aikikai in 1974, the tensions between Tohei and Doshu steadily increased. Tohei attempted to establish an exclusively ki training curriculum at the

Hombu, utilizing his methods, but Doshu made it clear that if Tohei were to remain chief Hombu instructor, he would have to do so on Doshu's terms, teaching as Doshu saw fit (Tohei, 1976: 89–90; Pranin, 1991: 121). This Tohei was not prepared to do. A draconian agreement was struck therefore. Writes Tohei:

> If the Aikido Headquarters was not going to teach Ki Development, I would have to teach it outside. But if I taught aikido outside in the position of Chief Instructor at the Aikido Headquarters, it would severely embarrass the organization. I made the following five promises to the Second Doshu:
>
> 1) No aikido techniques will be taught in Ki classes.
> 2) No aikido names will be used in Ki classes.
> 3) The facilities of the Aikido Headquarters will not be used for Ki classes.
> 4) No funds of the Aikido Headquarters will be used for Ki classes.
> 5) No aikido students will be invited to attend Ki classes.
>
> –Tohei, 1976: 90

In other words, Tohei's divorce from the Aikikai was to be absolute. This agreement led to the formation of Tohei's Ki no Kenkyukai in September of 1971 and the Ki Society. ". . . Doshu must have thought that I could not do Ki Development without using the name aikido or aikido techniques," Tohei writes. "I named my organization the Ki Society and taught only unification of mind and body, without teaching aikido techniques" (ibid). Still, Tohei retained a formal, though strained relationship with the Aikikai and Doshu.

In late summer of 1973, Tohei conducted a one-week seminar at the University of California, Fullerton, at which he requested his disciples be present (Tohei, 1975: 29). Suenaka and others were told to prepare for major changes, as Tohei was now making no secret of his plans to completely separate from the Aikikai; the only question remaining was when. The chief topic of discussion was the further expansion of the Ki Society and the particulars of Tohei's new ki training system. Central to this system was the philosophy that aikido was not to be performed or taught for purposes of self-defense, but solely as a vehicle for demonstrating the power and potential of ki. In order for this to occur—and again, to honor his agreement with Doshu—Tohei realized the technique itself must undergo a fundamental change. Consequently, he introduced a new body of techniques, both modified from existing aikido techniques and completely new, which he dubbed the "*taigi*," or body exercises. The body exercises were not techniques in the conventional sense, nor should they be confused with an attacker's movements (*aiki taiso*). Rather, the body exercises contained what Tohei felt were the essential techniques of what he would soon officially call Shin-Shin Toitsu Aikido.

Like his organizational peers, Suenaka received Tohei's updated teaching syllabus, including the body exercises. He recalls the first as seven sets of five basic techniques, similar to existing aikido technique but bearing different names. The primary difference was that the attacker (*uke*) and defender (*nage*) were to cooperate completely with one another in executing the techniques. There was to be no resistance at all from either party. If the defender moved, the attacker was to obligingly move with him and literally throw himself for the defender. Also, there was no *atemi*, no preemptive striking techniques, which Ueshiba clearly employed as an essential facet of his technique (Ueshiba, 1991), although less so in later years as his martial evolution made it largely unnecessary.

The significance of Tohei's introduction of the body exercises and the effect it had on the general perception of aikido cannot be underestimated. Cooperation between attacker and defender is essential when first learning aikido technique, as it is in any martial art. The attacker at first offers but token resistance, allowing the novice defender to feel the technique, to become familiar with the physical mechanics. Obviously, as the defender's skill increases, so too does the resistance offered by the attacker. But it is not resistance for its own sake; attacker and defender are still cooperating, in the true spirit of Aiki, and both are skilled enough to prevent injury to one another even if techniques are performed at full speed and with significant, "real" force. What Tohei was advocating effectively annulled aikido's practical self-defense efficacy. With the attacker offering no resistance, it is self-evident that the defender can never truly know the real authority or practical validity of his technique; by design, the body exercises had no conventional martial applications at all.

Tohei's introduction of the body exercise was met with mixed feelings by many of his senior students. While they all loved their teacher and felt tremendous loyalty to him, here they were being asked to dramatically alter their techniques in deference to this loyalty, in effect, to discard Ueshiba's teachings for what, regardless of good intentions, had become political reasons. Indeed, Tohei eventually went so far as to order his senior students to remove the founder's portrait from their dojos, a further sign of his utter separation from the Aikikai. This dramatic directive undeniably arose from a similar order from the Aikikai. According to Tohei,

> In March, 1974, an order was sent to all instructors and students in America that I was no longer to be welcomed into the dojos in America. I made my final decision to leave when I heard that the Aikido Headquarters had made the instructors in America remove my picture from the walls of their dojos.
> —Tohei, 1976: 90

Tohei's formal declaration of separation from the Aikikai came on May 1st of the same year, and with it his official announcement of the birth of Shin-Shin Toitsu Aikido (ibid).

For Suenaka, the conflicts created by Tohei's demands were too much to bear. While he believed that much of Tohei's ki teachings had merit, he felt he could not renounce his loyalty to Ueshiba's memory and teachings in deference to his loyalty to Tohei. In 1976, Suenaka officially resigned from the International Ki Society and formed the American International Ki Development and Philosophical Society (AIKDPS), teaching a synthesis of what he learned under both Ueshiba and Tohei, which he dubbed Suenaka-Ha Tetsugaku-Ho Aikido (Suenaka style, philosophical way). The use of the more modest *hu* to denote a branch of a style, rather than *ryu* to denote an exclusive style or system, was a deliberate choice. Aikido was not Suenaka's system, but Ueshiba's, yet the style was a conscious melding of Ueshiba's and Tohei's teachings, an offshoot, so to speak, of both. Similarly, using the word *tetsugaku* reflects Suenaka's belief in Tohei's ki training methods, excepting the body exercises, in concert with Ueshiba's philosophy of takemusu aiki, just as the name of Suenaka's organization, the AIKDPS, reflects Tohei's Ki Society influence. Ultimately, Suenaka was guided by Ueshiba's last words to him, in the months before his death: "Never stray from the Path of Aiki." Thus, in his severance from both the Aikikai and Ki Society, Suenaka brought the two back together, the martial and the spiritual, as Ueshiba intended.

So what place, then, does the ki that is at the heart of aikido really have in physical techniques? Is it, as some assert, simply universal love for all things, with no place in physical techniques, by definition, incompatible with a martial philosophy? This, by Tohei's estimation, would seem to be the view taken by the Aikikai and what led to his separation. Suenaka makes a specific distinction between ki in the broader sense of Universal love and ki as it pertains to the practical execution of proper aikido technique:

> Ki in terms of aikido means the latent energy within a person. For instance, if someone is excited, or if someone is afraid of something, his body automatically produces adrenaline to make him stronger, to make him faster. That's what ki is all about in aikido—the ability to call upon this energy, to utilize it and control it without having to be excited or scared and, in so doing, to perform a technique with the proper amount of strength necessary for that technique to work against a certain size person or in a certain situation. Of course, at the same time you have to utilize proper technique, to use the attacker's force also. I do not mean to say that ki is adrenaline, but it is like adrenaline. For aikido purposes, you can define ki as spiritual adrenaline. It is a very real energy, energy of purpose and of intent, of focus, of uniting body, mind and spirit together in one moment, to allow ki to flow through you and through your technique (personal interview).

"In our techniques we enter completely into, blend totally with, and control firmly an attack," Ueshiba wrote. "Strength resides where one's ki is concentrated and stable; confusion and maliciousness arise when ki stagnates" (Ueshiba, 1992: 93). Therefore, without a conscious application of ki and ki principles, aikido becomes simply the physical manipulation of joints and limbs, a battle of strength against strength, or speed against speed, a purely physical contest, contrary to Ueshiba's philosophy. On a more practical plane, it's a good way to get hurt or to cause unnecessary injury to your attacker, the same situation that led Ueshiba to place Aiki at the heart of his martial philosophy. Ultimately, aikido technique without ki is much less effective than aikido with ki, as Suenaka explains:

> I have met some people who have studied purely physical aikido for a number of years, who say, "Aikido does not need ki to work." These same people have no real power in their technique. They have no knowledge of the true mechanics of aikido, the subtlety. They move physically, and that's it. They use all muscle. If they're extremely strong, they might get it to work, but not likely. Even a weaker person will be able to resist against a stronger person who does not use ki in his technique, and of course, a stronger person won't be affected at all, and no matter how strong you are, there is always someone out there who is stronger. So strength alone is insufficient. But, if you know the mechanics of proper technique, and proper flow of ki, you can throw someone very easily, no matter how strong they are. Even if you have good technique, but no ki, it isn't aikido, and it won't be as effective (personal interview).

Accepting this, how then does one reconcile effective physical technique with the "softer" aspects of ki?

> It's true that aikido is an art that should enable you to be able to put down an attacker, for good if you have to. But that's not the aim of aikido. You have to resolve the situation, but in a way that will not harm the attacker. That's part of what Ueshiba meant by "the loving protection of all things." It doesn't mean you don't hurt your attacker at all, because aikido is a method of self-defense. It means that you do only what is necessary to gain control of a situation, causing as little harm to the attacker as you can in the process.
>
> Some people go to the opposite extreme, and say aikido should be only love, and not meant to hurt anyone. But if you practice a philosophy such as that, and you are attacked, then you have no means to protect yourself. And "the loving protection of all things" includes yourself and your loved ones. You must be able to make aikido work for yourself before you can make it work in any other situation (personal interview).

Thus, in aikido there must be a conscious development not only of physical technique, but of ki. This martial and spiritual development cannot occur separately for aikido practitioners: "The heart of martial valor is true bravery, wisdom, love, and friendship," Ueshiba wrote. "Emphasis on the physical aspects of warriorship is futile, for the power of the body is always limited" (Ueshiba, 1992: 59). Difficulty in reconciling martial intent and spiritual love on the mat and in daily life should not be viewed as a flaw in aikido itself, an "either–or" situation, but as a sure sign that the aikido practitioner is progressing on his or her journey towards takemusu aiki. In confronting this seemingly contradictory ideology, one draws that much closer to the perfection not only of martial technique, but of self. As expressed by Ueshiba, "The penetrating brilliance of a sword, wielded by a man of the Way, strikes at the evil enemy lurking deep within one's own body and soul" (Ueshiba, 1991: 29).

The effects of Tohei's split from the Aikikai and the events which presaged it had a profound and lasting effect on aikido technique. Many of Suenaka's peers soon followed his example, severing ties with the Ki Society to form their own organizations, or renewing ties with the Aikikai.

Whatever their reasons, this further division and restructuring of aikido alliances certainly was not conducive to a unified perception of the art and its underlying principles. Moreover, the introduction of the body exercises (*taigi*) into the mix and, more importantly, the philosophy they embodied, only added to the confusion. Whereas before, students who left the Aikikai to teach on their own essentially held fast to aikido's founding principles, with Koichi Tohei there was a complete and very public renunciation of aikido's martial foundation by the man who, perhaps more than any other, was responsible for disseminating aikido worldwide.

This renunciation has particularly affected aikido in the U.S., since Tohei aggressively expanded his Ki Society base there, most notably in California (like Suenaka, many of the first instructors there were introduced to aikido through Tohei in Hawaii). Although many Ki Society-affiliated dojos have reincorporated the martial aspect into their techniques, the two schools of thought remain. Yet through O-Sensei's example, we can see that this division is not proper and does not reflect the true spirit of aikido. Through Suenaka's example and others, we can see that reconciliation is possible.

Roy Suenaka
June 1986

Demonstration of Technique

Please note that all defensive movements begin in a natural stance, rather than a defensive stance. Techniques are performed fluidly, without pause. Special thanks to Chad Taylor for his assistance with photos.

Yokomen-chui shiho-namge hantai tenkan

CORRECT

1) After the attacker strikes, Suenaka moves to the opposite side. He steps back from the attacker at a 45-degree angle, out of range of the strike, while simultaneously redirecting it with his left hand. He thus propels the attacker off-balance and delivers a counter-strike at the same time.

2) Suenaka continues by sweeping the attacker's right arm away and out, capturing the attacker's wrist with his right hand and turning away, moving to the attacker's blind side and keeping him off-balance. His left arm moves beneath the attacker's right, bracing it and further preventing the attacker from bending his elbow, regaining his balance, or striking. Note how Suenaka maintains a proper distance (*ma-ai*).

3) Reverse angle view shows how Suenaka moves beneath the attacker's arm, turning 180 degrees while keeping the attacker's arm extended and the attacker off-balance.

4) Suenaka cuts the attacker's arm tightly into the attacker's shoulder, as if making a sword cut, leading the attacker even further off-balance and precipitating his fall. Notice that the cut is not taken to the outside, where it might dislocate the attacker's shoulder or break the elbow, and that Suenaka remains centered.

5) Having been kept off-balance from the beginning of the technique, the attacker falls to the mat. Suenaka remains upright and centered, maintaining his own balance.

INCORRECT

1) Suenaka blocks, rather than redirects, the attacker's strike, effectively preventing his use of the momentum generated by striking. He fails to step out to the side, resulting in improper distancing, leaving himself vulnerable to a counter-strike.
2) Suenaka moves outside as before, but without leading the attacker off-balance, again leaving himself open to a reverse technique or counter-strike.
3) Suenaka moves beneath the attacker's arm, raising it as he does so rather than pivoting below it, further returning the attacker's initiative. At this point, all the attacker need do to escape is cut his right arm downwards, throwing Suenaka backwards.
4) Suenaka pulls rather than cuts the attacker's arm into his shoulder. Because the attacker is not off-balance, and the technique used relies on strength rather than momentum, the move is ineffective.
5) Suenaka pulls the attacker down to the mat, taking the attacker's arm to the outside, risking injury. The success of the throw relies exclusively on strength. Suenaka is slightly bent at the waist, sacrificing some of his own balance to complete the throw.

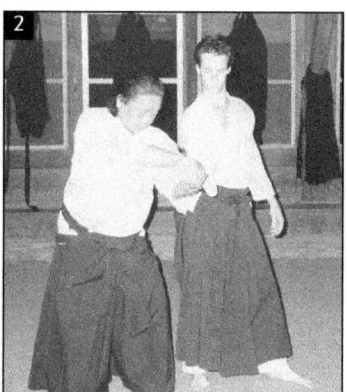

Mune-tsuki kote-gaeshi hansha tenkan

CORRECT

1) The attacker delivers a midsection strike. Suenaka immediately moves to the same side, redirecting the attacker's strike with his left hand while delivering a strike with his right. The attacker's momentum propels him forward.

2) Suenaka captures the attacker's wrist, beginning the wrist-cutting lock, and pivots, leading the attacker around him, off-balance. Note how Suenaka keeps the attacker's hand in front of him while remaining at the attacker's blind side.

3) Having successfully led the attacker off-balance, Suenaka slides his right foot backwards, whipping the attacker out before him, further destroying his balance. Simultaneously, Suenaka places his right hand atop the attacker's fingers, bending the wrist along its natural, inside anatomical arc and completing the kote-gaeshi lock.

4) Suenaka cuts the attacker's wrist downwards—again, like a sword cut—propelling the attacker off his feet and completing the throw.

INCORRECT

1) Suenaka moves to the attacker's blind side, but without leading the attacker off-balance or striking, risking neutralization or a counter-strike.
2) While turning outward, Suenaka drags, rather than leads the attacker, allowing him to get behind him, sacrificing control and again opening himself to neutralization or a counter-strike. The attacker still is not off-balance.
3) Suenaka cuts the attacker's wrist out to the side, against the joint, risking injury to the attacker. Improper distance and lack of lead allows the attacker to maintain his full balance and deliver a counter-strike, or himself move outside to neutralize the technique.
4) The attacker is forced to the mat by strength alone.

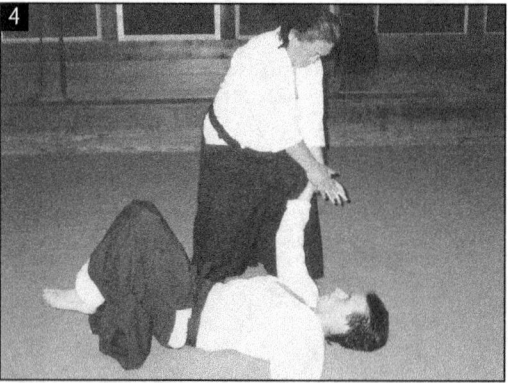

WRIST TURN-OUT

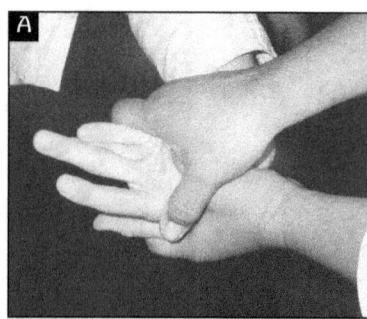
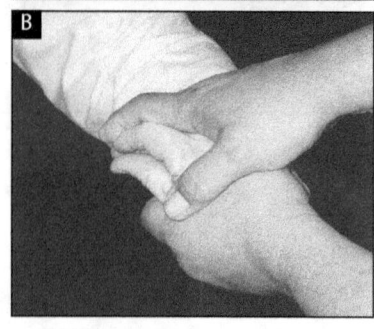

A) Incorrect Kote-Gaeshi Hand Position: The attacker's hand is forced unnaturally outwards. Lack of lead forces the defender to rely on strength and the pain of the outside lock to effect the throw.

B) Correct Kote-Gaeshi Hand Position: The attacker's hand is locked and bent backwards along the natural arc described by the fingers. With proper lead, this lock is always effective.

Shomen-uchi kokyu-nage hansha tenkan
CORRECT

1) The attacker delivers an overhead strike to the head. Suenaka side steps, redirecting the strike with his right hand and striking with his left.
2) Suenaka leads the attacker outside, capturing the momentum generated by the attacker's strike by sweeping his arm and allowing it to move him off-balance. Suenaka captures the attacker's head with his left hand as momentum naturally leads it there, guiding it into his shoulder, while continuing the lead with his right hand, arm out and palm upwards. Properly led, the attacker is unable to deliver a counter-strike.
3) With the attacker successfully led, Suenaka reverses direction, maintaining control of the attacker's head while using his right arm and shoulder to turn it, propelling him backwards.
4) Suenaka continues turning his right arm and shoulder while dropping his hips. It is the attacker's head, rather than his body, that is being thrown.
5) With the attacker off-balance, Suenaka releases the head and easily completes the throw.

INCORRECT

1) Suenaka blocks, rather than redirects the attacker's strike and fails to counter-strike or move to the attacker's blind side. The attacker maintains his balance and can easily counter-strike.
2) Suenaka moves outside and grasps the attacker's collar, rather than controlling his head at the same time, cutting the attacker's right arm downward. Again, the attacker maintains his balance.
3) The force generated by the downward cut forces the attacker to bend at the waist, aided by Suenaka pushing on the back of the attacker's neck with his left hand. The right hand at this point is essentially useless. Note the open, improper distancing.
4) Suenaka pulls the attacker upright with his left hand, restoring the attacker's balance and leaving himself open to neutralization or a counter-strike.
5) The attacker is pulled, rather than thrown, backwards.

CORRECT   *Katate-tori ikkyo hantai irimi*

1) The attacker grasps Suenaka's opposite wrist.
2) Suenaka shifts forward towards the attacker's blind side, using his left hand and the momentum generated by the attacker's approach to bend and lock the attacker's elbow and shoulder, essential for preventing a counter-strike.
3) Suenaka cuts downwards, off-balancing the attacker and allowing the momentum generated by the cut to move the attacker's arm in front of him and the attacker's head and shoulder below the point of control, making it impossible for the attacker to rise and regain his balance. Note the close distancing as Suenaka braces the attacker's arm and left shoulder against his lower abdomen and left thigh.
4) Suenaka slides inside on his left leg, propelling the attacker forward and onto the mat, where a submission may be employed.

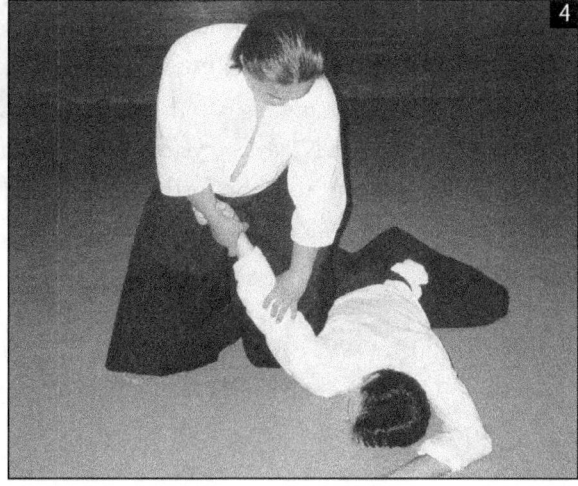

INCORRECT

1) Suenaka pushes on the attacker's elbow, risking injury to the join and leaving himself open to attack.
2) Suenaka's attempts to push the attacker off-balance, rather than cut the arm downwards. If the attacker spins to his left, he can easily lead Suenaka off-balance and neutralize the technique.
3) Suenaka pushes downwards on the attacker's arm, using strength to force him to the mat and in the process sacrificing his own balance. Note the wide, improper distancing.

Sources

As Morihei Ueshiba's life is already well-documented in numerous sources, some text references were not footnoted. For those wishing to read further, John Stevens' *Abundant Peace: The Biography of Morihei Ueshiba, Founder of Aikido*; Kisshomaru Ueshiba's *The Spirit of Aikido*; and Mr. Stevens' translation of O-Sensei's *Budo: Teachings of the Founder of Aikido* are recommended. Biographical information on Koichi Tohei was taken primarily from his *Book of Ki: Co-ordinating Mind and Body in Daily Life*, with additional background drawn from *The Aiki News Encyclopedia of Aikido*. Roy Suenaka's comments and recollections were taken from the forthcoming *Aikido no Kyohan*. All photographs are from Suenaka's personal collection.

Bibliography

Pranin, S. (Ed.). (1991). *The aiki news encyclopedia of aikido*. Tokyo: Aiki News.
Stevens, J. (1987). *Abundant peace: The biography of Morihei Ueshiba, founder of aikido*. Boston: Shambhala Publications.

· 3 ·

The Martial Yen:
American Participation in the Aikido Tradition
by Andrew Crawford, M.A.

Photo by Michael Spector.
Photos courtesy of Andrew Crawford except where noted.

Since the end of World War II, the Asian martial arts have been a part of American culture. Beginning with a few scattered practitioners and the occasional and apocryphal reference in movies (such as *The Manchurian Candidate*), they gained popularity and moved into the mainstream of American public scrutiny. Through the 1960s, the martial arts movement in the United States gained strength and popularity. The days when karate was truly a little-known and esoteric practice are long gone. It is unusual to find someone who is not at least familiar with the basic idea of the Asian martial arts, and it is not hard to find someone who has had experience in their actual practice. The word "karate," as a generic catchall for these martial traditions, is now part of the vocabulary of everyone over the age of five.

Why is there such a fascination with the fighting traditions of ancient Japan in modern America? Why do people become involved in long-term studies of these arts? What is the significance of the modern American's participation in a martial arts school? There are, of course, tangible physical and mental benefits to martial arts practice. It is now common knowledge that exercise is conducive to good health. Martial artists also learn to work efficiently in even the most stressful environments by maintaining a calm state of mind.

With these benefits also come risks. Personal injury amongst students is common. Few individuals escape occasional injury. Some suffer chronic or debilitating problems that result from practice. Since there are other forms of physical exercise and meditation techniques that may confer similar benefits, the decision to pursue these benefits through martial art study must be based on other factors.

More complete answers to these questions require a deeper knowledge of the martial arts themselves. There is no single reason for participation, no single attraction, rather a complex of motivations. We must discover in detail what the martial artist does. Only then can we hope to understand why individuals choose to participate in a martial art.

This article will focus on the martial art of aikido. The relevant aspects of aikido discussed are fairly representative of the other Japanese martial arts as well.[1] Although aikido, as such, did not come into existence until around 1942, it is heir to an ancient, except where noted martial tradition in Japan.

History and Background

Until the time of the "Tokugawa peace," the martial arts were a pragmatic practice in Japan. That is, they were intended specifically for use in combat to further the political ends of various rulers. The beginning of the Tokugawa Period in Japanese history marked the end of more than four centuries of bloody civil war. The new government, under the military leadership of Ieyasu Tokugawa, was able to take control and restore order to Japan.

During this long period of relative calm, several important changes took place. Gunpowder was introduced by the Portuguese. The Satsuma Rebellion in 1877 demonstrated decisively that the ancient traditions of martial combat were no longer relevant to the conduct of modern warfare.

With the peace, the perfectly honed fighting skills of the trained warrior were no longer in constant use. A standing army was maintained, but seldom was military action necessary. The fighting men were brought to the urban centers where they could be more easily controlled. They were encouraged to take up leisure pursuits to fill their time. The emphasis of many schools of combat slowly became more philosophical. The ideals of bravery, integrity, loyalty, frugality, stoicism, and filial piety were emphasized in these schools and supported by the government. This change in emphasis is marked by a difference in terminology. Older forms with a pragmatic orientation are referred to as *bujutsu* or "fighting arts." Newer forms are *budo* or "martial ways" (in the sense of "ways of life").

Toward the end of the nineteenth century, the Tokugawa Shogunate crumbled. Power was restored to the emperor and his advisors (feudal warlords and prominent nobility). It was during this period that aikido was born.

Aikido

Morihei Ueshiba, the founder of aikido, was a rural Japanese farmer. He is described in several accounts as a scholar and his studies are said to have included calculus, physics, and chemistry as well as philosophy and the martial arts. His development of aikido derived primarily from his studies of the classical martial arts and his religious beliefs. The primary influences for the development of aikido, therefore, are the Daito-ryu of Aikijujutsu and the Omotokyo.

Initially, Morihei Ueshiba was a practitioner of several traditional martial *ryu*, or styles. As a young man, Ueshiba met Sokaku Takeda. Takeda was the headmaster of the Daito-ryu and a well-known master of the martial arts. Under Takeda, Ueshiba underwent austere training (*shugyo*) as a classical *bushi* (warrior). He became an accomplished martial artist in his own right and was given permission to teach Daito-ryu Aikijujutsu by Takeda. Ueshiba continued to award Daito-ryu Aikijujutsu "proficiencies" through the early 1930s.

The changes in Ueshiba's teachings in the mid 1930s to 1940s prompted him to begin calling his style "Aiki Budo." These changes were principally the product of his spiritual enlightenment. At the time of his father's death, Morihei Ueshiba became involved with a millenarian movement known as the Omotokyo.

The Omoto religion was founded in 1892 by Nao Deguchi based on divine revelations she claimed to have received. The organization flourished under Onisaburo Deguchi (who had changed his name to become Nao Deguchi's successor despite a lack of agnatic kinship). Onisaburo preached the overthrow of the current government and symbolically declared himself emperor of Japan. Obviously, this was frowned upon by those in power and the Omotokyo was repeatedly subjected to forced dissolutions and imposed restraints.

It is the doctrine of the Omotokyo which seems to have influenced Morihei Ueshiba. The group's outlook is based in the traditional religions of Japan, but as with most of the "new" religions, there is a strong Christian influence. Omotokyo means "The Teaching of the Great Origin." The central tenet of the Omotokyo is that the final destruction of the world is imminent and the kingdom of heaven will be built on earth following Judgment Day.

It is, however, the secondary precepts of the Omotokyo that are of interest. They believe "man must live in religion; not one thing that man does is outside the sphere of true religion" (Thomsen, 1963, p. 128). The world is seen as a manifestation of an invisible God and man is seen as a receptacle for the divine. Ueshiba believed that he received the inspiration for much of his martial prowess from the *kami*, traditional Japanese deities. This does not appear to be uncommon. Sokaku Takeda also believed that he at least met kami (1989, October, p. 46).

"Man's purpose is to take the leading role in establishing the 'heavenly kingdom' on earth" (p. 135). Ueshiba claimed that "the prime object of aikido is to construct a paradise on earth by creating harmony in the world and making friends" (O-Sensei," 1984, November, 22–27). The Omotokyo is a religion which strongly emphasizes the international character of religion and its application to such ends as world peace.

Ueshiba is quoted as saying "aikido builds bridges in all countries and unites the world through harmony and love" (1986, June, 27). The parallel is clear. Members of the Omotokyo follow four guiding principles:

1) Purification, spiritually as well as physically, which is necessary in the life of the individual, family, community, nation and world.
2) Optimism, meaning the enjoyment of life with reliance upon God.
3) Progressiveness in active life, which is never confined to a narrow corner of life, but ever expanding, always exploring new possibilities.
4) Unification of the microcosmos (man) with the macrocosmos (God). (p. 135)

All four principles are reflected to some degree in the aikido of Morihei Ueshiba. Particularly clear is the connection of the first principle to aikido. Ueshiba believed that it was critical to practice *misogi* breathing and meditation for purification on a daily basis. Misogi remains a part of some aikido curricula to the present.

Unification of the microcosmos with the macrocosmos, or man with God, is also paralleled in aikido teachings. The existence of a supernatural force, known as *ki*, was postulated. Although ki is also described in terms of total physical harmony of the person, most practitioners understand it as a force separate from the individual. In order for aikido techniques to be executed correctly, the practitioner must allow this "universal energy" to flow through him. Redirecting an opponent's ki by using one's own remains a central tenet of many aikido organizations.

Another important part of the Omoto doctrine shared by Ueshiba's aikido is the principle of non-resistance (Sunadomari, 1989, July, p. 59). Aikido endeavors to eliminate conflict. As with all of the classical budo, the ultimate goal is not to fight. Aikido gives this particular emphasis in its philosophy and its technique. The aikido practitioner (*aikidoka*) is expected to be concerned for his attacker and to protect the attacker from harm while protecting himself. Toward this end the attacker is allowed to do what he wishes without resistance. The aikidoka merely moves in such a manner as to prevent harm to himself. While it may be necessary to restrain the attacker or cause him to distance himself from the aikidoka, these techniques are designed to minimize the possibility of permanent injury. Further, the mechanics of the techniques require that the aikidoka move in a way that is harmonious with the attacker, that is, not in direct conflict with his movements. Thus, the outcome of the technique is the result of the attacker's effort with minimal input from the aikidoka.

Morihei Ueshiba believed in the *kotodama*, a system of universal sounds which could be used to manipulate the physical world. He considered these sounds to be important in the misogi purification rituals he practiced and in other healing techniques.

In aikido, he presented the use of the *kiai*, a way of expressing the internal power of aikido by producing a loud shout. Ideally, such a shout is sufficient to unbalance and defeat an opponent.

The practitioners of Daito-ryu used the term "aiki" to refer to "self-defense" techniques, that is, techniques used only when one is attacked ("Tokimune Takeda," 1986, June, p. 24). In keeping with the Omoto philosophy, Ueshiba taught mainly those techniques which were for defensive purposes only. Thus, it became "aiki budo." In 1942 the name was officially changed to "aikido" (Pranin, 1986, June, p. 4).

Despite the clear influence of the Omotokyo, Morihei Ueshiba did not consider himself to be a religious leader:

> I could have entered the world of philosophy or religion.
> If I had mastered those ways, I could have reached a certain level.
> But I have always regarded budo as my mission. I am not a
> religionist but a budo man (Ueshiba, 1985, November, p. 29).

He also considered himself to be a farmer. "He believed in the idea of self-sufficiency and the combination of budo and farming" (1985, May, p. 16). His students do not feel that he forced his religious ideas upon them despite the critical role those ideas play in his budo ("Yasuo Kobayashi Interview," 1986, March, p. 10).

In the early years, Ueshiba selected his students in a traditional manner. He did not consider aikido to be "open" to the public. As in the traditional bujutsu and budo, he strictly controlled all teaching of the art. He taught aikido to some police, military, and government personnel but always had final say as to which specific individuals he would instruct. Since aikido was a martial art and dealt with life and death situations, secrecy was critical. He felt that indiscriminately revealing those arts would be immoral (Ueshiba, 1986, March, p. 15).

When approached by his son and other senior students, it was with "face red with anger, his veins standing out, and lips [turned] down at the comers trembling," that he reluctantly agreed to open aikido to the public:

> All right. It may be necessary for me to open contact with the general public.
> I will demonstrate the essence of Aiki if it will help to purify the muddy stream.
> I have already entrusted you young people with the future of this Path.
> As long as you don't stray from the Great Way of the True Mission
> to the benefit of mankind, I have no objection to what you do.
> You should make the most of this old man (p. 15).

Aikido continued to flourish in Japan despite some problems which arose from Ueshiba's political connection to the Omotokyo. Aikido weakened somewhat during the World War II period. Toward the end of the war enrollment in Ueshiba's school declined somewhat since most of the able-bodied males were involved in the war effort. Practice of all martial arts (save karate-do) was curtailed during the initial phase of the Allied occupation of Japan. Shortly, however, the restrictions were relaxed. This was a critical period for the spread of the martial arts. Allied service men stationed in Japan had the opportunity to observe traditional schools of bujutsu and budo and some were able to train in one or more styles. These people brought the first taste of the martial arts back to Europe and America. Ueshiba's higher-ranking students were in poor financial shape due to Japan's drained economy. Many asked permission of Ueshiba to teach aikido outside of Japan with the hope of being able to earn a living. A very few were asked to go abroad to spread aikido. Thus, aikido and the other traditional fighting arts of Japan spread to America.

Japanese Society

The traditional fighting arts are intimately connected with modern Japanese culture. This is often overlooked. In her book, *Japanese Society*, Chie Nakane does not draw a connection between the martial ways of earlier Japanese societies and the modern "structures" she finds in Japan. There is, however, a clear influence which remains to this day and can be seen in any social or ethnographic study of modem Japanese culture.

Nakane describes the structure of Japanese society as a number of groups set against one another. She cites a prevalent feeling of hostility for individuals from groups other than one's own. A single loyalty to a single group is "uppermost and firm" in the minds of each Japanese individual. Furthermore, she describes a system of absolute ranking based on age, popularity, sex, ability, but primarily status. Leaders have strong personal ties with their followers but almost no connection with their peers. The only connection among peers is through a common leader. Nakane values "the strength of this structure [which] lies in its effectiveness for centralized communication and its capability of efficient and swift mobilization of the collective power of its members" (1970: 63). The parallels with the former feudal system are clear. She even tells us that violation of the social order is very costly for the individual (socially) just as it was for the samurai of old (who generally died for violating the social order.) According to Nakane, the "roles of individual members are readily adjustable to changing situations . . . the individual has the advantage of great freedom of action . . . [thus] maximizing the potential ability of individual members" (p. 81). As the samurai were allowed great freedom of action in accomplishing their assigned tasks (notably on the battlefield) the modem Japanese is allowed the freedom of methodology to accomplish the ends required of him. Adaptation is an important key for a successful warrior. As Draeger notes, "survival is innate to the bujutsu, itself the study of self-defense, and thus the classical martial arts and their ryu survived the onslaught of time" (1973: 24). The ancient martial ways are still a part of Japanese society.

Careful attention to the words and behavior of many martial arts instructors indicate that these cultural values are maintained by Japanese *sensei* ("teachers") in America. The attention to ranking can be seen in the following quote from a letter written by a prominent Japanese instructor teaching in America: "Problems start to arise when organizations come to the fore. It is human relationships which matter, relationships between teachers and students and juniors and seniors" (Pranin, 1986, June, p. 32).

There are clear influences of Japanese cultural traditions on martial arts organizations in the United States today. The concern with social position can be seen in the various systems that have been introduced for ranking practitioners of the martial arts. A system of colored belts is used to mark one's position relative to others in the organization. Rank depends on length of membership and degree of conformity to expected norms, partially in the sense of increasing proficiency. There is a pronounced factionalism among martial artists in the United States.

Discussions among students of different schools, instructors and arts often take on a character of boasting and denigration. Arguments about which instructor, school, or art is better are common.

The Martial Arts as Religion

Many practitioners and historians do not consider the martial arts a form of religion. However, authors of books about the religious systems of Japan invariably address the bushido traditions. One, Robert Bellah, in his book *Tokugawa Religion*, goes as far as calling bushido a "manifestation of religion" (1957: 90–98). There are many interesting similarities between bushido and religion in general. Besides the obvious classical functional definitions which could be applied there are other interesting correspondences with contemporary religious functionalism. In Edwin Friedman's book *Generation to Generation: Family Process in Church and Synagogue* for example, he cites four connections between the preacher and his congregation. These are: 1) the "multigenerational forces" behind the religious tradition, 2) involvement of the congregational leader during rites of passage, 3) the length of time over which a specific spiritual leader becomes familiar with his congregation (often spanning several generations himself), and 4) the frequent occurrence of individual congregational leaders demonstrating leadership in areas other than spiritual. These characteristics put the congregational leader in an ideal position for "pastoral counseling" according to Friedman (1985: 1–10). Interestingly, these are also four of the ideal characteristics commonly expected of a martial arts instructor.

As with most religious congregations, there are strong social bonds formed within a group of martial artists who practice together. There are many interesting interrelationships occurring within dojos that cut across normal social boundaries. There is a great diversity of economic and social as well as cultural background among members of the martial arts community. However, these individuals interact socially outside of the dojo.

There have been several marriages within the groups that I have observed. Invitations are often issued to the entire group to attend these and other rites of passage. There is an interesting sense of solidarity. Professional and academic recommendations of persons from one's dojo to persons outside the dojo, who may have other social ties to the person preparing the recommendation, are common. In general, it seems that members of the dojo make their specialized professional skills available to one another free of charge or "wholesale."

Many of the old Japanese ritual traditions continue to be observed in modem martial arts groups and appear to foster group cohesiveness. There is a certain amount of formal conduct expected from students. Students are expected to bow to the instructor and to each other at certain points during practice. There are two different forms of bowing, both of which must conform to precise specifications. A standing bow is appropriate before and after practicing with a particular partner, or in return for brief instruction given to an individual by the instructor. The more formal kneeling bow is used in a ceremony which opens and closes each class session and is used after receiving instruction from the instructor as a group or before standing in response to the instructor's summons. Bowing is returned by the instructor. The student(s) must execute a bow at least as formally as the instructor. If an instructor bows in a kneeling position, the students must also bow in a kneeling position. To bow from a standing position to a kneeling instructor would be very bad manners. The converse is not true, however. A student's bow should also begin before and end after his superior's. Traditionally, the depth of the bow is considered to be important as well.

Students are not allowed to argue with the instructor (especially during class).

There are also prohibitions on the use of certain phrases or words. For example, one is never to say "I know" in response to a suggestion or other instruction. The use of the word "wrong" is forbidden and must be replaced with "*chigao*," the Japanese word meaning "different." Students who are late are expected to wait for permission to join the class from the instructor, and students must ask special permission of the instructor to leave the practice area during class even for a moment. Although there are no immediate sanctions for violations of these norms and individual infractions are largely ignored, one who is clearly not trying carefully to observe them will come to be viewed as rude and shortly be ostracized from the group.

One particular ritual that was clearly intended to help maintain the group identity and merits some attention took place at a funeral for the chief instructor of a dojo. His death left many things uncertain for the group and they found themselves in a sort of transitional period. The instructor's death isolated the rest of the group from its national affiliation. The connection technically still existed, but there were no strong personal ties between the remaining group members and the larger organization. The group was also in immediate danger of losing its training facility due to some conflicts with the owner that the instructor was no longer there to mediate. Finally, there was some concern that the ranking student, who automatically became the new chief instructor, would be unable to fulfill his obligation since he was unwilling (and financially unable) to become a professional martial arts instructor. At the wake, the deceased instructor's ashes were sprinkled into cups of hot tea and consumed by the students following the example of the new chief instructor who explained that it had the symbolic implication of continuing the deceased instructor's life through each of his students. This ritual appears to have been intended to assure the members of the dojo of the group's continuity and solidarity even through these difficulties.

During the *rei* ceremony, students usually line up according to rank and or seniority before bowing to the *shomen* and afterwards to the teacher.

Another interesting practice that is observed during each class is the rei ceremony. The rei ceremony is a bowing ceremony, but it is more than a show of respect. The instructor announces the beginning of class by clapping his hands twice. The students line up in order of their seniority and recognized rank within the dojo. In some dojos this attention to rank is quite important and senior students will physically shove lower-ranking students out of line to gain their proper place. In other dojos, the students only try to follow the general pattern but do not worry about being in exactly the correct position so long as they are next to other students wearing the same color belt as they. In the more formal rei ceremonies, the instructor kneels in the formal position facing away from the class. This is the sign for the students to sit, one at a time, from highest ranking to lowest ranking. There is thereafter a pattern of bowing, often accompanied by clapping to attract spiritual attention, first to the founder or deities of the dojo, and then to the instructor.

At the end of the class this ceremony is repeated, sometimes accompanied by short periods of meditation (*mokuso*). In many groups, the final rei ceremony is accompanied by a procession in which each student bows to every other student, usually exchanging ritual thanks ("*Domo arigato gozai masu*" or "Thank you very much"). This part of the ceremony involves a formal method of moving on one's knees and is organized so that the more senior a student is, the less he has to move in this manner. During this portion of the ceremony new or visiting members formally introduce themselves to any students that they do not know by exchanging names and perhaps shaking hands. These introductions take place although the students may have already practiced techniques together during the class.

Above: Students sit quietly at attention as the instructor demonstrates techniques or discourses on related topics. Below: Competent instructors often blend theory and practice while demonstrating aikido techniques. Photo by Michael Spector.

There may also be a creed for the dojo, written by the chief instructor, which is recited in either the beginning or ending rei ceremony. In one such ceremony, at the instructor's signal, the ranking senior student recites the "*dojo kun*" or "principles of the school" one at a time with the rest of the students repeating each after him. In another rei ceremony, the code is recited simultaneously with the instructor. The codes reflect expected normative behavior or sentiments expressed in generalized terms. One dojo code states "seek perfection of character, be faithful, endeavor to excel, respect others, refrain from violent behavior." These codes are recited by the senior student and students. This following is an example of a creed made by students recited in unison with their instructor:

> Let us have a universal spirit
> that loves and protects all creation
> and helps all things to grow and develop.
> To unify mind and body
> and become one with the universe
> is the ultimate purpose of my study.

Obviously this creed also has strong implications for promotion of group solidarity.

In almost any traditional dojo, there can be found an altar or shrine to the founding deities of the school. This practice dates back to the earliest martial ryu. In aikido, this is called the *shomen*, meaning "head." This altar is usually a recessed area in the wall or a low table of some sort. A picture of Morihei Ueshiba (the founder of aikido) usually occupies a prominent position on or above the shrine. In some instances, a smaller image of the founder of a specific dojo may be placed below the central image. Generally, this is done by the founder's students after his death. To place a picture of oneself or to allow such an image to be placed in the shrine would be regarded as extremely inappropriate. Often fresh flowers are brought and put on the shrine in vases. Sometimes heavy hand bells (*suzu*) or sets of "clap sticks" used in chanting and meditation ceremonies can be found on the shrine. Often, a set of traditional Japanese swords (*daisho*) will also be a part of the shomen. In some of the more traditional schools, particularly in Hawaii and Japan, incense is burned on these altars.

As with the shrines of most religions, there is a special etiquette that must be followed in dealing with the shomen. The shomen is regarded with the same respect as higher ranking instructors. It is inappropriate to turn one's back to or expose the soles of one's feet to the shomen at any time. It is also considered impolite to turn one's back or the soles of one's feet to any instructor, but special attention is given to avoid treating the shomen in this manner. An exception to this rule is made when one is fixing one's gi. In fact, it is considered bad manners not to turn one's back to the shomen when rearranging one's clothing. All members of the dojo, including the instructor, bow to the shomen during the formal rei ceremony (described above) that opens and closes each class.

It is expected that individuals will execute a standing bow to the shomen when entering or leaving the dojo and when entering or leaving the practice space (or mat). Along with the formal rei ceremony that opens and closes classes, this serves to demarcate a period of time. Instructors and many senior students indicate that one must put aside everything else in one's life while one is practicing. This is critical for proper execution of martial techniques being taught and for the safety of the students. After all, the martial arts were originally designed for killing and injuring opponents and inattention can be disastrous. The similarity to many formal religious ceremonies is clear. Demarcation of a period of sacred time is integral to most religious rituals.

Left: A bow to the shomen during the formal rei ceremony opens and closes each class. This symbolically demarcates a period of "sacred time" used for dedicated practice and acknowledges the heritage of the art. Above: Individuals respectfully bow to each other before and after practicing together.

On some occasions certain rituals may be conducted during practice. Many of these are considered forms of meditation. One of these is commonly conducted early in the morning, but only at training camps. During this particular ritual, all students meditate while performing a breathing exercise. Air is taken in through the nose and is released while vocalizing a short "ahhh" sound. This vocalization is not synchronized, and when there are many people involved the sound is described as "the universal sound."

In another meditation ritual that is conducted more frequently, the students are lined up and seated in the seiza position as they would be for the formal rei ceremony. The students close their eyes and breathe in through their noses and out through their mouths (usually without vocalization). In this case the breathing is synchronized. The instructor may clap to signal inhalation and exhalation or he may use the "clap sticks" kept on the shrine. When the instructor is ready to end the exercise, he claps several times in rapid succession during an exhalation and, after a pause, claps once more to signal an inhalation and the end of the meditation.

"Practice makes perfect"—as two aikidoka illustrate by their techniques executed with the speed and grace associated with this style. Photo by Michael Spector.

Some instructors also conduct chanting ceremonies. Ideally, each student will have a heavy bell for this ceremony. Most schools have one or only a few such bells that are kept on the shomen. When the number of students is greater than the number of bells, the bells are shared and the students without bells are told to pretend that they have a bell. The instructor begins by ringing the bell, which produces a definite and singular "clink," in a slow and regular rhythmical pattern. With each downstroke of the bell a syllable from the following phrase is chanted: "*Toho kami, ami ta me*" (i.e. "To-ho-ka-mi-a-mi-tame"). The chant becomes progressively faster. At several points the instructor alters the chant so a larger section of the phrase is recited with each downstroke ("*Toho-kami-amitame*," then "*Tohokami-amitame*," and finally "*Toho-kamiamitame*"). As the chant accelerates, it becomes increasingly difficult to keep up. More and more concentration and physical effort is required. This is particularly true for those who are ringing the bells. For this reason, the ceremony is often explained as an exercise to build up muscles and concentration. Although this is no doubt partially true, it is also obvious that there are religious implications particularly once one becomes aware that the chanted phrase is an invocation of the deities.

The awarding of new ranks is also conducted during practice. At the beginning or ending of a practice session, the sensei awarding the new rank calls the student to be promoted before the class. The student is expected to come forward, walking on his knees (*suwari waza*) and receive his certificate from the instructor. The student is also expected to bow to the sensei and to the shomen at this time. If the student's new rank allows the wearing of a new color of belt, the instructor may also present the belt at this time. The student then removes his old belt, folding it into eights, and puts on the new belt while the class watches.

Students are also taught to perform certain personal rituals in addition to bowing to the shomen when entering and leaving the dojo and practice space. Aikido involves some training with traditional weapons: the jo, a staff about four feet long, and the *bokken* or *shinai*, which represents the *katana* or traditional sword of the samurai. Most students own their own weapons. Each time a student picks up a weapon, he is expected to bow to it. During practice, this may be synchronized in a group. A bokken or shinai is placed on the right side of a seated student while he is receiving instruction. This indicates that the student is not preparing to attack. When individual practice begins, the weapon is transferred to the left side of the body. Traditionally, weapons were considered to be the soul of the samurai. Touching another person's weapons was considered adequate insult for murder. In the modern martial arts, this taboo is maintained. As with many points of etiquette, however, the modern sanctions are not nearly so severe.

Other personal rituals include the treatment of the *gi* or practice uniform. The gi has important symbolic value. It is white to represent purity of the soul. Some martial arts styles use a black gi to represent the impurity associated with dirty or dishonorable fighting methods. As with the formal bowing ceremonies, the gi also serves to delineate practice time. The belt used to tie the gi is often folded into eighths when it is removed after practice. The student then bows to the belt while facing in the direction of the shomen.

As part of their training uniform, black-belt students (*yudansha*) wear a long, skirt-like, pleated pair of pants called a *hakama*. When removed, this is also folded in a highly formalized and complicated way. In addition to teaching tidiness, this procedure is explained by one practitioner as a method of meditation used to focus and calm the mind after a training session.

Individuals often interact in the dojo as a social unit:
one-on-one (above) or as a group (right). Photo by Michael Spector.

Closely connected with the shomen and its associated ritualism is the idea of divinities. Special terminology is used to refer to Morihei Ueshiba. He is rarely spoken of by his given name among aikidoka. Instead, he is called "the founder" or, more frequently, "O-Sensei," meaning "Great Teacher." This special terminological deference also extends to his son, Kisshomaru Ueshiba, who is still alive. The son is referred to as *Doshu*, meaning "Grand Master of the Way." Traditionally, the next head of a martial order was the son of the previous head. This is known as the *soke* system of succession. The use of these terms is an extension and intensification of the respect that is accorded to all instructors. When referring to an instructor in polite conversation, it is considered necessary to use either the title "*sensei*" or "*san*" (the Japanese equivalent of "mister") with his name. Female instructors are addressed as "sensei."

Inexplicable or even supernatural powers are frequently attributed to O-Sensei and other masters of the traditional martial arts. Sokaku Takeda is described by his senior students and many who have met him as having been able to read minds and perform unbelievable physical feats. Similar powers are attributed to O-Sensei. Accounts of specific incidents abound. In one such account he is described as having been able to shoot "a white light" from his eyes. Those who practiced with him report that he had progressed to a level "beyond technique." He was able to throw opponents with the slightest of efforts, by merely pointing, for example. Most of his teaching was highly esoteric and much of it remains unclear even to his senior students. Some practitioners, particularly his senior students, maintain that he was a *kami* or "deity." As noted earlier, the tenets of aikido also posit the existence of a universal force known as ki which may be manipulated by practitioners.

A good argument can be made for describing the martial arts in general and aikido in particular as religions. Formalized rituals are conducted, doctrine is taught, and there is a belief in supernatural beings and forces. Some practitioners describe aikido as a religion and a few even admit that the religious aspects are the central attraction for them.

While this is not a complete description of the dynamics of social interaction in the martial arts, it is clear that martial arts dojos qualify as social groups. It is likely that one of the important factors in obtaining and retaining members in martial arts organizations is this secondary social function. It has been suggested that the psychological needs of people in European society include social interaction and a sense of belonging. This need is often met by organized religion. Sociologists have long observed that the practice of organized religion has been in steady decline in the United States for several decades. A void has arisen in the lives of many Americans. They experience an isolation and alienation that sociologists have characterized as "anomie." Participation in secondary social groups, particularly those with religious dimensions, seems to be the remedy for many people. Perhaps this is one reason for the American fascination with the martial traditions of Japan.

Participation in the group is empowering. Members are able to obtain social positions within the group that are denied to them in broader society. A factory worker stuck in a position with no upward mobility may study the martial arts and, with time, become a respected instructor. The social role as a martial artist becomes more gratifying than any position open to him or her in the broader society.

It is possible for a member of a martial arts group to find other members that fulfill specific social needs of his. People who begin practicing at the same time often develop a sort of fraternal relationship. They feel closer to each other than they do to those who started practicing before or after they did. The role of the instructor or senior student as a nurturing parent figure has already been mentioned.

This gratification of social needs in the alternate social group is enhanced by participation in rites designed to give the member power over people in the broader social setting. As trained fighters, martial artists are in a position of superiority over the average American at a primal level. For some practitioners, this sense of superiority extends beyond even the physical realm to include supernatural dimensions.

Most martial artists refrain and are discouraged from using their skills to gain leverage in other social settings. They don't "beat up" or threaten their bosses, coworkers, or neighbors with their fighting abilities. For many schools, one of the central ideals is to control one's environment and oneself so that one's martial skills will never be needed in actual combat. Students learn the ways of combat so they may never have to fight.

Nevertheless, the sense of power (illusory or real) certainly serves to reassure one in unpleasant situations. It is satisfying to know that, while one may be relatively powerless in a particular social situation, one is capable of physically dominating one's current social superior.

The martial arts are many things for many people. They are a way to better physical and mental health through discipline and physical training. They provide a social environment that may be more pleasant than its alternatives. They offer social and spiritual support. Some of these factors may be more relevant than others for particular individuals. It is unlikely, however, that any single factor is determinate. The factors that maintain an individual's interest in the martial arts are also likely to change over time. The draw of power may spark a person's initial interest while the social environment may induce one to continue practicing. The attraction of the ancient arts of war for the modern American is complex. It is truly an involving and enduring interest.

Social ties are made soon after one starts classes.

Notes

[1] ... as far as I know. My background includes a prolonged study of aikido encompassing several schools and a shorter study of a karate group. I have had some experience with practitioners of other arts.

[2] The information presented on Japanese history is from the viewpoint of an American martial arts practitioner. This is the way that I believe many martial artists understand Japanese history.

Bibliography

Draeger, D. F. (1973). *Classical bujutsu*. New York: John Weatherhill.

Draeger, D. F. (1973). *Classical budo*. New York: John Weatherhill.

Draeger, D. F. (1973). *Modern bujutsu and budo*. New York: John Weatherhill.

O-Sensei radio interview transcript. (1984, November). *AikiNews*, 64, pp. 22–27.

Pranin, S. (1986, June). Aikido and Daito-ryu: The unacknowledged symbiosis. Editorial. *AikiNews*, 71, pp. 3–4, 39.

SokakuTakedaBiography.AikiNews, 74 (1987, April): 38–42, 49; 75 (1987, August): 36–40; 76 (1987, December): 40–44; 77 (1988, April): 50–54, 58, 63; 79 (1989, January): 48–53; 80 (1989, April): 32–38; 81 (1989, July): 34–40; 82 (1989, October): 42–48.

Storry, R. (1978). *The way of the samurai*. New York: W. H. Smith.

Sunadomari, K. Morihei Ueshiba: Founder of aikido. *AikiNews*, 72 (1986, September): 32–37; 73 (1986, December): 26–30, 38; 74 (1987, April): 50–54, 66; 75 (1987, August): 52–56; 76 (1987, December): 52–56, 63; 77 (1988, April): 28–33; 79 (January, 1989): 42–47; 80 (April, 1989): 58–63; 81 (1989, July): 56–61; 82 (1989, October): 64–69.

Thomsen, H. (1963). *The new religions of Japan*. Tokyo: Charles E. Tuttle.

Tokimune Takeda: Conversation with the son of Sokaku Takeda. *AikiNews*, 71 (1986, June): 20–26; 72 (1986, September): 20–27, 50; 73 (1986, December): 18–22, 50–51.

Turnball, S. R. (1977). *The samurai: A military history*. New York: Macmillan.

Ueshiba, K. The founder of aikido Morihei Ueshiba. *AikiNews*, 61 (1984, May): 11, 23; 62 (1984, July): 19–20; 63 (1984, September): 24–25, 30; 64 (1984, November): 17, 20; 65 (1984, December): 30–31, 33; 66 (1985, February): 16–17; 67 (1985, May): 16–17; 68 (1985, August): 24–25; 69 (1985, November): 29; 70 (1986, March): 15; 71 (1986, June): 27, 36.

Yasuo Kobayashi interview: In the classic Hombu style. . . (1986, March) *AikiNews*, 70, pp. 5–14.

· 4 ·

Use of the Knife and Short Staff in Aikido Training
by Kimberley Taylor, M.Sc.

All photos courtesy of K. Taylor and the University of Guelph Aikido Club.

Introduction

The knife is the least understood of all weapons used in aikido practice, and this reflects, to a certain extent, its place in the other budo as well. Even in the West, the knife is an object of some suspicion and ill repute, perhaps because it is so effective and easily concealed.

Knife attacks (*tanto tori*) can be a powerful method of training in aikido. While empty-handed practice can be simply empty practice, beginning students are rarely sloppy when defending themselves against a knife, even a wooden one. If knife practice is always treated with a certain seriousness, the student's concentration will increase each time it is used. Unfortunately, knife practice in aikido sometimes gets little attention or respect. The knife is grabbed and shoved at the defender (*nage*, the one who throws the attacker in aikido practice) to be taken away and then handed back once more. Too often, little in the way of care is shown when using the knife in practice.

A short overview of the knife as an historical artifact of Japan will be given here, followed by some notes on the use of the knife in aikido practice. The main emphasis will be on empty-handed defense against the knife since this is the usual situation in class. A discussion of how the attacker (*uke*, the one who takes a fall in aikido practice) should attack with the knife is provided, along with a short discussion of short staff (*jo*) against knife. A final section on how a defender might use the knife after obtaining it from the attacker is provided for further thought.

No attempt has been made to catalogue all the possible responses to a knife attack; instead a few representative techniques against some typical attack patterns are described. These techniques are roughly classified according to the defender's initial movement. Aikido is a young art, but it is not homogenous and there are several different "streams" being practiced today. This has led to difficulty in the interpretation of Japanese terminology. In this paper I have tried to use the definitions supplied in the text *Aikido* by Kisshomaru Ueshiba (1985), the son of the founder of aikido, Morihei Ueshiba. In any case, English translations of the terms are provided for clarity.

FIGURE 1: Japanese Names of Sword Parts

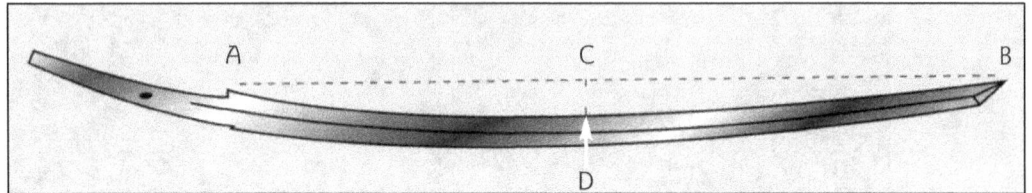

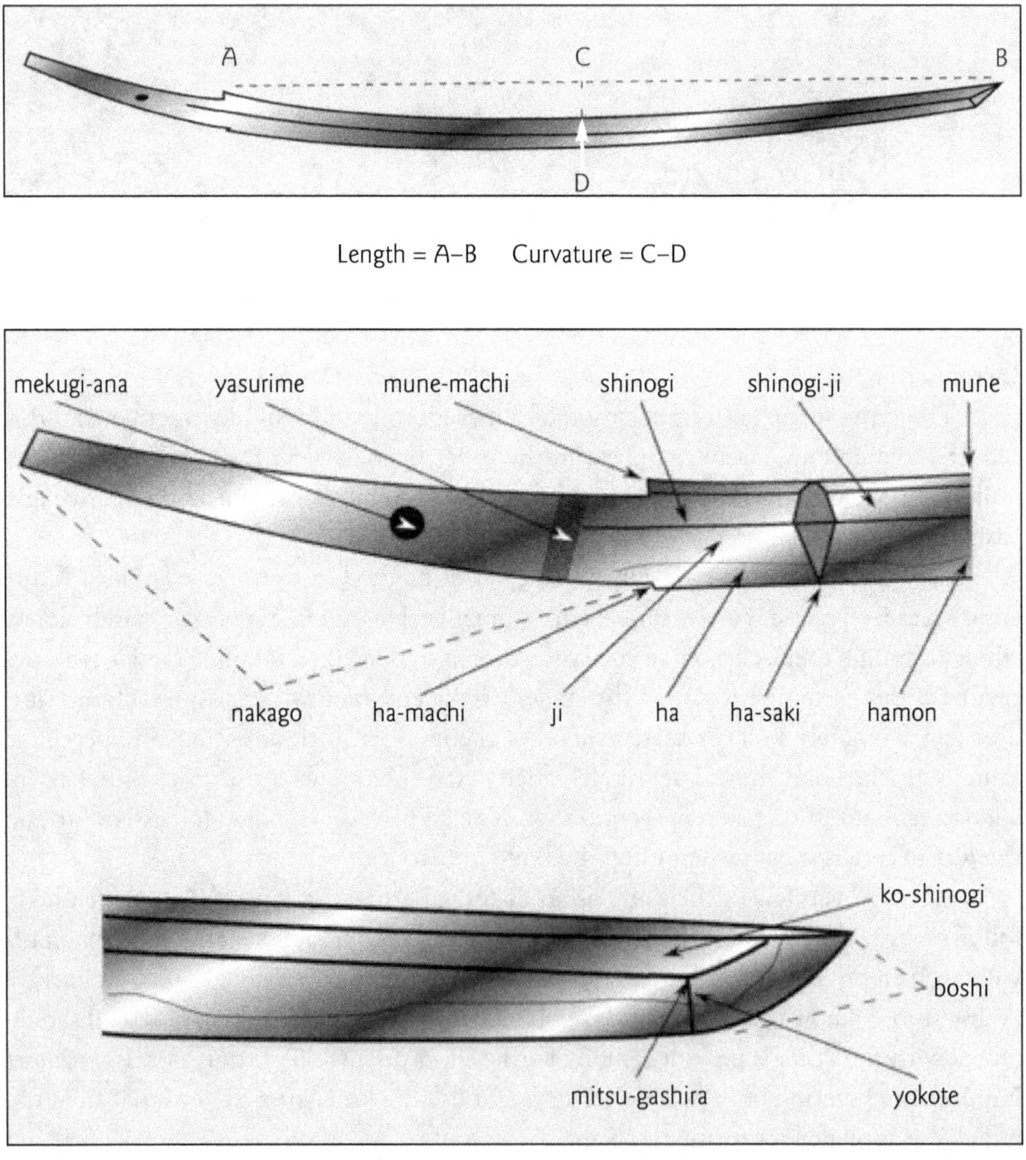

Length = A–B   Curvature = C–D

The Tanto in Japanese History

Japanese knives come in as many styles as do those in the West. They are used for hundreds of everyday purposes from carpentry to cooking. The knives of the samurai, those meant for fighting, are placed in several general categories (Sato, 1983; Yumato, 1958; Ogasawara, 1970). All edged weapons that are less than one *shaku* (about one foot) are classed as knives (*tanto*). Those from one to two shaku are short swords (*shoto*) and those over two feet are long swords (*daito*). Rather than following the curve of the blade, this measurement is made in a straight line, from the back notch at the guard (*munemachi*) to the tip (See Fig. 1). Knives that are mounted the same way as a sword are called *tanto*. They usually have a cord-wrapped handle and a guard (*tsuba*) (See Fig. 2). Knives without guards are called *aikuchi*, and this is actually the type that is most often used in aikido practice. Other knives include the *kwaiken*, which was usually carried by women for their protection. Fighting knives were often mounted like swords with cord-wrapped handles of plain wood or metal. Their edges were sometimes shaped like that of a sword, and at other times with only one bevelled side making an edge rather like a chisel.

FIGURE 2: Tanto Handle Fittings

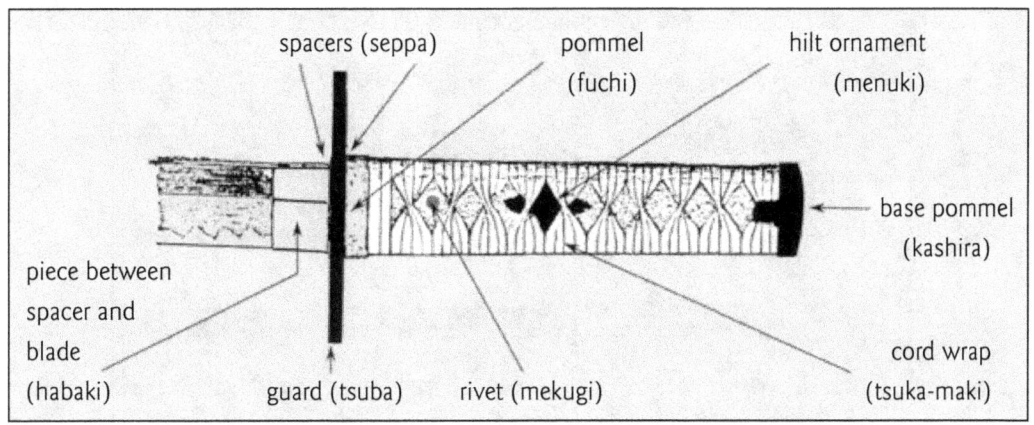

Figure 3 shows several edge patterns. Some knives had a widened tip which provided strength enough to penetrate armor. All of these various forms have been named and classified by collectors and more information can be obtained from the books by Sato, Yumato, and Ogasawara.

FIGURE 3: Blade shapes

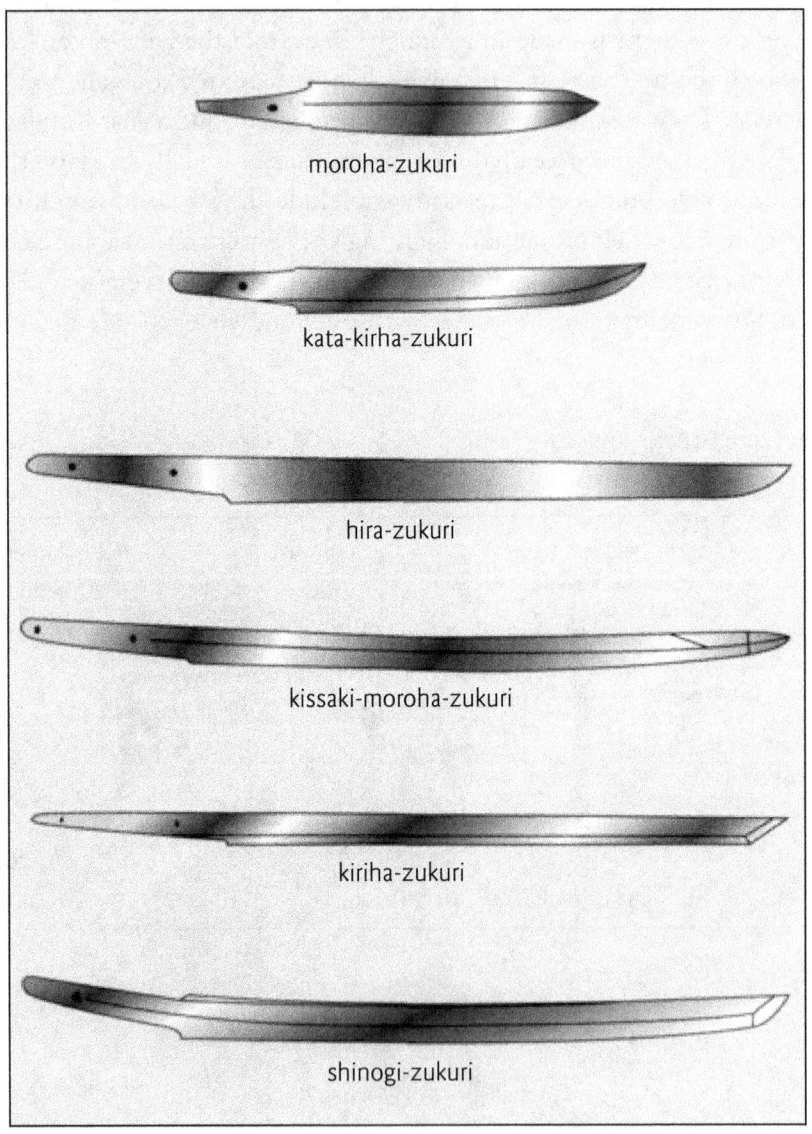

The *tanto* or *aikuchi* is the style we are mainly concerned with here. This form consists of a single V-shaped edge, a straight or evenly curved back and a point formed by cutting the metal back on an angle at the tip. Details on the construction of swords and tanto can be found in Kapp, et al. (1987).

The *Nihon Shoki*, a book from the mid-700's CE, in mentioning a *tosu*, contains the first reference to Japanese knives (Sato, 1983). This small knife was used in an assassination attempt on the Emperor Suinin. Legal codes of the time seem to indicate that the tosu was a symbol of rank carried by the upper classes, both men and women. This symbology is later echoed by the sword in the age of the samurai. From the Heian Era (from 782 CE) to the early Kamakura (1185 to 1333), the long tachi sword was usually paired with a shorter blade called a *koshigatana*, which was mounted as an *aikuchi*. In the early Kamakura the tanto style of fittings appeared.

The tanto became very common around the thirteenth century during the Mongol invasions and was paired with the long tachi blade. This 24 to 25 centimeter (cm)-long *tanto* had no ridges and was narrow with a slight curve. It is thought that the tanto came into use for the close-quarters fighting, which was necessary due to the Mongol close-quarter battle methods, and for fighting on ships. Up to this time Japanese battles had been rather loose affairs mainly involving individual warriors on horseback. The tanto of this time were manufactured using the same process as was used for the sword. Various hardnesses of laminated steel were forge-welded and hardened (heated and quenched in water) using a clay coating along the back of the blade to delay cooling, which created a blade with a flexible spine and a hard edge.

At the start of the fourteenth century, the tanto became longer (27–30 cm) and wider with less curve. Some of the more famous knives of this time are the Hocho Masamune or "Masamune kitchen knife" blades (Fig. 4). In the later part of this century, the tanto disappeared and a thick, curved companion sword called the *odabira* replaced it. This sword is similar to the other weapons of the Nambokucho Era (1333–1391), which all seemed to grow to enormous size. This was the era of the *o-dachi*, swords up to five feet long which were carried across the back and used with cord wrappings down most of the blade (Sato, 1983).

In the later Muromachi Era (1392–1572), a period of wars, a new type of blade developed as swords again shrank to a more practical size. The *uchigatana* were of two general sizes, the katana of over 60 cm and the shorter *wakizashi*. These blades, which were placed through the belt, were known from the Kamakura Era but were considered lower-class weapons as they were best suited for foot soldiers. In the Muromachi period, the upper classes adopted them and the tanto also reappeared, though shorter and narrower than before. By the end of the era a new type of tanto was popular, being about 15 cm long and carried under the clothes (*kwaiken*). There were also double-edged knives at this time.

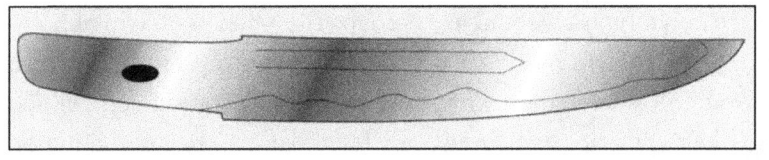

FIGURE 4:
Honcho Masamune

In the Momoyama (1573–1599) and the Edo (1603–1868) periods, the *daisho* (long/short) paired blades were fully adopted and the tanto virtually disappeared as a major weapon. There were more than enough old knives to fill the demand and as a result few new ones were forged. During the Pacific War, the Japanese government supplied naval officers and the Kamikaze fighter pilots with dirks in the style of the tanto or aikuchi (Fuller and Gregory, 1986). In recent years a few smiths in Japan have begun making traditional tanto once again, mainly for the collector's market. Western knifesmiths are also making this Japanese style of blade (Maynard, 1986).

Tanto Jutsu

Many of the old martial arts traditions (*ryu*, which were mostly founded in the late Muromachi and Edo periods) taught *tanto jutsu* (knife techniques) for both offense and defense. In a sword-oriented school the knife may have been taught as a defensive weapon against a sword, or it may have been used for a surprise attack as the fight moved to close quarters. The Sekiguchi-ryu tradition of *iaido* (the art of drawing the sword) includes several forms which use the tanto against an attacking sword. Modern *naginata* (a pole-arm weapon) schools also use the tanto as a supplementary weapon for situations in which the opponent gets inside the range of the naginata. The jujutsu schools which arose during the Edo period often included tanto in the curriculum.

The tanto was used primarily for thrusting, but techniques were also included for blocking and slashing although the blade was not heavy or long enough to be as effective as the sword in this last application. Some ryu also taught knife and spike throwing. The straight-pointed items were called *shuriken* as opposed to the "star" shapes which were called *shaken* (Gruzanski, 1968), a definition that has become reversed in the West, with the "throwing stars" now being called shuriken. There is some question as to whether a tanto would have been of much use as a throwing weapon, beyond its value as a distraction, but stories exist of their use.

With these several sources of instruction in knife techniques, it might have been expected that a separate *do* (*michi* or "way," implying a way of life) style would have arisen for this weapon just as *kendo* arose from the *kenjutsu* or *jodo* from *jojutsu*. This, however, does not seem to have been the case as the tanto never managed to become as respectable as the sword, naginata or jo. The tanto was never quite seen as an instrument of spiritual forging but remained simply a weapon.

Practice Knives

Many different styles of practice knives are available for use today. Rubber knives in the Western style are readily obtainable and are perhaps the safest tool available. In recent years, the Japanese tanto style has been popular as a working knife in North America. Made from hard stainless steel, these knives are easily cared-for weapons, which may appeal to those who like to practice dangerously. By far and away, the most common practice knife used in the aikido dojo is a wooden blade in the shape of an aikuchi. It is generally 11–14 inches long and curved, with the same shape as a *bokken*.

MAKING A PRACTICE KNIFE

These wooden blades are easily made with a few basic tools and the instructions provided here for the ambitious student.

Lay a curve of appropriate width (1.25 inches at the handle to one inch at the tip) and length on a piece of wood 3/4 to one inch wide (Fig. 5). Cut this out with a saw. Now cut a wedge out of the tip so that the back (concave side) is longer than the edge side (Fig. 6). This creates the point, more angle means a sharper tip. Clamp the handle and use a drawknife, spokeshave or rasp to take the corners off at about forty-five degrees creating three straight planes across the back (see Fig. 7).

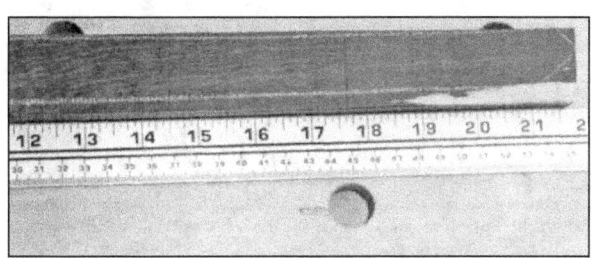

FIGURE 5:
Knife pattern laid out on a piece of Africa Blackwood (usually used for bagpipes). This tip style is based on the bokuto used in the Niten Ichi Ryu sword style.

FIGURE 6:
Cutting the tip for the knife.

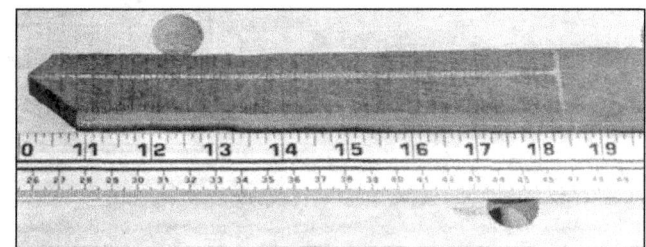

FIGURE 7:
Layout for shaving.

The angled planes run on the blade portion only and the back plane (the original sawed surface) gets narrower toward the tip. The handle, being about one hand width from the butt end, can be cut like the back planes at this time and rounded over later. Turn the blade over so that the convex or edge side is up. Draw a line down the center to keep your lines straight and shave the sides from this center line back to the edge of the forty-five degree planes you just cut (Fig. 8). At the same time make the blade sides narrow slightly toward the tip. The last thing to do is to round over the handle to a comfortable grip (Fig. 9). Sand and finish with a wood oil such as Tung Oil and you are ready to practice (Fig. 10). This same method is used to make wooden *bokuto*.

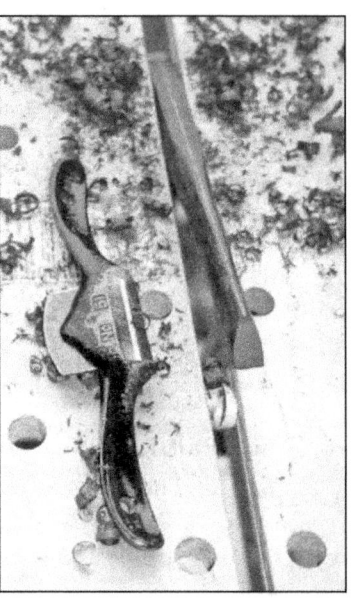

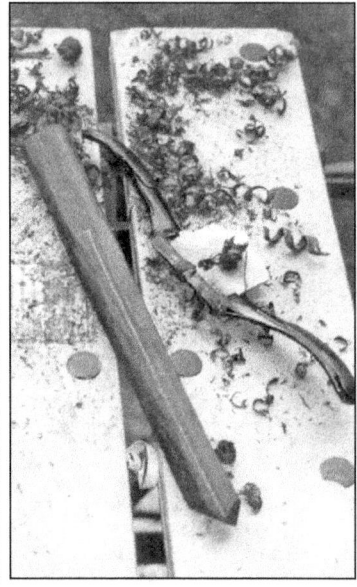

FIGURE 8:
Cutting the edge planes with a spokeshave.

FIGURE 9:
Handle rounded, all planes shaped and ready to sand.

FIGURE 10:
Belt-sander with a soft pad on the bed so that curves may be sanded. Sanded with 50- to 80-grit belts.

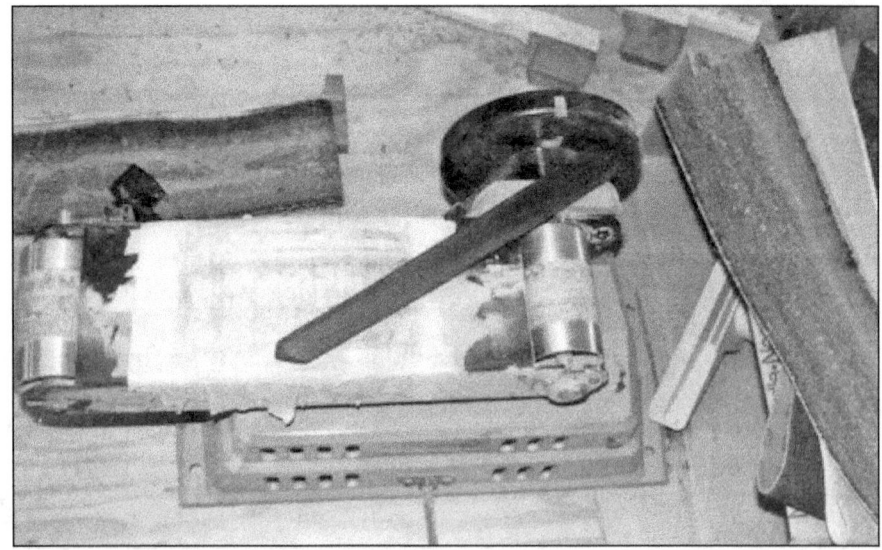

Attacking with the Knife (tanto ukemi)

Every aikidoka is eventually required to attack with a knife. It should be remembered that some people, for personal reasons, have a profound fear and dislike of knives. Since practice with the tanto is so useful to the art, some thought must be given as to how to include these people in training. Pay close attention to the etiquette of handling the blade and never play around with it during a practice session. Keep the practice serious but try not to be ominous.

A gradual approach to the knife may be needed for fearful students. Let newer students see knife techniques being performed. Later, let those who are most fearful attack with the tanto, finally let them handle attacks which are very slow and careful before going on to fully active practice.

Etiquette

The first time you pick up any weapon for practice you should face the high point of the room, hold the weapon up with both hands (palms up), the edge toward yourself, tip to the left and arms extended as if offering the blade. Hold the weapon at eye-level and keep it at this height as you bow from the waist (Fig. 11). Straighten up and then lower the blade to the carry position. This is an excellent way of reminding yourself that the wooden stick now represents a very dangerous weapon. The bow is to request assistance in understanding the use of the art and a prayer that no harm will come to you or your partner. It is the same as the bow at the start of the class. The blade is held with the edge toward yourself and the tip to the right so that it is in the least threatening position, which is also the most polite manner.

The wooden practice blade must always be treated as if it were a real knife. This means never handling the edge, fooling around with it, throwing it or carelessly dropping it onto the mat. When putting it down, place it so that the edge faces toward the wall of the dojo and never toward someone else; the tip should not face toward the *kamiza* (the high point or altar shelf). When carrying it, keep the tip pointed toward the ground until you are ready to attack. By the same token keep the edge aimed at yourself when not using the weapon.

FIGURE 11:
Mr. Lenny Seed of the University of Guelph Aikido Club, showing a standing bow.

Ordinarily, when not practicing techniques, you should hand the tanto to someone else, handle first, holding the back of the blade in your palm so that if the other person pulls on the knife it doesn't cut you (Fig. 12). It is more correct to hand the knife over using both hands to show that you have no aggressive intentions. Hold the handle with one hand and the blade with the other (palms up), making sure that the edge is pointed toward yourself. Make a small bow as you hand it over (Fig. 13). When receiving a blade, do it with two hands and immediately turn the blade edge to face yourself.

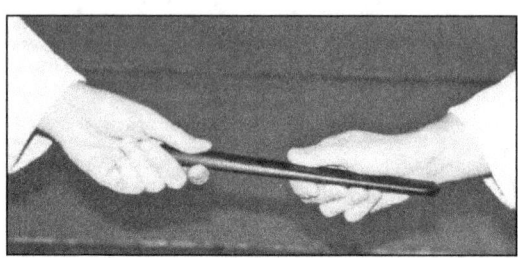

FIGURE 12: Handling over the blade safely.

FIGURE 13:
Mr. Lenny Seed handling the tanto to Pat Senson in a formal manner during practice at the University of Guelph Aikido Club.

During active practice when you are returning the knife to the attacker (*uke*), you should put it down on the floor between the two of you, with the edge pointing at yourself and the tip off to one side. It is neglectful to simply hand a blade to your attacker, thus putting yourself immediately into range of an attack.

Keep in mind that at some time in the future you may be asked to attack with a real knife. You are now training the proper instincts for that time. Be aware of what the edge and the tip are doing and where they are facing, especially when you are doing a breakfall or a roll with the knife in your hand.

At all times you must demonstrate that you have complete control of the weapon. If you do not, your instructor may feel the need to take it away from you for the sake of your own safety. This is not likely to be a pleasant experience.

Holding the Tanto

There are two general grips for holding the knife, one far more common than the other. The usual grip is to take the hilt and pull it up into the palm with the little and ring fingers. The thumb and remaining two fingers are wrapped loosely to provide control (Fig. 14). This grip is the same as that used for the sword and the staff and for holding someone's arm. In a less common grip (in the Japanese martial arts) the index finger and the thumb are used for gripping. This puts the front of the hand close to the guard in a forward grip and is used to provide a stable base for a thrust (Fig. 15). This grip is not recommended for practice with Japanese weapons.

FIGURE 14: Gripping the tanto with the little finger.

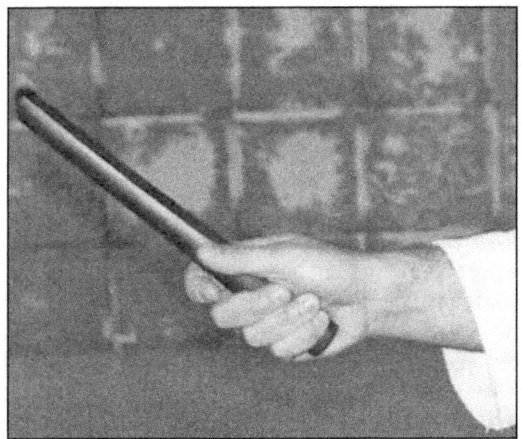

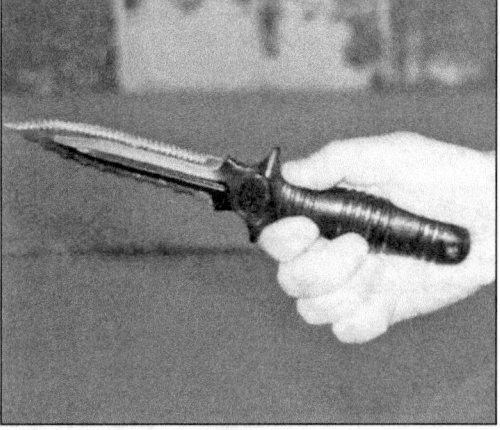

FIGURE 15: A fencing-style grip utilizing the thumb and index finger.

Tanto Positions

There are essentially four ways of positioning the tanto. Each way will determine what strikes can be made and from what angle. It is important to note that a tanto is not an exotic weapon like a push-knife which has a T-shaped grip and is used in a punching motion. The tanto is the same as a kitchen knife with a guard. The common practice knife is a guardless aikuchi but the presence or absence of a guard makes no real difference in the attack.

The tanto can be held with the point facing "forward" (or up) from the thumb and index finger side of the hand, or facing "backward" (or down) from the little finger side. In addition the edge may face up the arm "toward" your body or "away" from the body. These combinations create the four basic grips on the knife.

1) By far the most natural and flexible grip on the knife is the "forward" and "away" position which is the same as a sword grip. The knife may be thrust forward and all slashes except the floor to ceiling vertical cut can be made easily (Fig. 16).
2) By spinning the handle 180 degrees, the edge is now facing upward ("toward" your body). This grip allows thrusts to be made and a floor to ceiling rip is possible. Other slashes are now difficult (Fig. 17).

FIGURE 16:
Grip #1, tip forward and edge away from the arm. This is the "sword grip."

FIGURE 17:
Grip #2, tip forward and edge toward the arm.

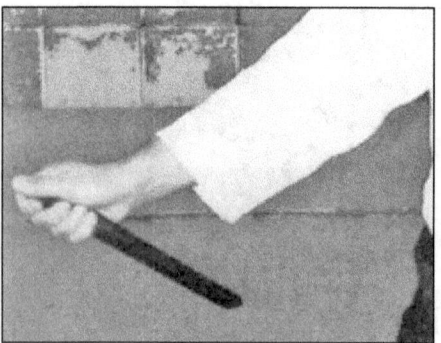

FIGURE 18:
Grip #3, tip facing "back" and edge facing away from the arm.

3) Placing the knife in the hand so that the tip points "backward" from the little finger edge of the hand and the edge points down ("away" from the body) allows one to fold the knife up along his forearm (Fig. 18). Slashes from all directions except the downward vertical are possible. Forward thrusts (one-handed) are difficult on the horizontal axis but can now be delivered from above or from the sides. On the other hand, low horizontal thrusts are now easily made to the rear.

4) Spinning the blade 180 degrees so the edge faces "toward" the body gives a tanto position that allows only thrusts from above and the sides. No slashes are possible from this position. This is the "movie madman" grip (Fig. 19).

FIGURE 19: Grip #4, tip facing "back" and edge facing toward the arm.

Other hand positions tend to be a little exotic and are usually variations of the four described above. These are the strongest grips for attacking with the knife. A good *uke* (attacker) should be able to switch from one grip to another without having to use two hands to do it. This allows him to shift attacks smoothly as needed. A small amount of practice will be sufficient and is a good exercise in knowing where the edge is at all times.

Tanto Attacks

The knife can be used to thrust and to slash. For both the attacker and the defender the thrust (*tsuki*) is slightly more dangerous. The thrust leaves the attacker more open since he is usually leaning forward now and has given the defender an arm to grasp. The thrusting attack, if it connects, will do more damage than the slash since the tip has a much greater chance of reaching a vital organ. Most thrusts will be aimed at the stomach or solar plexus, the middle level (*chuden*). In some cases the thrust may be at the neck or the face, the upper level (*joden*).

As when you are punching, knife thrusts should be an honest attempt to make contact with the defender (*nage*). Presumably if it were a fake, the defender would not react. Attack with commitment and the intent to score a hit, but remain under control to avoid causing injury to the defender and also to avoid having to perform a fall (*ukemi*) when you are seriously off balance.

A slash, which will cut skin and possibly muscle, is less immediately dangerous to the defender. A number of slashes, however, can result in severe loss of blood. The attacker, by keeping the attacking arm close to the body for most of the attack, is less exposed to a counterattack by the defender. There are two points at which the defender can counter a slash: before it reaches the target and on the follow-through after a miss. The attacker should be aware of this and be ready to perform a fall when needed.

When slashing, the tip and two or three inches of the edge at the tip are the cutting surface. Knives are not chopping tools like an axe, but must be drawn across a surface in order to cut. The attacker should move accordingly. There are eight traditional angles of attack depicted by lines drawn horizontally, vertically, and the forty-five degree angles to these. In addition, some attacks may be a combination of two or more angles as a slash and return slash are made. It is also possible to slash and return with a thrust.

The attacker should always remember that the techniques in tanto waza are often more direct and hence more quickly applied than in unarmed practice. In addition there seems to be a basic attitude change in most defending persons when facing a tanto. The defender is much more willing to be rough during the throw. This is usually a good thing, since facing a knife is much more dangerous than facing an unarmed attack, but the attacker must be ready to adjust his fall accordingly.

TANTO WAZA — Specific Technique Practice

Several attacks and possible responses are given below. These are by no means the only techniques that may be used against the knife but they will provide a good idea of what is possible. The techniques are classified according to the attack and the defender's opening defensive move.

Unarmed Defender Against a Knife

These are the most common attacks and some common responses when the defender is unarmed. As a general rule, it is a good idea for the defender to get between the attacker's center of gravity and the knife. This will disrupt the flow of power to the knife and allow the defender to control the blade. The defender can cut the power from either side of the attacker's arm. If he is on the inside of the arm he must be aware of the attacker's free hand which can be used to continue the attack. A better place for the defender to be is the outside of the attacker's arm, so he should be aware that the attacker may unexpectedly switch from the inside to the outside during a technique. In general, the inside (*uchi*) is the front (*omote*) and the outside (*soto*) is the rear part (*ura*) of the techniques. We will assume the attacker is holding the knife with his right hand for these discussions. The defender is in *hidari hanmi gamae* (a left foot forward, half turned stance) (Fig. 20a).

I. MIDDLE-LEVEL ATTACKS (Chudan Thrust)

This thrust may be made with the tanto held in grip number one or two. The techniques may also be used against a rising slash with the blade held in grip number two. The defender must note at some point during the execution of the technique which grip the attacker is using, since the final knife removal often requires the defender to grip the back of the blade. The techniques can all be done without checking on this until the last second. A final check is always necessary since it is easy for the attacker to spin the knife from grip number one to two and back while his hand or wrist is being held.

I-21. Ura Tenkan. Ura tenkan means to move to the rear. The defender moves to his left front, turning on the toes of the left foot 180 degrees, and swings the right foot around behind the attacker. The defender places the left hand on the side (Fig. 20b), then top (Fig. 20c) of the attacker's right arm before moving into an elbow lock (*hiji shime*), forcing the elbow down toward the ground (Fig. 20d). As the attacker hits the mat, the defender follows and removes the knife by flexing the attacker's fingers and wrist up his forearm to open the hand. If the attacker is using grip number one, the defender can slide down the fingers and strip the blade out of his hand by gripping the back of the blade (*mune*) (Fig. 20e).

I-21. The same opening move (Figs. 20a to 20c) can also lead into *kote gaeshi* (wrist [out] turn). The defender grasps the top of the attacker's right hand and then twists the wrist outward (Fig. 21a) as the attacker turns toward the defender. In this case the defender throws the attacker and then uses the same hand grip to remove the knife if the attacker has not already been forced to let it go (Fig. 21b). If the defender is still standing as he does this, both partners should be aware that the knife may be dropped down on top of the attacker.

I-22. Ura Tenkan. Using the same initial body move, the left hand may take the attacker's wrist from underneath (Fig. 22a). In this case the left forearm is not raised as the attacking arm is deflected, but the hand remains aimed at the mat. As the attacker turns to face the defender, the defender may move under the attacker's arm to apply *sankyo* ("third technique") (Figs. 22b-c). At this time the defender may hold sankyo with his left hand and use the right to strip the knife by the back of the blade (Fig. 22d). Again, this defense strip depends on the attacker employing grip number one. A knife may be grabbed by the edge safely, but if any pulling motion is applied, the edge will cut into the hand so this strip is not recommended if the attacker is using grip number two. Instead, the attacker may be taken down into the sankyo pin and then forced to release the blade (Fig. 22e) before the pin is applied (Fig. 22f). The defender takes down the attacker (starting in Fig. 22c) by stepping forward with the

right foot, pulling the attacker's elbow forward with the right hand, and dropping the attacker's shoulder against the defender's knee as he drops to the mat.

I-23. Starting the same way as in technique I-22, the defender may simply apply a corner drop (*sumi otoshi*) (Fig. 23a) as the attacker turns toward him. The defender will keep hold of the arm as the attacker falls and may then drop a knee onto the inside of the upper arm to cause the attacker to drop the knife (Fig. 23b). The attacker should be ready for this and drop it earlier. If the defender lets go as he throws, the attacker may roll out and return to attack, recognizing that on the street he would likely have an injured arm at least.

I-24. Omote Ushiro Aski

Omote ushiro ashi means to remain in front of the attacker and withdraw a foot. The defender may withdraw his left foot and turn his hips into a right-foot forward stance (*migi hanmi gamae*) as he matches the speed of the thrust and grasps the attacker's wrist with the right hand, palm down (Fig. 24a). By withdrawing his right foot the defender can continue the attacker's motion and turn his arm over while moving to the outside (Fig. 24b) so that a *nikyo* pin may be applied (Fig. 24c). By pinning the elbow down onto the mat and bending the hand toward the attacker's head, the defender can force the attacker to drop the knife (Fig. 24d). If the defender has pinned the attacker with his elbow on the ground in nikyo, the defender can lift the elbow up and apply a *gokyo* pin to force the knife free (Fig. 24e).

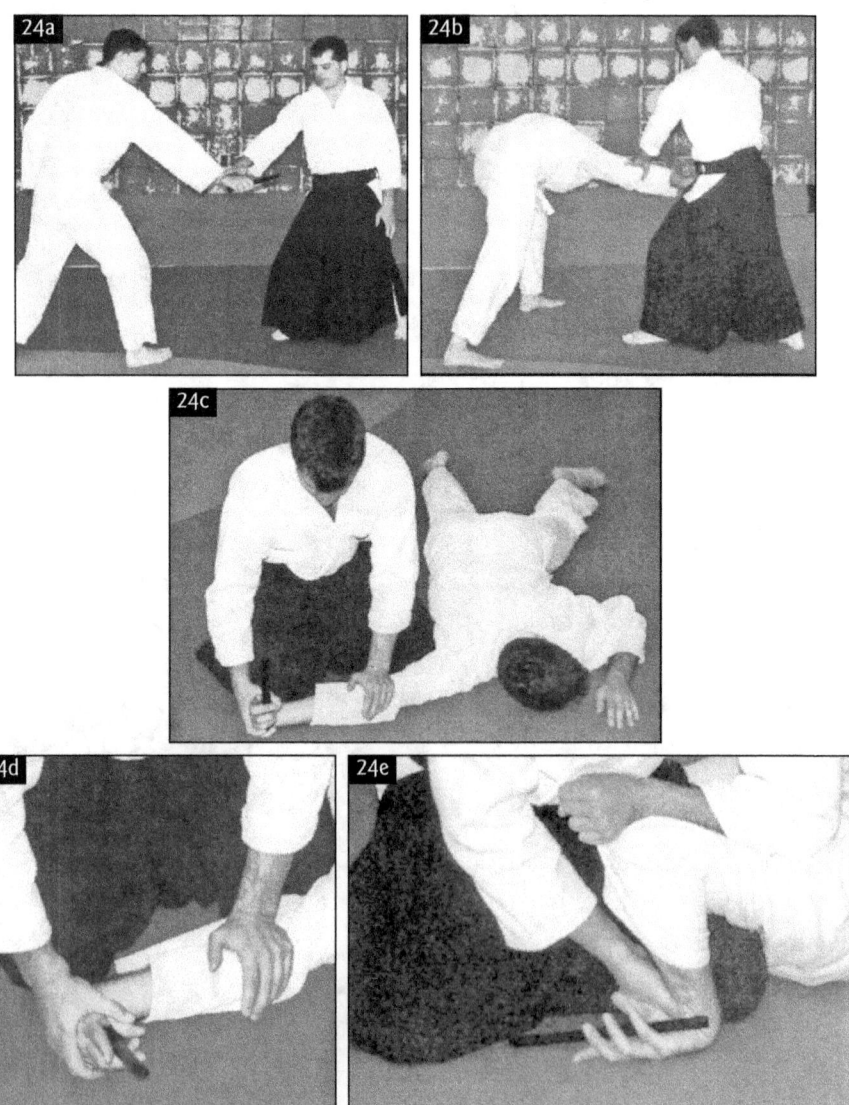

I-25. Sankyo may be applied in the same situation (Fig. 24b) if the defender switches from the right hand to the left hand as he moves to the outside of the arm (Fig. 25a). It is usually safer to perform this switch after moving to the outside and taking firm control of the attacker's balance (Fig. 25b).

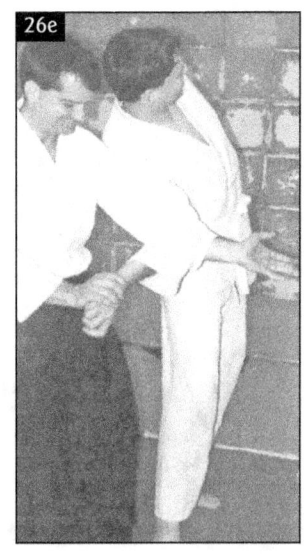

I-26. Omote Ushiro Ashi. By stepping back into a right-foot forward stance (*migi hanmi*) and grasping the attacker's wrist from the underside with the right hand (Fig. 26a), the defender can then shift to the outside of the arm and bring the left arm up under the attacker's elbow to apply *ude kime nage* (Fig. 26b). The defender may step across the attacker's front (Fig. 26c) or to the rear (Fig. 26d) position and throw in the same direction as the attacker's movement. The attacker should be careful if trying to flex the biceps to get out of this throw as the defender may suddenly apply the rest of the technique slamming the elbow forward and twisting the shoulder badly (Fig. 26e).

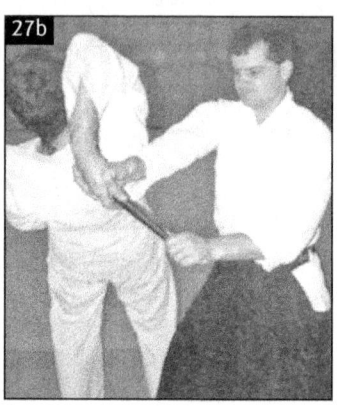
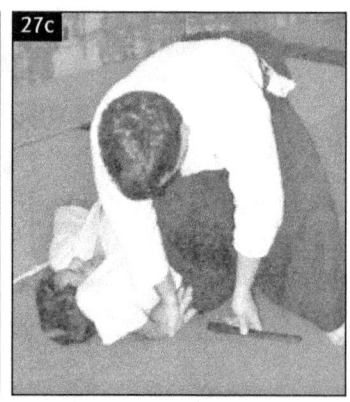

I-27. Shiho Nage (four-sided throw) can be applied from this attack, instead of *ude kime nage*, by passing under the arm instead of locking it out (Fig. 27a). From the locked position at the attacker's shoulder, the knife may be stripped out with the left hand (Fig. 27b), or the defender may throw the attacker down while keeping hold of his wrist, and on the ground he may push the attacker's elbow down beside his right ear while pulling the wrist outward to twist the shoulder and pin him as the knife is stripped (Fig. 27C).

I-28. From the same attack and initial move (Fig. 26a), as the defender moves to the outside of the arm, he may elect to step deeply behind the attacker (Fig. 28a). By reaching over the left shoulder and grasping the attacker's right lapel, the defender can apply a choke from behind (*ushiro kubi shime*) (Fig. 28b). Continuing the choke, the defender can pull the attacker straight back into a sitting position with his left knee in the attacker's back and the right knee down on the mat (Fig. 28c). The defender can now throw the attacker face down by turning to the right and pulling the attacker's right arm back. The defender will end up with his left knee on the attacker's back, employing a choke while the attacker's right arm is being pulled back and up (Fig. 28d). If the attacker does not release the knife, a nikyo movement can be used to force his hand open (Fig. 28e).

I-29 and I-30. Other Entries

Entering into the attacker's front side (*irimi*) on the initial movement is not recommended as this puts the defender in range of the attacker's left hand (Fig. 29a). However, this entry is practical when the defender is striking at the attacker's throat or face with the right arm while stepping forward with the right foot, since the striking arm will also serve as a block to any attack from the attacker's left hand (Fig. 29b).

Moving in *kaiten* (turning 180 degrees on the balls of the feet with no foot shift, sometimes called *tenkai-ashi*) instead of tenkan to get to the outside of the attacker may be more practical if the attacker is moving with great power and speed (Fig. 30). This position is also achieved if the entering move is made to the left side.

II. UPPER-LEVEL ATTACKS (Jodan Attacks)

The attacker may thrust to the face or throat using grip numbers one or two. He may also slash downward using grip number one or even stab downward using grip numbers three or four. The angled slashes to the side of the head are similar to those to the front of the head, which means that the response need only be modified slightly for these attacks. The attacker must be careful any time he strikes toward the defender's head as even a blunt weapon can injure the eyes.

II-31 and II-32. Ayumi Ashi Irimi Tenkan Ikkyo Ura

When attacked, the defender moves into a right-foot forward stance and enters to the attacker's right side, riding his hand up by placing the back of the right wrist on the attacker's right wrist and controlling his elbow with the left hand (Fig. 31a). Stepping in with the left foot to the attacker's rear and then turning, the defender puts the attacker down onto the mat in an ikkyo pin (Fig. 31b, c, d). The first movement from the defender may also be a slide step in with the left foot, in which the left hand brushes the knife to the side and into the defender's right hand before throwing the attacker by stepping behind him (*tenkan*) (Fig. 31e-g). In Figure 31g it appears that the defender has broken his posture by bending over. However, Figure 31c shows that the rear leg provides postural stability as the defender adjusts his body to control the attacker, who is shorter.

The defender may, after turning the attacker's arm so that he bends at the waist (Fig. 32a), slip the left hand over his arm. The defender can then grab his own right wrist (Fig. 32b). By turning in *kaiten* or *tenkan* to the left, the defender will throw the attacker in a *shihonage*-type technique which is very powerful and locks the attacker's knife hand at the same time (Fig. 32c). The same movement with his left arm will allow the defender to apply an elbow lock as well.

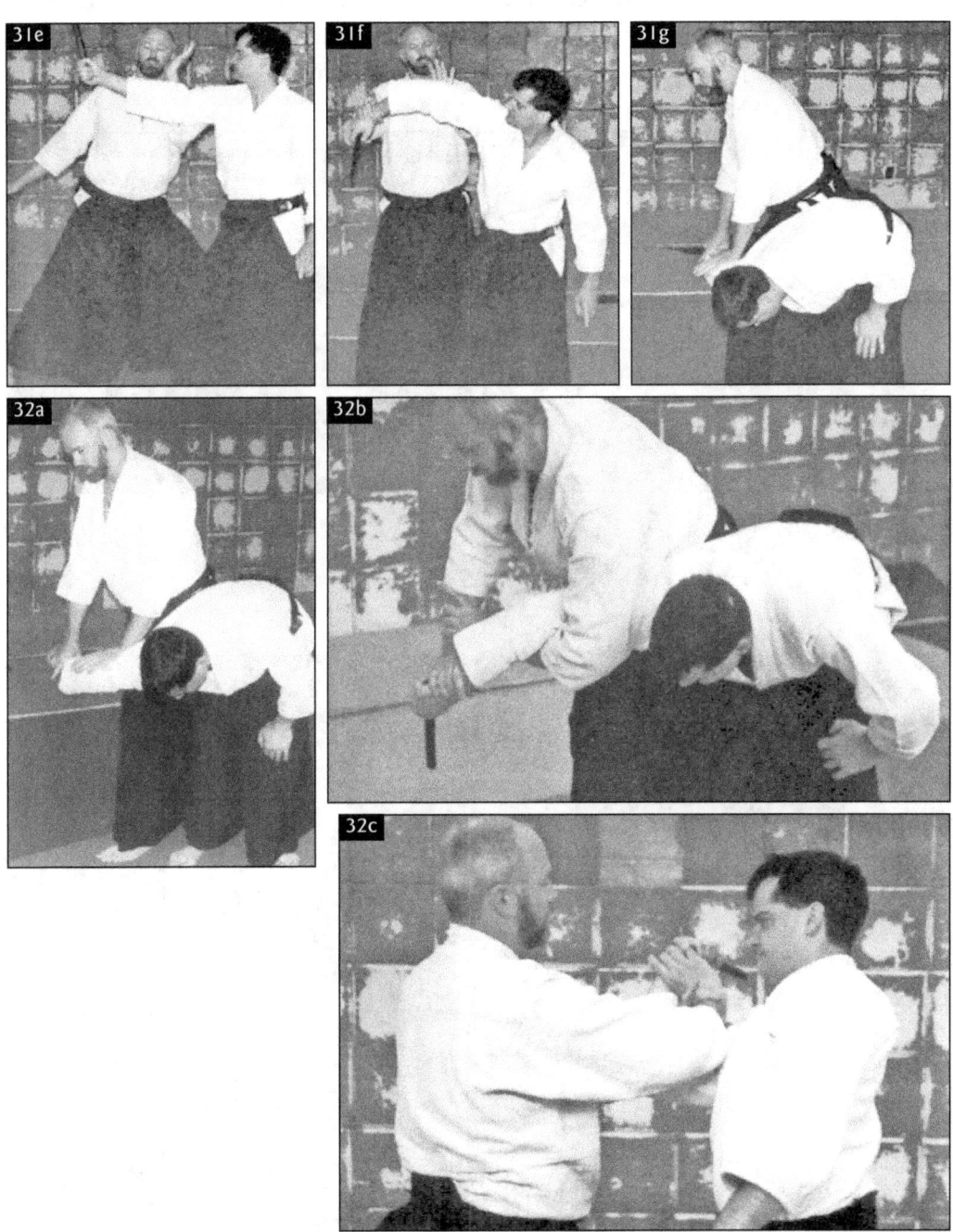

II-33 and II-34. Irimi Ura and Irimi Nage

By sliding out to his left with the left foot (Fig. 33a) and then stepping in with the right while reaching past the attacker's neck with his right hand, the defender can throw in *irimi nage* (Fig. 33b). The defender must stay close to the attacker's chest to avoid having the knife raked across his right ribs as the attacker falls (Fig. 33c). As the attacker hits the ground, the defender may reach back and around the attacker's right arm, hold it straight, change knees and use the leverage to push the attacker's shoulder upward in an arm bar/lock (Fig. 33d). By moving around the attacker's head, the defender can roll the attacker over onto his stomach.

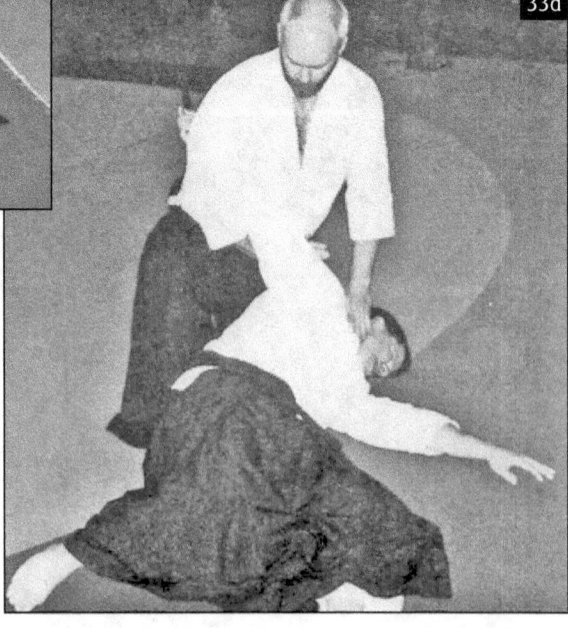

Ura Irimi Tenkan. A second irimi nage may be executed by sliding diagonally into the attacker's right side, putting the left hand on the back of his neck. The right hand then grasps the attacker's wrist from below (Fig. 34a) while the defender steps behind the attacker (*tenkan*) to break his balance (Fig. 34b). Without letting go of his right wrist, the defender reverses direction and raises his right arm across the attacker's throat carrying his right hand and the knife with it as well to throw the attacker down with irimi nage (Fig. 34c).

II-35. Ushiro Ashi and Ura Ude Kime Nage

The defender may change feet or step back with the left foot, then meet the descending arm with his right arm, bringing it down to the right, keeping the hand on top of the attacker's wrist (Fig. 35a). The defender will then bring his left arm up under the attacker's elbow and throw in *ude kime nage* (Fig. 35b).

II-36. Ura Gokyo

By sweeping the attacker's arm out to the left with his left arm (Fig. 36a), the defender can grasp the inside of the attacker's wrist with the right hand (Fig. 36b). The defender may then bring the arm up and over to his right, controlling the attacker's elbow with his left hand, and apply a gokyo pin after throwing him down as in *ikkyo* (Figs. 36c, d).

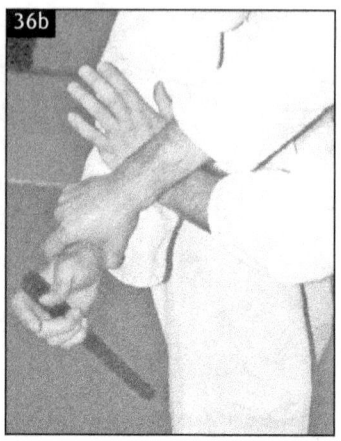

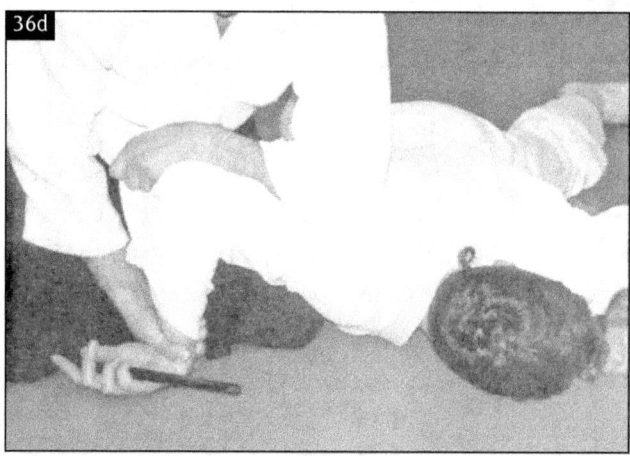

II-37. Ushiro Ashi Omote Shihonage

Stepping back with the right foot allows the defender to sweep the attack down on his left side with the left arm (Fig. 37a). By bringing the arm across low to his front and being careful to stay out of range of the blade (Fig. 37b), the defender can then move into *shihonage* and throw the attacker down (Fig. 37c). If the defender keeps hold of the attacker's hand, the knife may simply be knocked loose as he hits the mat. If it is not in position for this, the defender can strip it by forcing the attacker's right elbow down beside his right ear as he draws the attacker's hand out and bends it at the wrist.

II-38. Ushiro Ashi Omote Nikyo

Stepping backwards into a *migi hanmi* stance (right foot forward) lets the defender sweep the attacker's arm down with his right hand (Fig. 38a). The defender may now move back to his right by sweeping the attacker's arm up and over to that side and stepping in to throw while controlling the attacker's elbow with the left hand (Fig. 38b). It is not a good idea to attempt the wrist lock of nikyo when facing a knife (Fig. 38c).

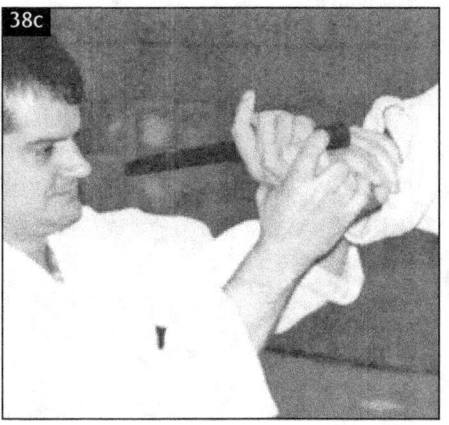

III. HORIZONTAL SLASH TO THE INSIDE (yoko giri)

In this case the attacker slashes with the tanto from his right to his left, holding the knife in his right hand.

III-39. Ushiro Ashi Shihonage

The defender can move with the swing, changing foot positions as he guides the attacker's wrist with his hands (Fig. 39a) and then grasps and guides the attacker's arm across the front (Fig. 39b) and into *shihonage*, either to the inside or outside positions (Fig. 39c).

III-40. Irimi and Uchi Hiji Shime (inside elbow lock)

By stopping the wrist with the left hand (Fig. 40a), then sliding the right arm over the arm and grasping his own wrist (Fig. 40b), the defender can apply an elbow lock from the inside of the attacker's arm. The defender must then turn to his left to throw the attacker down before the attacker strikes with his free hand (Fig. 40c). The defender will fold the attacker's arm up behind the attacker's back as the defender steps behind the attacker (*tenkan*) while keeping the knife in front of himself (Fig. 40d).

III-41. Irimi Tenkan, Gokyo, Nikyo or Soto Hiji Shime

By stopping the swing with his left hand, the defender can grasp the attacker's right wrist with his own right hand, palm down (Fig. 41a). The defender then moves the attacker's arm up and over to the right to get to the outside (*soto*) of the attacker's arm and applies a *gokyo* pin or an elbow lock (*hiji shime*). If the defender grabs the back of the attacker's hand he can now apply *nikyo* pin (Fig. 41b). In this case the weaker grip (resulting from a bent wrist) is reinforced if the left hand is used to help move the arm up and over (Fig. 41c).

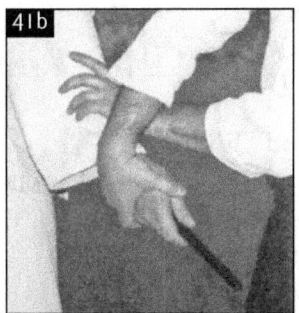

IV. HORIZONTAL SLASH TO THE OUTSIDE

The attacker slashes or stabs from his left side toward his right. This is most likely as a return strike from the previous horizontal strike.

IV-42. Irimi Tenkan and Ushiro Kubi Shime

As the attacker starts the slash, the defender steps into control his elbow with the right hand (Fig. 42a) and slides his left arm around the attacker's neck to grasp his lapel (Fig. 42b). The defender now unbalances the attacker to his rear while applying a choke and pulling his right arm back. As the attacker goes to the ground, the defender drops to one knee so that the left knee is now in the center of the attacker's back. By turning to the right as described earlier, the defender can drop the attacker face down while retaining control of the knife hand.

IV-43. Irimi Tenkai (Kaiten) and Hiji Shime

By sliding into the attacker's rear, the defender can block the attacker's arm above the elbow and at the wrist (Fig. 43a) and then grasp the wrist with both hands to apply a lock to his right elbow (*hiji shime*) (Fig. 43b).

IV-44. Gyaku Kube Shime (reverse neck lock).

Using the same opening motions as in Figure 42a, the defender can control the attacker's right hand with his own right hand and slide his left arm in front of the attacker's throat (Fig. 44a). By bending the attacker backward as if to execute an entering throw (*irimi nage*) (Fig. 44b), the defender will come to a position where he can wrap his arm around the attacker's neck and grasp his own belt (Fig. 44c). By pushing toward the attacker's torso, the defender can completely unbalance the attacker.

IV-45. Ayumi Ashi Irimi, Irimi Nage

The defender may simply step in and throw the attacker with the right arm by executing an entering throw (*irimi nage*) (Fig. 45). This is a very powerful throw since the attacker is partially turned away as it is applied. As is evident from the above discussion, some of the techniques applied against a tanto attack can be quite dangerous and the attacker must be even more on guard than usual against a sudden locking of his joints.

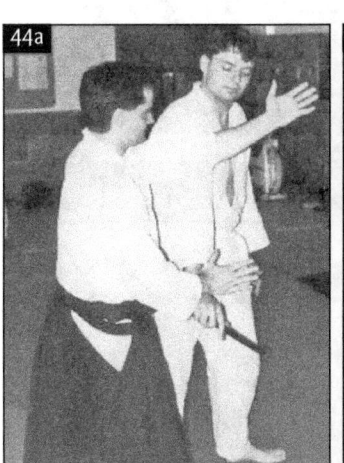
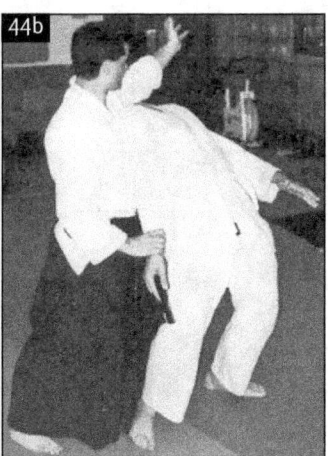

V. SMALL STAFF (jo) AGAINST KNIFE (tanto)

V-46. The most obvious way to use a *jo* (four-foot staff) against a knife attack is to take advantage of the reach in a jo and simply strike at the attacker's wrist (Figs. 46a–f). While these techniques can be practiced (with care and proper control) in a class, more varied practice is also possible.

The attacker should never simply jump in and run himself onto the jo. Instead, he should wait until the defender moves the tip off of the attack line and then immediately use the *suki* (opening). The defender should get ready for the technique and then deliberately create an opening for the attacker. We will assume that the attacker stands with his right foot forward (*migi gamae*) with the knife in his right hand and that the defender stands with his left foot forward (*hidari gamae*) with the jo poised for a middle attack (*chudan*) thrust.

Jodan Tsuki

A simple technique and one a bit more complicated are given for comparison.

V-47. Irimi Ura.

The defender may drop the jo and then slide into the attacker's right side as he thrusts with the knife. Using the front of the jo, the defender can ride down the attacker's right arm (Fig 47a) and then move the jo up to his neck to throw him in irimi nage (Fig 47b). The defender should use his left forearm against the attacker's neck rather than the jo to prevent accidental injury. The middle and back end of the jo should be used against the attacker's upper arm to prevent him from slashing at the defender as he falls.

V-48. Ushiro Ashi, Omote

The defender may elect to slide his left foot back and reverse the jo's ends to sweep the attacker's arm over to the left (Fig. 48a-b). As his arm stops, the defender may grasp the attacker's knife hand with his left hand (Fig. 48c) and then sweep the jo under the attacker's arm, placing it against the outside of the attacker's elbow and his throat (Fig. 48d). By allowing the attacker's arm to bend upward, the defender can then apply leverage against the attacker's elbow, throat and wrist to throw him down to the left (Fig. 48e). Needless to say, extreme care must be taken with this technique to avoid injuring the attacker's nose or throat. The increased leverage given by the jo can also cause problems if inexperienced students are involved.

Chudan Tsuki
V-49. Irimi Omote, Uke Nagashi (enter to the front, receive and deflect).

The defender can slide into the attacker's front and deflect the thrust to the left by dropping the tip of the jo and raising the right arm in the usual way (Fig. 49a). By sliding in fairly deeply, the defender can be in a position to place the attacker's right wrist on the left shoulder, drop the jo from the right hand and re-grip the other end which is lifted up on the outside of the attacker's upper arm (Fig. 49b). By applying pressure with the jo on the attacker's triceps, locking his elbow out and moving toward him while turning to the right, the defender can throw the attacker down onto his stomach (Fig. 49c). The defender must, of course, be careful not to let the attacker pull his arm back while throwing him or he could slash the defender's neck (Fig. 49d).

V-50. Ushiro Ashi, Omote

The defender may give the attacker an opening by pulling the jo back so that the left hand is at the end of the jo (Fig. 50a). As the attacker thrusts, the defender withdraws his left foot and swings the right end of the jo to block the attacker's arm downward to the left (Fig. 50b). As the attacker is unbalanced in this direction, the defender can then continue the movement with the end of the jo to catch the attacker's legs at the calves and complete the throw by straightening up and away from the tanto as the attacker slashes upward (Fig. 50c). Of course, a more efficient and practical way of executing this technique would simply be to hit the attacker's hand hard enough to make him drop the knife, making for a short practice.

The four techniques just illustrated are probably sufficient to illustrate that moving into throw the attacker with the jo rather than simply smashing his wrist exposes the defender to the knife. While there is nothing wrong with practicing in this way, the defender should understand that he is deliberately giving up a considerable advantage by moving in. It is not recommended that beginners practice in this manner because the risk to the attacker is simply too great.

Other techniques can be executed which will force the defender to use the jo in a nonstriking fashion. The attacker may grab the jo with his free hand and then thrust or slash with the knife, forcing the defender to deal with the grasp on the jo at the same time as he is trying to avoid the knife (Fig. 51).

Use of a Knife for Defense

Aikido is often considered unique amongst martial arts for its philosophy that the defender is responsible for the safety of the attacker as well as himself. With this ideal in mind, it would seem that the defender should simply throw the knife as far away as possible if he takes it from the attacker during a technique. By the same reasoning, the defender would not have a knife in hand at the start of a technique. All this assumes of course that a knife cannot be used except in a cutting or stabbing way. A few notes on the possibility of using a knife in a nonlethal way are given here in the hope that this weapon may eventually be "rehabilitated." It would go a long way toward removing the ambiguity of the use of the tanto if true aikido practice could be carried out while holding the weapon as well as simply defending against it. Of course, the use of the sword to kill opponents (even if imaginary) in such arts as iaido and kendo did not stop those arts from becoming *do* forms, but this article is not the place for that ethical discussion.

The tanto has a blunt end on the handle, one dull edge and a straight or shallowly curved blade. This allows for several non-cutting uses which can be derived from such arts as *tessen-jutsu* (fan techniques).

In any of the gripping positions, the handle can be used for striking. If held in grip number one or two, a "hammer-fist" type of strike may be used (Fig. 52a). If grip number three or four is used, the strike may be thrust forward as if thrusting with a jo (Fig. 52b). Since the end of the handle (*tsuka gashira*) is quite solid, strikes can be made to less vulnerable targets on the attacker, such as large muscle and bone. This will result in pain but not in injury beyond bruising. The handle can also be used to press into such sensitive points as the breastbone to control the attacker during a technique (Fig. 52c) or the back of the hand to release a grip (Fig. 52d).

Normal punching strikes can also be performed with the knife in the hand. The fingers, wrapped around the handle are in a much more secure position and are less likely to be broken on contact with a target than when they are simply doubled up in a fist. The blade edge may be turned back away from the attacker to avoid cutting him when punching although this motion will not result in much of a cut anyway (Fig. 53).

If the tanto has a longish handle, a range of techniques which involve pressing the attacker's bones are possible. If the attacker grasps the defender's right wrist with his left hand while the defender is holding a tanto in grip number one (Fig. 54a), the defender could simply move the handle so that it is laying across the top of the attacker's wrist. If the defender has placed his right hand, palm down, on the inside of the attacker's wrist, then he can cross his left hand underneath and grab the end of the handle thus trapping the attacker's hand with an "X" hand formation and the handle (Fig. 54b). The defender can now lever the handle down onto the attacker's wrist bones and force him to the mat (Fig. 54c).

The same technique can be performed with the flat edge of the blade rather than the handle. The attacker grabs as described above and the defender responds by spinning the tanto grip to number two with the edge facing upward. The defender now turns his palm upward to lay the blade of the tanto across the top of the attacker's wrist from the inside. With his left hand the defender crosses underneath his right and grabs the blade near the back portion near the blade tip (Fig. 55). The defender's left hand is palm up as he grabs the back of the blade.

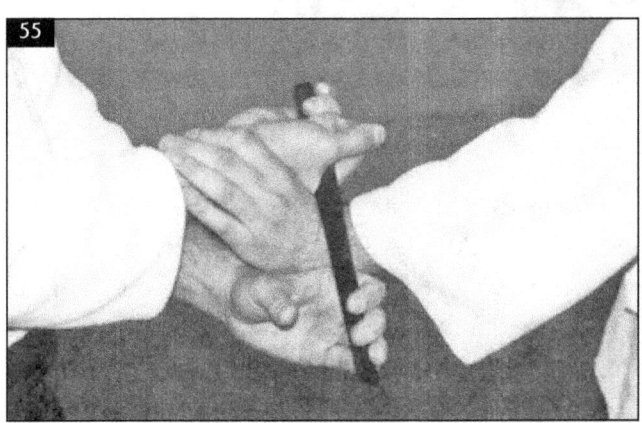

By slightly twisting the edge upward as he pulls back and down with his body, the defender levers the sharp corner at the back of the blade into the attacker's wrist bones. A similar type of trapping can be done when the knife is held in grip number three. For instance, if the defender has taken a blade away from the attacker while applying sankyo (Fig. 56a) but has not yet pinned the attacker, the defender may simply use the back of the blade to hook the attacker's elbow (Fig. 56b-c) rather than throwing the knife away and using his hand. If the defender is already holding a knife, the same kind of trapping can be used on the attacker's wrist while executing an ikkyo hold (Fig. 57).

If, while desiring to apply an ikkyo hold, the defender finds that the knife is in the wrong hand, but still in grip number three, he might elect to press on the elbow with the edge of the knife anyway (Fig. 58). Pressing with a knife blade will not cut the elbow since this type of blade is designed to cut (on a pull) rather than to chop.

Concluding Remarks

In this chapter the use of the tanto in aikido practice has been discussed. Unarmed responses to attacks with a knife against middle-level and upper-level thrusts and against horizontal slashes have been described. For these attacks, the defender's initial movement, stepping forward in irimi or tenkan to get inside the attack and stepping back to remain outside striking range, has been used, along with the defender's holding the defending hand palm up or down, to generate the initial defensive motions that lead into classical aikido techniques. Since the techniques of aikido are said to be limitless, no attempt was made to catalogue them. Instead, this simple breakdown of opening movements was used to provide a framework for the discussion. Other movements combined with other attacks would, of course, lead to still more techniques. The use of the jo against a knife was discussed briefly to indicate some further possibilities of knife practice.

The use of the knife by the defender was also introduced to provoke thought. With this discussion of the tanto it is hoped that the reader can see many other possibilities for this rather neglected weapon. It is curious that the knife, which is a weapon still being used on the streets, has less respect than the sword in aikido practice. With the right attitude and some thought to the techniques, there is no reason the practice of tanto techniques cannot become another *do* form. I provide these comments for those more qualified than myself in the hopes that they will undertake this development.

I would like to express my deep thanks to Len Seed and Pat Senson of the University of Guelph Aikido Club who posed for the photographs. The University of Guelph Aikikai was founded in 1980 by Dr. Peter Yodzis and Mr. Bruce Stiles. Stiles Sensei is still chief instructor at the club. The author and Mr. Seed were members of that original class.

Bibliography

Fuller, R., & Gregory, R. (1986). *Military swords of Japan, 1868–1945*. London: Arms and Armour Press.

Gruzanski, C. V. (1968). *Spike and chain: Japanese fighting arts*. Rutland, Vermont and Tokyo: Charles E. Tuttle.

Japanese Sword Museum. *The manual for appreciating the Japanese sword*. Tokyo: Nippon Bijutsu Token Hozon Kyokai.

Kapp, 1., Kapp, H., & Yoshihara, Y. (1987). *The craft of the Japanese sword*. Tokyo: Kodansha International.

Maynard, R. (1986). *Tanto: Japanese knives and knife fighting*. Burbank, California: Unique Publications.

Ogasawara, N. (1970). *Japanese swords*. (D. Kenny, Trans.). Osaka: Hoikushi Publications.

Sato, K. (1983). *The Japanese sword*. (J. Earle, Trans.). Tokyo: Kodansha International.

Ueshiba, K. (n.d.). *Aikido*. Tokyo, Japan: Hozansha Publication Co.

Yumato, J. M. (1958). *The samurai sword: A handbook*. Rutland, Vermont, and Tokyo: Charles E. Tuttle Co.

· 5 ·

Toward a Semiosis of the Martial Arts:
Aikido as a Symbolic Form of Communication
by Eliot Lee Grossman, J.D.

All photographs by Krishna Malhotra.

Introduction

Aikido is often paradoxically described by its practitioners as a "nonviolent martial art" dedicated to world peace. Aikido founder Morihei Ueshiba searched for many years to discover the "true essence" of *budo* until he had a mystical revelation that "true budo is love." While Ueshiba's esoteric explanations of aikido principles were often incomprehensible to his students, he always insisted that aikido had an important lesson to teach humanity; a lesson to be understood through the body by the practice of aikido techniques.

It is the thesis of this article that we can arrive at a deeper understanding of aikido if we consider it to be a *symbolic form of communication*, as well as a martial art, and utilize the science of semiotics to translate the "message" encoded in the "body language" of aikido techniques. This article begins by providing a brief description of aikido and semiotics and then proceeds to utilize Jakobson's classic model of the communicative process to present its discussion of aikido as a form of symbolic communication. The article concludes by "decoding" the "message" of aikido by analyzing a typical aikido technique as if it were a conversation between attacker and defender and then translating that "conversation" from "body language" into the natural language of English speech.

This article includes a technical section with photographs of aikido techniques which illustrate the major points made in the text. If our hypothesis is correct, that aikido uses body kinesis to communicate its philosophy, as well as to constitute its system of self-defense, then semiotic analysis should prove effective in enhancing our understanding of aikido's underlying principles.

Aikido: A Modern Martial Art

Aikido is a modern martial art created by Morihei Ueshiba (1883–1969) based upon his study of various classical samurai arts, including jujutsu and the arts of the sword and spear (Ueshiba, K. 1985: 146; Yamada, 1996: 3). The term "aikido" is a combination of three Japanese words: *ai* (harmony), *ki* (life energy, the energy of nature), and *do* (path or way). "Aikido" may be translated into English as "the way of harmonizing life energy" or "a way of life through harmony with nature."

Unlike those martial arts which emphasize striking or blocking and counter-striking an opponent, aikido emphasizes evading the attack and using its energy to throw and/or control the attacker (Kobayashi, 1992b: 4; Saposnek, 1985: 179).[1] Aikido is also distinguished from other martial arts by its particular philosophical teachings, a product of Ueshiba's relationship with the Omoto sect of Shintoism and his spiritual experiences which occurred during his search for the "true essence of budo" (Stevens, 1987: 17–37; Ueshiba, K., 1985a: 150–154; Ueshiba, M. 1996: 10–14; Kimura, 1997: 42–45).

The following is illustrative of Ueshiba's spiritual experiences during the course of his training: "One day a naval officer visiting Ayabe decided to challenge Morihei to a kendo match. Morihei consented but remained unarmed. The officer, a high-ranking swordsman, was naturally offended at this affront to his ability and lashed out at Morihei furiously. Morihei easily escaped the officer's repeated blows and thrusts . . . . Following the contest, Morihei went out to his garden . . . Suddenly Morihei started to tremble and then felt immobilized. The ground beneath his feet began to shake, and he was bathed with rays of pure light streaming down from heaven. A golden mist engulfed his body . . . and he himself assumed the form of a Golden Being. Morihei perceived the inner workings of the cosmos and further perceived that 'I am the Universe!' The barrier between the material, hidden, and divine worlds crumbled; simultaneously Morihei verified that the heart of budo was not contention but rather love, a love that fosters and protects all things" (Stevens, 1987: 32–33).

Ueshiba continuously modified aikido and its techniques over the course of his life, gradually emphasizing harmony and flowing movements while de-emphasizing physical strength and aggressive movements (Ueshiba, K., 1985b: 36). The changes in techniques were also accompanied by changes in the name of the martial art that Ueshiba was developing, from *aikibujutsu* (harmony of ki martial art) to *aikibudo* (harmony of ki martial way) to *aikido* (Ueshiba, M., 1996: 11–12, 14, 18; Ueshiba, K., 1987: 82; Bekku, 1997: 23).

While present-day aikido instructors differ in the extent to which they attempt to teach the philosophical aspects of aikido in addition to its techniques, Ueshiba taught his aikido as a complex philosophical system whose techniques were often explained as the movements of various Shinto deities or manifestations of the sacred sounds of the mystical science of *kotodama* (Ueshiba, M., 1993; Stevens, 1995; Gleason, 1995).

Ueshiba left behind a number of statements which suggest that he believed that aikido, in addition to providing a highly effective system of self-defense and a rigorous discipline for individual spiritual development, had an important message to teach all of humanity (Saotome, 1989: 208–209). However, the enigmatic nature of many of Ueshiba's teachings makes it difficult to determine precisely what the content of aikido's message might be and how aikido might transmit that message (Ueshiba, M., 1985: 23; Summerhawk, 1997: 8; Tohei, 1997: 8; Stevens, 1985: 12).

Reisel emphasizes that it is through the practice of aikido that the aikidoist receives Ueshiba's message: "Master Ueshiba did not leave us a treatise on how to practice Aikido, all neatly spelled out in a book. He hid it in his art, in his techniques. As you practice, so shall you uncover his philosophy . . . He said his Aikido was to teach Human Beings to be one family. He never said how. He didn't have to. The art says it for him by talking to our bodies. It's up to us to let our bodies speak to our minds and hearts" (Reisel, 1985: 154).

This viewpoint is supported by one of Ueshiba's *aikido doka* (aikido poems) in which he reminds us: "Ai-ki cannot be exhausted/By words written or spoken/Without dabbling in idle talk/Understand through practice" (Ueshiba, K. 1987: 76).

It is the hypothesis of this article that aikido's message is indeed transmitted to our bodies through the practice of aikido techniques and that we may utilize "semiotics," which studies symbolic forms of communication, to decode aikido's message so we may consciously, as well as unconsciously, receive and assimilate it.

Semiotics and Kinesics

Semiotics is the science which investigates symbolic forms of communication. Semiotics studies natural languages as well as other forms of communication, such as ritual, ceremony, dance, theatre, mass media, and advertizing. Many semioticians believe that all of human culture has a communicative aspect and, accordingly, semiotics may be used to investigate any human activity or cultural product. Some semioticians have investigated such seemingly non-linguistic phenomena as foods or fashions as if they were languages, seeking to discover their grammar and vocabulary.

The basic concept employed in semiotics is the "sign." A sign is anything which stands for something else. The process by which a sign stands for something else is call "signifying" or "signification." For example, the word "cat" stands for a particular animal which meows. An automobile in a television commercial may stand for sexuality, power, or social status. A statue of a blindfolded woman holding a set of scales can stand for justice. Each of these items, the word "cat," the automobile, and the statue, is a "sign" when it is used to "signify," as in the foregoing examples.

Semiotics, also called "semiology," was invented independently of each other by the French linguist Ferdinand de Saussure and the American philosopher and logician Charles Sanders Peirce in the early 1900's: "Although its origins can be traced back as far as Plato and Augustine, semiotics as a self-conscious theory emerged only at the beginning of this century, in the writings of Charles Sanders Peirce and Ferdinand de Saussure. It received fresh impetus in 1958 with the publication of Claude Levi-Strauss's *Structural Anthropology*, which applied Saussure's principles to the study of primitive cultures, but it achieved maturity only when it was consolidated with psychoanalysis. That consolidation was effected by Jacques Lacan. However, it was implicit from 1900, when Sigmund Freud gave us *The Interpretation of Dreams*" (Silverman, 1983: 3).

Semiotics studies the "sign," which Saussure defined as a "two-sided psychological entity" consisting of a sound image (the "signifier" or "signal") and a concept (the "signified" or "signification") (Saussure, 1986: 66–67).[2] Peirce proposed a "triadic" theory of the sign, consisting of the elements of "sign," "object," and "interpretant." Although Peirce employs a number of differing definitions of these elements and their mutual interrelationships, the essential principles of his theory are: (1) that signification requires an object ("sign") that functions significatively; (2) that the object acting as a sign represent another object; (3) that the object acting as a sign "determines" an "interpretant" (Greenlee, 1973: 23).

According to Peirce, a "sign" is "anything which is so determined by something else, called its Object, and so determines an effect upon a person, which effect I call its Interpretant, that the latter is thereby mediately determined by the former" (Hardwick, 1977: 80–81). While Peirce's "triadic" theory of the sign provides a useful theoretical model for decoding the meaning of the signs of aikido, his arcane and archaic terminology renders Peirce's theory rather enigmatic to a modern reader unfamiliar with semiotics. Accordingly, in this chapter we shall use a model of the sign, inspired by Peirce's pioneering work, but in which the terminology has been simplified and modernized as follows: A "sign" *refers* to an "object;" the "sign" *expresses* a "meaning;" the "meaning" *reflects* the "object."[3] This model may be visually illustrated as follows:

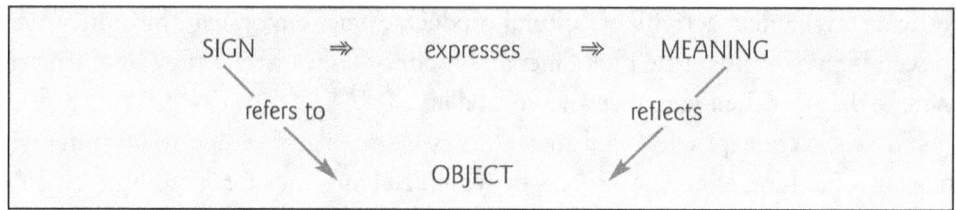

The theoretical basis for this investigation is Eco's pansemiotic hypothesis that, "the whole of culture *should* be studied as a communicative phenomenon based on signification systems" (Eco, 1976: 22). According to Eco, "[t]his means that not only *can* culture be studied in this way but . . . only be studying it in this way can certain of its fundamental mechanisms be clarified" (Id.). Hawkes explains the basis for this hypothesis as follows: "As the work of Levi-Strauss and others indicates, any aspect of human activity carries the potential for serving as, or becoming a sign . . . As Umberto Eco says, a sign is anything that can be taken as significantly substituting for something else. Accordingly, nothing in the human world can be merely utilitarian: even the most ordinary buildings organize space in various ways, and in so doing they signify, issue some kind of message about the society's priorities, its presuppositions concerning human nature, politics, economics, over and above their overt concern with the provision of shelter, entertainment, medical care, or whatever. All fives senses . . . can function in the process of semiosis: that is, as sign-producers or sign-receivers. The uses of perfume, of the texture of a fabric in clothing, the ways in which the tastes produced by cooking signal status, location, identity, foreigners are manifold" (Hawkes, 1977: 134).

Barthes (1968: 41–42) describes this phenomenon as the "semantization" of culture: "This semantization is inevitable: as soon as there is a society, every usage is converted into a sign of itself; every raincoat is to give protection from the rain, but this use cannot be dissociated from the very signs of an atmospheric situation. Since our society produces only standardized, normalized objects, these objects are unavoidably realizations of a model, the speech of a language, the substances of significant form. To rediscover a non-signifying object, one would have to imagine a utensil absolutely improvised and with no similarity to an existing model . . . a hypothesis which is virtually impossible to verify in any society."

If we also accept Barthes' position that semiology, "aims to take in any system of signs, whatever their substance and limits; images, gestures, musical sounds, objects, and the complex associations of all these, which form the content of ritual, convention or public entertainment," then, just as Barthes has undertaken semiological investigations of such cultural phenomena as fashions, food, cars, furniture, and photography, as though they were languages (Barthes, 1968: 9–11, 25–30; Silverman, 1983: 25–32), we should be able to investigate the martial art of aikido as if it were a language (Saotome, 1989: 2; Greenlee, 1973: 28–29).

Kinesics, a branch of semiotics founded by Ray Birdwhistell (1952, 1970), studies nonverbal communication or "body language." According to Birdwhistell, "body motion is a learned form of communication which is patterned within a culture and which can be broken down into an ordered system of isolateable elements" (1970: xi). In the course of his investigations, Birdwhistell discovered that, "there are body behaviors which function like significant sounds, that combine into simple or relatively complex units like words, which are combined into much longer stretches of structured behavior like sentences or even paragraphs" (Id.: 80). Since the "signs" which are the subject of our investigation are the body motions which comprise aikido techniques, we shall find it useful to employ various concepts from kinesics.

One of Birdwhistell's insights is that there is a basic distinction between two kinds of kinesic signs, which he denominates "formal" and "parakinesic" signs. "Formal" signs function in body language in the same manner that words, sentences or paragraphs function in verbal communication. "Parakinesic" signs amplify, emphasize or modify the "formal" signs and/or say something about the context of a given communication. For example, gestures or other body movements may function as "parakinesic" signs to interrupt another speaker or request him or her to be still so the subject can speak; to emphasize or terminate a conversation; or to allow or prohibit others to enter the conversation (Birdwhistell, 1970: 117).

Discourse analysis is a relatively recent branch of semiotics which is concerned with the study of the social uses of language.[4] Among the variety of approaches which have emerged in this field is "critical discourse theory" (see, e.g., Pecheaux, 1982; Foucault, 1995; Thompson, 1984; Eagleton, 1991; Macdonell, 1986; Anderson, 1988; Fairclough, 1989; Gimenez, 1989). Critical discourse theory is concerned with investigating the relationship between meaning and power: how power socially constructs meaning and how meaning is mobilized to sustain or transform unequal relations of power (Fairclough, 1989: 1–14; Anderson, 1988: 15–24; Thompson, 1984: 1–15). We shall apply critical discourse theory to the "communicative interaction" of individual combat in which an aikidoist must be able to successfully transform an asymmetrical power relationship with a larger and stronger attacker (Ueshiba, K., 1987: 40).

The Semiotics of Aikido

The cultural phenomenon to be investigated in this article is aikido. Aikido is a martial art consisting of a system of bodily movements (techniques); principles for their proper execution and application; an underlying meta-theory; and a system of etiquette and ritualized behavior which prescribes various requirements for the physical space within which the art is practiced and the distribution and clothing of the bodies of its practitioners within that space.

Jakobson's Model of Communication

As a general framework for this investigation we shall adopt Jakobson's classical model of communication (Waugh & Monville-Burston, 1990: 16; Hawkes, 1977: 83) in which a "message" in a particular "context" is transmitted by a "speaker" to an "addressee" in a "code" by means of a particular "contact" between them:

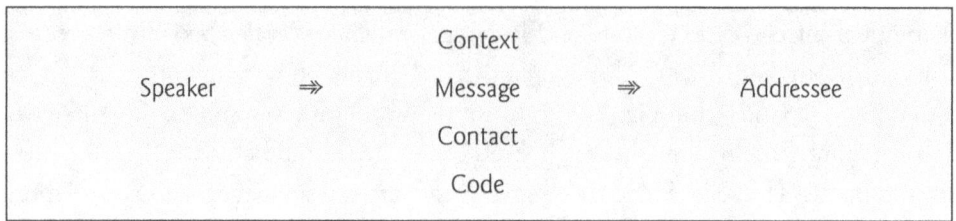

The Dojo: The Context of Aikido

The context for aikido practice is the practice hall or *dojo* (literally "the place for study of the way") where aikido is taught. Aikido is a "way of life," but our discussion is limited to the dojo by this article's length. The dojo is a ritually demarcated and organized space. Aikido practitioners ritually demarcate the dojo's boundaries by making a standing bow upon entering and leaving. Within the dojo, the practice area is demarcated by the same bowing ritual. Thus, aikido practice is marked off as a special activity—different from those of every day life—by the ritual recognition of the special nature of the space within which the art is practiced (Donohue, 1991: 165–178; Stevens, 1985: 25; Saotome, 1989: 204–206).

The Shomen (Altar)

The dojo is spatially organized by reference to an altar whose location identifies the front of the practice area. The altar commonly consists of a photograph of Ueshiba, a scroll with "aikido" written in Japanese ideograms, and a bouquet of flowers. We shall utilize our "triadic" theory of the sign to aid in determining the meaning of the altar.

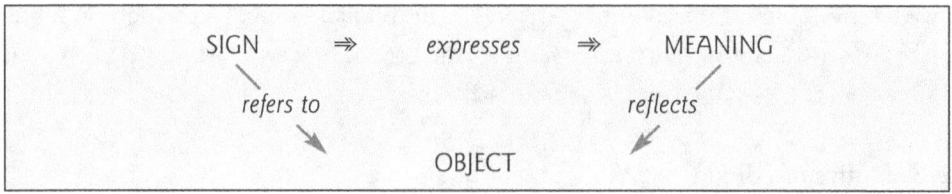

We can hypothesize that the photograph of Ueshiba as a "sign" *refers* to its "object" (the person of Ueshiba), and *expresses* its meaning, while the meaning of the sign *reflects* its "object" (the person of Ueshiba). The meaning of this "sign" is that the "founder" of aikido, photographed in a formal pose, is a figure to be respected. We may insert this into our visual model as follows:

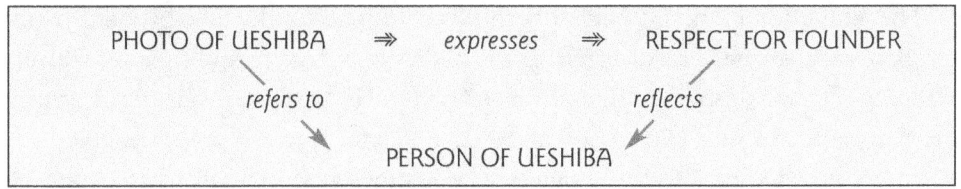

In Peirce's taxonomy of signs, Ueshiba's photograph would be considered an "iconic" sign because the relation between it (photograph of Ueshiba) and its object (person of Ueshiba) is one of resemblance (Silverman, 1983: 19; Hawkes, 1977: 128–129).

The scroll's flowing and harmonious calligraphy in which "aikido," the name of the martial art as written in Japanese ideograms, is a "sign," which *refers* to its "object" (the martial art named "aikido") and *expresses* its "meaning," which is that aikido is the way of flowing and harmonious use of energy. The "meaning" of the scroll's calligraphy *reflects* the martial art of aikido. This may be visually represented as follows:

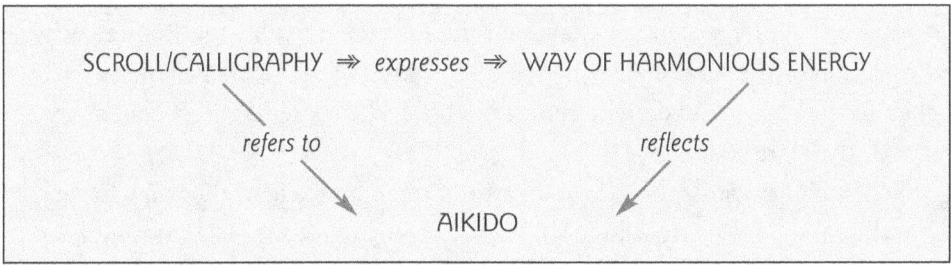

In Peirce's taxonomy of signs, the scroll and its calligraphy would be considered a "symbol" because the relation between sign and object in languages and other notational systems is established by a social convention (Silverman, 1983: 20; Hawkes, 1977: 129).

The bouquet of flowers is a "sign" which *refers* to nature as its "object" and *expresses* the "meaning" that we should honor and respect the world of nature with which it is our duty to harmonize by learning and applying aikido principles. The "meaning" of the bouquet *reflects* nature as the object of this sign. This may be visually represented as follows:

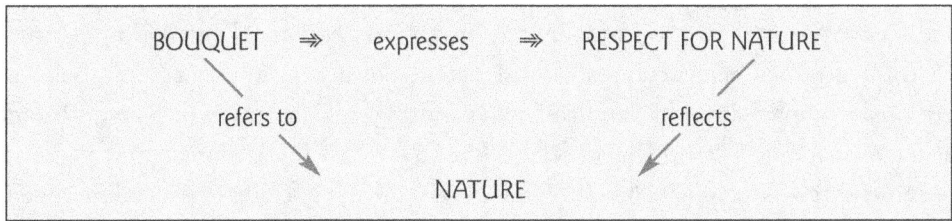

The bouquet of flowers may be considered a "symbol" in Peirce's taxonomy of signs because the use of floral bouquets to perform the ceremonial function of showing respect is established by a social convention (Silverman 1983: 20; Hawkes 1977: 129).

The altar also functions to organize the interior space of the dojo by identifying the front of the practice area and distributing the bodies of instructor and students within the dojo's space. The word "shomen" literally means "front" in Japanese. Thus, at the beginning and end of practice sessions, instructor and students sit facing the front of the practice area and perform a seated bow to the shomen. The instructor, seated directly in front of the shomen, then turns to face the students who exchange bows with him or her. Classes are taught with the instructor demonstrating techniques standing in front of the shomen, facing the class, while the students sit facing the shomen.

The Bow

In addition to demarcating the dojo and practice area as ritual spaces, the bow also functions to order the practice of aikido in the dojo and regulate the conduct of instructor and students during practice, reinforcing relations of mutual respect. Aikido classes begin and end with the instructor and students sitting in *seiza* and bowing to the shomen and to each other. Instruction generally proceeds with the instructor selecting a student to provide an attack so that the instructor may demonstrate a particular technique. When the demonstration of the technique is concluded, instructor and student bow to each other and then to the class members who return the bow. The students then break up into pairs to practice the technique.

Each pair of students then takes an area of the practice mat, they bow to each other and practice the demonstrated technique, alternating roles as *uke* (attacker, literally, the one who "receives" the technique) and *nage* (defender, the one who executes the technique). When the instructor signals by clapping his or her hands that practice of this technique is at end, each pair of students exchanges bows and returns to sit in line facing the shomen to observe the instructor demonstrate the next technique.

Repeated bowing during aikido classes plays an important role in the social construction of an atmosphere of seriousness and mutual respect between students and instructor and among the students themselves. Such an atmosphere is of utmost importance in practicing an art whose techniques, both attacks and defenses, can cause pain, serious injury or death (Ueshiba, M., 1996: 38; Saposnek, 1985: 25–26).

When properly executed, aikido techniques place the attacker, who is the recipient of the technique, in a position of vulnerability to the defender. The aikido practitioner, while throwing an attacker, can readily dislocate the attacker's joints or break their limbs, intentionally or inadvertently, or unleash a devastating strike against which an off-balanced attacker is unable to defend (Saposnek, 1985: 189–190). Thus, mutual trust is essential between the attacker (uke) and defender (nage) during aikido practice. The repeated bowing continuously reaffirms each student's respect for the other, reinforcing an atmosphere of mutual respect which minimizes potentially dangerous "macho" behavior while defusing any conflicts that might arise if one practice partner were inadvertently to cause pain or injury to another (Saotome, 1993: 245).

Because the circumstances under which and the manner in which one bows is established by a social convention, the bow may be considered a "symbol" under Peirce's taxonomy of signs (Silverman, 1983: 20; Hawkes, 1977: 129).

The Uniform: Gi, Belt, & Hakama

Aikido is practiced by persons who are ritually attired. The traditional *gi*, consisting of loose-fitting pants and tunic-style jacket, in either its karate or judo version, is worn in aikido classes, identifying the student as a practitioner of a Japanese martial art.

Each student also wears a belt around his or her waist whose color corresponds to their level of accomplishment in the art, according to a highly-structured system of examinations. While different aikido schools or styles may utilize different ranking systems or corresponding colors, beginning students generally wear a white belt, advanced students wear a black belt, and intermediate students may wear white belts or belts in other colors. Aikido students may also wear over their gi a *hakama*, the warrior's skirt worn by medieval Japanese samurai as part of their traditional dress. In some aikido schools, wearing the hakama is a privilege reserved for advanced students. In others, all students above the level of "white belt" wear hakama.

The gi immediately identifies the person wearing it as a student of an Japanese martial art. The belt's color locates the student within the hierarchy of aikido with regard to their level of accomplishment in the art, determined by formal examinations which result in the awarding of a rank with the right to wear a belt of a corresponding color. The hakama recalls the samurai values which it was Ueshiba's purpose to preserve for modern society in the form of the modern martial art of aikido (Saotome, 1989: 211). The aikidoist's uniform, consisting of gi, belt, and hakama, may be considered a "symbol" under Peirce's taxonomy of signs because its components are established by a social convention (Silverman, 1983: 20; Hawkes, 1977: 129).

Uke and Nage as
"Speaker & Addressee" of the Message of Aikido

In aikido practice students exchange the roles of attacker (uke) and defender (nage), with an appropriate aikido technique being executed by nage in response to a particular attack by uke. As we shall see when we apply Jakobson's schema to analyze such an interaction, both uke and nage also exchange roles as "speaker" and "addressee" of the message of aikido.

The "Contact" for Communication in Aikido

The "contact" between "speaker" and "addressee" of a message is that which makes possible a given communication. In the case of our investigation, the "contact" is the class in which aikido is practiced and, within that class, the practice of a given aikido technique.

The "Message" of Aikido

The "message" in Jakobson's communication model is the verbal sequence emitted by the "speaker" to the "addressee." In the case of our investigation in which the signs to be studied are physical body movements rather than verbal sounds, we shall define the "message" as consisting of the sequence of communicative body movements performed by the "speaker" to be received by the "addressee."

The "Code" in Aikido

The "code" utilized in aikido consists of the physical body movements of uke and nage during practice of a particular attack and corresponding aikido technique to defend against that attack. In order to decipher this code we shall hypothesize that aikido has the same basic "syntagmatic" and "paradigmatic" structure proposed by Saussure for language. According to Saussure, the "syntagmatic" structure of a language is a horizontal dimension which determines the linear order in which linguistic units may be combined to form meaningful utterances. For example, "the cat ate the rat" is meaningful, but "the ate rat cat" is not meaningful. The "paradigmatic" (or "associative") structure of a language is a vertical dimension which determines which linguistic units may be substituted for each other in a given syntagmatic complex and render a meaningful utterance. For example, in the statement "the cat ate the rat" the terms "dog," "lion" or "monkey" may be substituted for "cat," but "ran," "slept" or "baseball bat" may not be (Saussure, 1986: 89–99; Barthes, 1968: 58–88).

It is a working hypothesis of this investigation that all aikido techniques have the same formal structure. That structure consists of eight elements which are listed at left.[5]

ATTACK
⇓
EVADE
⇓
HARMONIZE
⇓
LEAD
⇓
LOSE BALANCE
⇓
THROW
⇓
FALL
⇓
CONTROL

In this chapter, we shall closely analyze one particular attack and defending aikido technique to illustrate this hypothesis. Photographs of several more techniques which have the same structure are included to provide additional supportive data. The formal structure described above, showing the insertion within it of uke's and nage's bodies, is visually represented in the diagram to the right.

Sequence	UKE	NAGE
1	attack	-------
2	-------	evade
3	-------	harmonize
4	-------	lead
5	lose balance	-------
6	-------	throw
7	fall	-------
8	-------	control

We shall make use of shared insights by Barthes and Eco in deciphering the meaning of aikido's kinesic signs. The physical body movements which comprise aikido techniques fall within the category which Barthes (1968: 41) calls as "sign-functions" in that they have the utilitarian function of providing a means of self-defense in addition to their communicative function as signs. As Barthes explains:

> Many semiological systems (objects, gestures, pictorial images) have a substance of expression whose essence is not to signify; often, they are objects of everyday use, used by society in a derivative way, to signify something: clothes are used for protection and food for nourishment even if they are also used as signs. We propose to call these semiological signs, whose origin is utilitarian and functional, *sign-functions.*
> – Barthes, 1968: 41

Eco makes a similar point while discussing architectural "signs." Using the example of a staircase, Eco explains that within the code of architecture an object with given characteristics (a staircase) may act as a sign by communicating to the observer its possible function (climbing up). This is a cultural datum which can be established independently of the observer's behavior or presumed mental reaction (Eco, 1989: 333–334).

The significance of these shared insights is the following. If Eco's description of the "architectural sign" is assumed to be true of "function-signs" in general, we may hypothesize that the kinesic "function-signs" which constitute aikido techniques also communicate their possible function. That being the case, the object designated by such a sign is precisely its utilitarian function and the sign's meaning will reflects that function. This is the key to deciphering the meaning of the kinesic signs of aikido. We shall derive their meaning with reference to their function as a means of self-defense.[6]

The form of aikido techniques and their manner of execution bears a direct relationship to their function of providing an effective method of self-defense. In Peirce's taxonomy, a sign which has a "real" rather than an arbitrary or conventional connection to its object is an "indexical sign." Since the object of a sign-function is its utilitarian function, and the utilitarian function of aikido's kinesic sign-functions is to provide a means of self-defense, they may be considered "indexical signs" (Silverman, 1983: 19; Hawkes, 1977: 129).

TECHNICAL SECTION
Munetski Kotegaeshi: straight punch to abdomen / wrist turn throw

Aikido Practice as Communicative Interaction

With the necessary theoretical elements in place, we may now undertake our semiotic analysis of aikido techniques. For the purposes of this chapter, the technique to be analyzed is *munetski kotegaeshi*, a wrist throw defense against a straight punch to the solar plexus. The basic movements of this technique consist of the following:[7]

A-1 Uke (r., Jim Chandler) takes a step toward nage (l., the author) and strikes at nage with a straight punch to the solar plexus.
(Function: Attack)

A-2 Nage steps off the line of attack at a 45-degree angle and steps to uke's right.
(Function: Evade)

A-3 Nage turns clockwise 180 degrees to face in the same direction as uke, slides the forearm of the hand which is closer to uke down uke's outstretched punching arm, bringing nage's hand, palm down, into position atop uke's fist.
(Function: Harmonize)

A-4 Nage steps forward, using contact with uke's fist to lead uke forward and slightly downward, off-balance.
(Function: Lead)

Attack
⇓
Evade
⇓
Harmonize
⇓
Lead
⇓
Lose Balance
⇓
Throw
⇓
Fall
⇓
Control

A-5 Uke loses balance.
(Function: Lose balance)

A-6 Nage grasps uke's fist and turns 180 degrees counter-clockwise, twisting uke's wrist to point the fist back toward uke, at the same time bringing nage's free and, palm down, on top of the fist, sliding it over uke's fingers while lowering uke's hand, throwing uke to the ground.
(Function: Throw)

A-7 Uke falls backwards to the ground.
(Function: Fall)

A-8 Nage points uke's fist toward uke's face, inserts the web of his free hand into uke's elbow joint, walks past uke's head from one side to the other of uke's body, thereby turning uke face down. Nage kneels next to uke, placing uke's outstretched arm between nage's legs. Nage turns uke's hand palm up inserting it in nage's elbow joint as nage crosses his own arm in front of his chest. Nage crosses his other arm across uke's outstretched arm in the opposite direction, securing uke's arm for the pin. Nage turns his hips toward uke's head, taking the slack out of uke's shoulder joint, pinning uke to the ground.
(Function: Control)

Munetski Kaiten-nage

straight punch to abdomen / windmill throw

Shomenuchi Irimi-nage

downward strike to head / entering throw

Katatedori Ikkyo Omote
wrist grab/first teaching move in front of attacker

Tachidori Shomenuchi Zenpo-nage
sword taking downward cut to head / forward throw

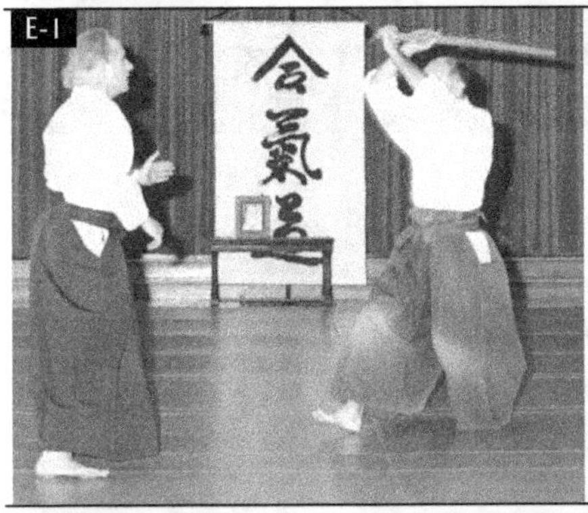
E-1

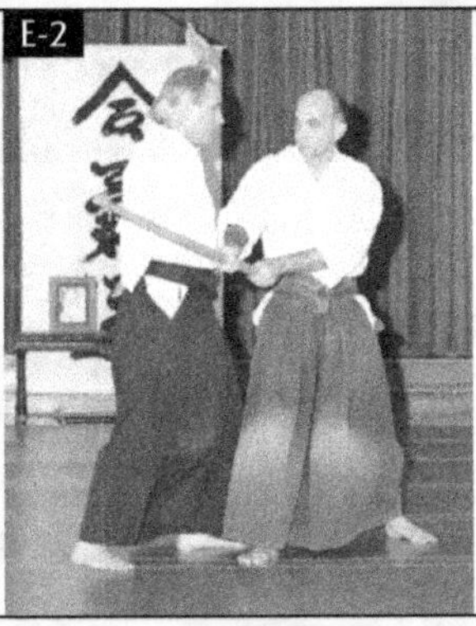
E-2

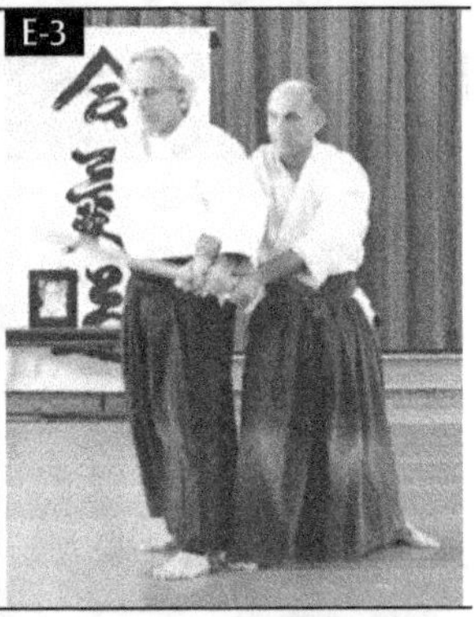
E-3

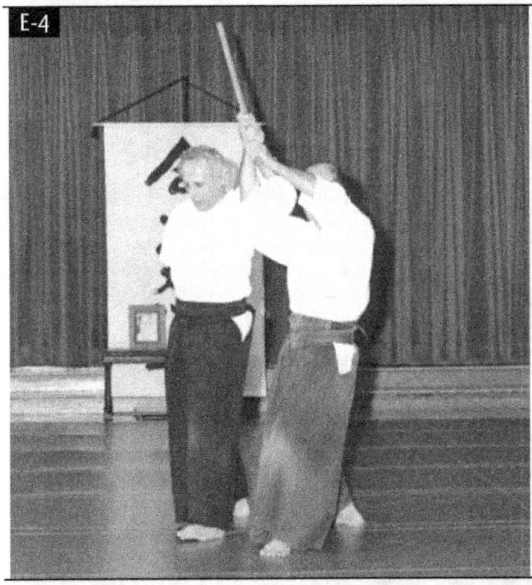
E-4

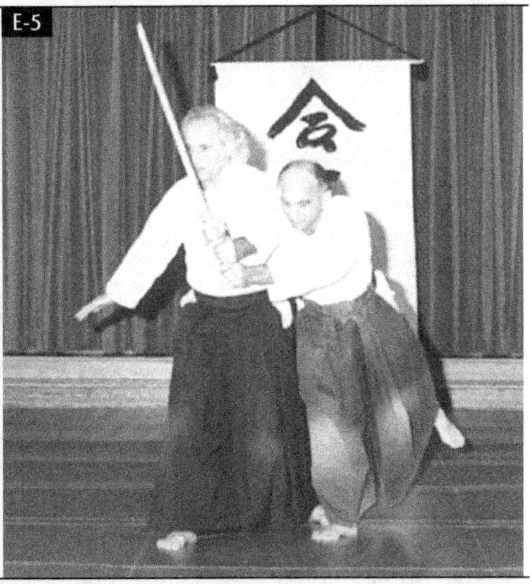
E-5

E-6

E-7

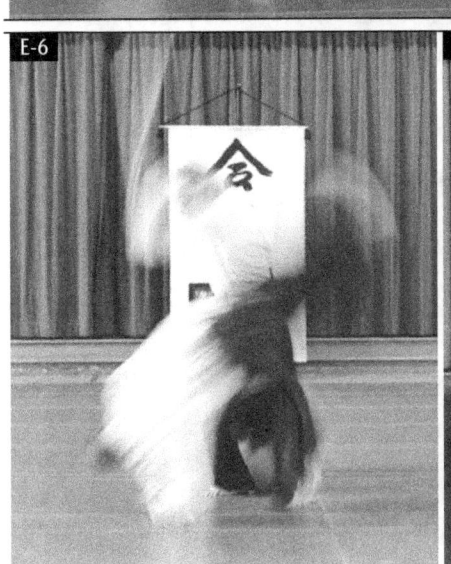

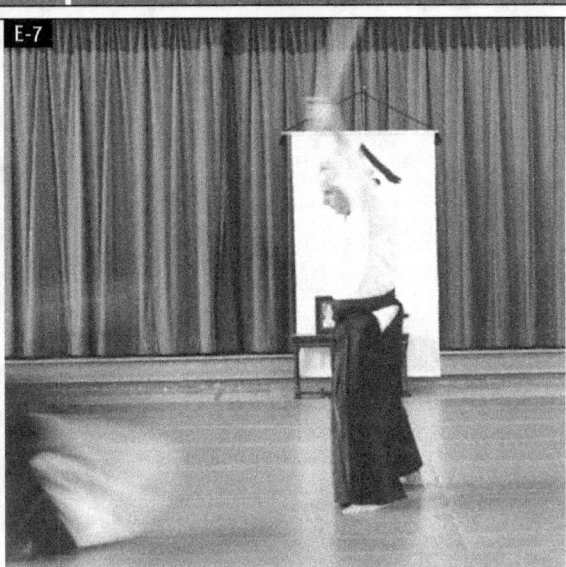

The analysis of munetski kotegaeshi confirms our earlier hypothesis that the basic syntagmatic structure of aikido techniques consists of the eight steps of:

Attack ⇒ Evade ⇒ Harmonize ⇒ Lead ⇒ Lose Balance ⇒ Throw ⇒ Fall ⇒ Control

Employing Barthes' and Eco's shared insight that the object designated by a sign-function is the utilitarian function of the sign, we may now attempt to decipher the meaning of each of these eight kinesic sign-functions as follows:

1. **Function**
   Attack
   Speaker: uke
   Addressee: nage

1. **Meaning**
   Kill!

When uke attacks nage, the function of uke's body movements is to strike nage with sufficient force to disable or kill. "The original intent of bujutsu was to kill an enemy with one blow" (Ueshiba, M., 1996: 38).

2. **Function**
   Evade
   Speaker: nage
   Addressee: uke

2. **Meaning**
   I decline to be the target
   of your violence.

When nage receives the message that uke is attacking, nage sends his own kinesic message to uke. Nage's body movements function to evade the attack by stepping off the line of force to take a position inside uke's guard where uke's own body blocks uke from being able to strike nage.

3. **Function**
   Harmonize
   Speaker: nage
   Addressee: uke

3. **Meaning**
   We are one.

Nage blends his movements with uke's movements and turns to face in the same direction as uke. Uke and nage's energy (*ki*) is now flowing in the same direction and they are in harmony with each other in a state of "oneness" (Ueshiba, K., 1987: 63; Kobayashi, 1985: 3).

While the communicative meaning of the preceding three stages of the technique (attack, evade, harmonize) may be derived in a relatively simple intuitive fashion, the remaining stages (lead, lose balance, throw, fall, control) resist ready translation. In order to understand their function as kinesic signs we shall find it necessary to employ Birdwhistell's concept of "parakinesic" signs which do not translate as words, sentences or paragraphs, but rather as kinesic punctuation marks which modify, emphasize or amplify the "formal" kinesic signs. From this perspective, we may propose the following meaning for these signs:

4. **Function**	4. **Meaning**
Lead	Parakinesic sign whose function
Speaker: nage	is to take control of uke's body
Addressee: (none)	so that uke's message can no longer be transmitted.

Having avoided uke's attack and harmonized with uke's body movement, nage is now in a position to take control of uke's body and lead uke to a point of disequilibrium where uke is off-balance and thus unable to utilize the kinesic code in order to transmit uke's message of violence. In order to do this, nage cannot resort to physical force, which would be sensed by uke and resisted, thus turning the interaction into a tug-of-war in which the physically stronger of the pair would necessarily be victorious (Saito, 1973: 16). Instead, nage breaks uke's balance by removing the target and blending with uke's attacking movement in such a manner that uke does not sense that nage has taken control of uke's body until uke has already lost his balance and is no longer in a position to resist. Thus, this parakinesic sign is "sent" by nage but is not "received" by uke.

With this movement, nage now dominates the kinesic code. Uke may no longer transmit his message because uke has lost the ability to utilize the kinesic code. Rather, nage may now utilize his control over uke's body to cause uke to transmit *nage's* message of nonviolence, rather than *uke's* violent message.[8]

5. **Function**	5. **Meaning**
Lose balance	Parakinesic silence:
Speaker: uke	Uke has lost the code
Addressee: (none)	and can no longer transmit his message.

There are times in conversation when silences have the same importance as spoken words. A "pregnant silence" is a common expression for such a situation. There are also situations which are so shocking that one may be at a loss for words. This particular moment in the interaction between uke and nage ("lose balance") may be interpreted as such a "kinesic silence": uke has lost the ability to utilize the code and cannot transmit his message; nage has taken control of the code but has not yet emitted his message. It is as if uke, in a conversation, had received so great a surprise he or she was rendered "speechless."

6. Function Throw Speaker: nage Addressee: (none)	**6. Meaning** Parakinesic sign: Nage causes uke's body to transmit nage's message.

Here nage uses the technique of *kotegaeshi* to throw uke to the ground. This is a parakinesic sign whose function is to cause uke's body to transmit nage's message. The technique itself does not send a message to uke because if it were detected by uke it might be resisted.

7. Function Fall. Speaker: nage. Addressee: uke.	**7. Meaning** Uke falls to the ground with the force of (and because of) his own attack, i.e., it is self-defeating to attack others.

Uke's body responds to nage's throw by falling to the ground with the force of uke's own attack on nage. Nage makes uke's body transmit nage's message: Uke falls by the force of his own attack, thus demonstrating that it is self-defeating to attack others.

8. Function Control. Speaker: nage/uke. Addressee: uke.	**8. Meaning** Formal kinesic sign: Uke is under control of nage. Parakinesic sign: Nage controls uke.

This sign consists of the body movements of both nage and uke. Nage has uke pinned to the ground. Uke cannot get up and is vulnerable to a shoulder dislocation. Nage's movements may be considered to constitute a "parakinesic" sign by which nage terminates the "conversation" with uke. Uke's movements constitute a "formal" kinesic sign that conveys the meaning that uke, as a result of uke's own attack on nage, is now under control of nage and vulnerable to whatever devastating counter-attack that nage might wish to unleash.

The relationship between the bodies of uke and nage in the final stages of this aikido technique is reminiscent of Foucault's semiotic analysis in *Discipline and Punish* (1995: 3–69) of the relation between a medieval king and a prisoner suffering torture pursuant to the king's command. Foucault hypothesizes that the prisoner's body functions as a sign to signify both the crime committed and the absolute power of the king in imposing punishment. In aikido, nage causes uke's body to signify the counter productivity of violence and the superiority of harmony and nonviolence.

There is admittedly a relative indeterminacy or opaqueness inherent in any attempt to translate from one semiotic system to another, whether it be from non-linguistic systems to natural languages, as in this article, or from one natural language to another (Niranjana, 1992: 55).

It is not the contention of this chapter that the translation herein of the kinesic signs of aikido techniques into the speech of natural language is *the* correct translation, but rather that it is *a* correct translation. Just as there have been numerous different translations of some literary works into a particular natural language, there may be more than one "correct" translation of the signs of aikido from the semiotic system of kinesics to the semiotic system of a natural language such as English.

It is, however, the hypothesis of this chapter that any translation of the kinesic signs of aikido into natural language must be consistent with the utilitarian function of those signs—i.e., to constitute an effective system of self-defense—in order to be within the range of tolerance of a "correct" translation. The fact that there may be more than one "correct" way of translating a particular communication from one semiotic system to another is not a peculiar theoretical problem for the translation attempted in this chapter, but rather an essential given of any translation because of the very nature of translation itself as a project concerned with the communication of meaning.

Analysis of the Discourse of Aikido

To better understand how nage is able to dominate the "code" of individual combat and deprive uke of the means of transmitting a message of violence, it is necessary to consider the kinesic signs of aikido as not merely constituting "messages" but also being "discourses" in the sense the term is employed by such theorists as Foucault. For Foucault, a "discourse" is not merely "a set of linguistic data linked together by syntactic rules of construction." Rather, discourses are "games, strategic games of action and reaction, of question and answer, of domination and retraction, and also of struggle. Discourse is this regular conjunction of linguistic data on one level, and polemics and strategies on another" (Foucault, 1986: 15).[9]

Foucault's concept of discourse, which includes as its fundamental element the struggle for power, is well-suited to analysis of individual physical combat as a confrontation between competing discourses. Foucault states that discourse is "not simply that which translates into struggles or systems of domination, but rather that for which and by means of which one struggles, that power that one desires to make one's own" (Foucault, 1971: 5).[10]

In the confrontation between uke and nage, uke tries to dominate the code and violently impose his discourse over nage. Nage uses aikido's code to avoid the imposition of uke's discourse and take control of uke's body so that uke can no longer emit any other discourse than that of nage. Thus, each struggles to take over the discursive process as a form of struggle for power. The objective of the aikido practitioner's discourse is to utilize the power implicit in the harmony of the universe to control an attacker and deny him the opportunity to express a violent discourse which by its very nature is in contradiction to this state of harmony.

Pecheux's concept of the conditions and process of production of discourse may also be employed to gain a better understanding of the interaction between uke and nage (Pecheux, 1995: 82–113). Among the "conditions of production" of kinesic discourse is the human body as a "means of production" of the kinesic signs constituted by body movements. When nage takes control over uke's body by leading uke to a state of disequilibrium, nage effectively changes the conditions of production of discourse by expropriating from uke the means of production of uke's discourse. As uke loses balance, is thrown by nage, and falls to the ground, the process of production of discourse also changes—uke's body now functions as a means of production of nage's competing discourse.

Uke struggles to maintain an unequal relationship of power with nage by using physical force to impose uke's violent discourse on nage. Nage utilizes the nonviolent discourse of aikido to overthrow and transform those power relations by changing the conditions and process of production of discourse in such a way as to deprive uke of the means of producing his discourse and, instead, causing uke to transmit the discourse of nage.

Conclusion

Aikido, a modern martial art invented by Morihei Ueshiba to preserve and transform the virtues of the warrior traditions of medieval Japanese society, provides not only an effective means of self-defense and a rigorous discipline for personal and spiritual development, but a message for humanity of the superiority of nonviolence as a means to deal with situations of conflict. Aikido's non-violent philosophy is manifested in its techniques which may be considered to have a communicative as well as a martial function, whose meaning may be deciphered by resort to semiotics. The key to decoding the message of aikido is recognizing that the kinesic "sign-functions" constituted by the bodily movements of aikido techniques designate as their object their utilitarian function of providing a means for self-defense.

While exchanging roles as *uke* (attacker) and *nage* (defender) in the course of aikido practice, aikidoists transmit and receive through their bodies the competing discourses of violence and nonviolence, continuously learning the self-defeating nature of aggression and the superiority of controlling conflict by avoiding confrontation and finding an appropriate means of harmonizing with its source. Ideally, in a "real" confrontation outside the dojo, the aikidoist will instinctively react in accordance with this training and provide a similarly instructive lesson to any attacker.

> **Acknowledgment**
>
> The author wishes to dedicate this chapter to his teacher, the late Roderick T. Kobayashi Shihan. The author also wishes to thank Kimberly Taylor, Deborah Klens-Bigman, Beth Shibata, and Rosy Zúñiga for critiquing a preliminary draft; Krishna Malhotra for shooting the photographs which accompany the article; Jim Chandler for assisting in demonstrating the techniques in the photographs; and Julieta Haidar for introducing the author to the study of semiotics. The opinions and any errors in the article are the responsibility of the author.

Notes

1. While strikes may be used in aikido, their usual purpose is to unbalance rather than injure the opponent (Saotome, 1993: 229).
2. For a basic introduction to Saussure's theories for those unfamiliar with semiotics, see Gordon (1966).
3. In seeking to employ a model of the "sign" accessible to the lay reader, the author realizes that he risks offending the philosopher or semiotician who may, for example, object to the use of the term "meaning" in place of Peirce's neologism "interpretant." While less theoretically precise, the term "meaning" is readily understandable in everyday speech. Its use in the triadic model of the sign employed in this article does not imply that the author adheres to the philosophical idealism which Peirce sought to avoid by employing his particular terminology.
4. For a basic introduction to discourse analysis for those unfamiliar with the field, see Fairclough (1989) and Anderson (1988).
5. The final "control" step of pinning the opponent is an option in those techniques where the attacker is thrown or taken down close to the defender, but is unavailable in those techniques where the attacker is thrown a distance away from the defender.
6. Peirce's triadic theory of the sign, combined with Barthes' concept of the "sign-function" and Eco's insight that the object of some signs is their "utilitarian function," provide a necessary context and reference point for the translation of the kinesic signs constituted by aikido techniques by referring us to their utilitarian function as a means of self-defense. This is crucial for our investigation because, unlike Birdwhistell, we do not have a verbal component of our "communicative interaction" to provide the necessary context and reference point (Birdwhistell, 1970: 96, 224–227).
7. There are numerous "correct" ways of executing this techniques. See, e.g., Sosa and Robbins (1987: 94–95), Yamada (1996: 73–75), Ueshiba, K. (1985a: 54–55), and Saotome (1989: 144–145).
8. The "nonviolent" message of aikido is that violence is self defeating. One who attacks another makes himself or herself vulnerable to a devastating counterattack. A better way to deal with violent conflict is to avoid it, harmonize with the source of conflict, and control the situation without oneself having to resort to violence (Ueshiba, K.,

1987: 54).
[9] English translation by the author.
[10] Idem.

Bibliography

Anderson, R. (1988). *The power and the word: Language, power and change*. London: Paladin Grafton Books.

Barthes, R. (1967). *Elements of semiology*. (A. Lavers & C. Smith, Trans.). New York: Hill and Wang.

Bekku, M. (1997). Interview with Shoji Nishio. *Aikido Journal*, 24(3), 22–24.

Birdwhistell, R. (1970). *Kinesics and context: Essays on body motion communication*. Philadelphia: University of Pennsylvania Press.

Birdwhistell, R. (1952). *Introduction to kinesics*. Washington, D.C.: Department of State, Foreign Service Institute.

Donohue, J. (1997). Ideological elasticity: Enduring form and changing function in the Japanese martial tradition. *Journal of Asian Martial Arts*, 6(2), 10–24.

Donohue, J. (1991). *The forge of the spirit: Structure, motion and meaning in the Japanese martial tradition*. New York: Garland Publishing, Inc.

Eagleton, T. (1991). *An introduction to ideology*. London: Verso.

Eco, U. (1989). *La estructura ausente*. (F. Serra Cantarell, Trans.). Barcelona: Editorial Lumen. (Original work published in 1968).

Eco, U. (1976). *A theory of semiotics*. (Translated). Bloomington, IN: Indiana University Press.

Fairclough, N. (1989). *Language and power*. London: Longman Group U.K. Ltd.

Foucault, M. (1995). *Discipline and punish: The birth of the prison*. (A. Sheridan, Trans.). New York: Random House. (Original work published in 1975).

Foucault, M. (1986). *La verdad y las formas juridicas*. (E. Lynch, Trans.). Mexico City: Editorial Gedisa Mexicana, S.A. (Original work published in 1978).

Foucault, M. (1971). *El orden del discurso*. Mexico City: Ediciones Populares de la Facultad de Filosofia y Letras, UNAM. Available in English as "Orders of discourse" in *Social Science Information 10* (April 1971): 7–31; and in R. Young, (Ed.), (1981), *Untying the text: A post-structuralist reader*, London: Routledge.

Gimenez, G. (1989). *Poder, estado y discurso: Perpectivas sociologicas y semiologicas del discurso politico-juridico*. Mexico City: UNAM.

Gleason, W. (1995). *The spiritual foundations of aikido*. Rochester, NY: Destiny Books.

Gordon, W. (1996). *Saussure for beginners*. NY: Writers and Readers Publishing, Inc.

Greenlee, D. (1973). *Peirce's concept of sign*. The Hague: Mouton.

Hardwick, C. (Ed.). (1977). *Semiotic and significs: The correspondence between Charles S. Peirce and Victoria Lady Welby*. Bloomington, IN: Indiana University Press.

Hawkes, T. (1977). *Structuralism and semiotics*. Berkeley, CA: University of California

Press.

Hoopes, J. (Ed.). (1991). *Peirce on signs: Writings on semiotic by Charles Sanders Peirce.* Chapel Hill, NC: University of North Carolina Press.

Jakobson, R. (1980). *The framework of language.* Ann Arbor, MI: Michigan Slavic Publications. (Original work published in 1956).

Kaptchuk, T. (1983). *The web that has no weaver: Understanding Chinese medicine.* Chicago: Congdon & Weed, Inc.

Katchmer, G. (1993). *The tao of bioenergetics.* Jamaica Plain, MA: YMAA Publication Center.

Ketner, K. (Ed.). (1995). *Peirce and contemporary thought.* New York: Fordham University Press.

Kimura, I. (1997). The Omoto religion and aikido: Spiritual and physical instincts—Interview with Yasuaki Deguchi, grandson of Omoto founder Onisaburo Deguchi (Part 15). Aikido Journal 24(4), 42–44 (and preceding installments).

Kobayashi, R. (1992a). *Aikido doka: Poems of Morihei Ueshiba.* Los Angeles: Aikido Institute of America.

Kobayashi, R. (1992b). Aikido, the eternal path of peace and wisdom [1985] in D. Wedell, (Ed.), *The first eleven years: Essays of R. Kobayashi from the first eleven years of the seidokan communicator.* Los Angeles: Aikido Institute of America.

Kobayashi, R. (1985). *Introduction to aikido.* Los Angeles: Seidokan Headquarters.

Macdonell, D. (1986). *Theories of discourse: An introduction.* Oxford: Basil Blackwell, Inc.

Niranjana, T. (1992). *Siting translation: History, post-structuralism, and the colonial context.* Berkeley, CA: University of California Press.

Pecheux, M. (1982). *Language, semantics and ideology.* (H. Nagpal, Trans.). New York: St. Martin's Press, Inc. (Original work published in 1975).

Pecheux, M. (1995). *Automatic discourse analysis.* (D. Macey, Trans.). Amsterdam: Rodopi. (Original work published in 1969).

Ratti, O. & Westbrook, A. (1973) *Secrets of the samurai: A survey of the martial arts of feudal Japan.* Rutland, VT: Charles E. Tuttle Co.

Reisel, M. (1985). A turn to balance, in R. Heckler, (Ed.), *Aikido and the new warrior.* Berkeley, CA: North Atlantic Books.

Saito, M. (1973). *Traditional aikido: Sword, stick and body art–volume 2, advanced techniques.* (W. Witt, Trans.). Tokyo: Minato Research and Publishing Co.

Saotome, M. (1989). *The principles of aikido.* Boston: Shambhala Publications.

Saotome, M. (1993). *Aikido and the harmony of nature.* Boston: Shambhala Publications.

Saposnek, D. (1985). Aikido: A model for brief strategic therapy, in R. Heckler, (Ed.), *Aikido and the new warrior.* Berkeley, CA: North Atlantic Books.

Saussure, F. (1986). *Course in general linguistics.* (R. Harris, Trans.). Chicago: Open Court. (Original work published in 1915).

Silverman, K. (1983). *The subject of semiotics.* New York: Oxford University Press.

Sosa, B., & Robbins, B. (1987). *The essence of aikido: The non-aggressive art of self-defense*. Burbank, CA: Unique Publications.

Stevens, J. (1995). *The secrets of aikido*. Boston: Shambhala Publications.

Stevens, J. (1993). *The essence of aikido: Spiritual teachings of Morihei Ueshiba*. Tokyo: Kodansha International Ltd.

Stevens, J. (1987). *Abundant peace: The biography of Morihei Ueshiba, founder of aikido*. Boston: Shambhala Publications.

Stevens, J. (1985). *Aikido: The way of harmony*. Boston: Shambhala Publications.

Summerhawk, B. (1997). A tale of two senseis: Michio Hikitsuchi sensei and Yasuo Kobayashi sensei. *Aikido Today Magazine, 11*(1), 8–9.

Sugawara, T. & Xing, L. (1996). *Aikido and Chinese martial arts: Its fundamental relations*. Tokyo: Sugawara Martial Arts Institute, Inc.

Thompson, J. (1984). *Studies in the theory of ideology*. Berkeley, CA: University of California Press.

Tohei, K. (1997). The only thing that Ueshiba sensei taught of true value was how to relax. *Aikido Journal, 24*(2), 6–9.

Tohei, K. (1976). *Book of ki: Coordinating mind and body in daily life*. Tokyo: Japan Publications.

Tohei, K. (1968). *This is aikido*. Tokyo: Japan Publications.

Ueshiba, K. (1985a). *Aikido*. Tokyo: Hozansha Publishing Co., Inc.

Ueshiba, K. (1985b). Interview with Doshu, in R. Heckler, (Ed.), *Aikido and the new warrior*. Berkeley, CA: North Atlantic Books.

Ueshiba, K. (1987). *The spirit of aikido*. (T. Unno, Trans.). Tokyo: Kodansha International.

Ueshiba, M. (1985a). Excerpts from the writings and transcribed lectures of the founder, Morihei Ueshiba, in R. Heckler, (Ed.), *Aikido and the new Warrior*. Berkeley, CA: North Atlantic Books.

Ueshiba, M. (1991b). *Budo: Teachings of the founder of aikido*. (J. Stevens, Trans.). Tokyo: Kodansha International.

Waugh, L. & Monville-Burston, M. (Eds.). (1990). *Jakobson on language*. Cambridge, MA: Harvard University Press.

Westbrook, A. & Ratti, O. (1970). *Aikido and the dynamic sphere*. Tokyo: Charles E. Tuttle Co.

Yamada, Y. (1996). *Ultimate aikido: Secrets of self-defense and inner power*. Seacaucus, NJ: Carol Publishing Group.

Yang, J. (1996). *The essence of Shaolin white crane: Martial power and qigong*. Jamaica Plain, MA: YMAA Publication Center.

Yang, J. (1991). *Muscle/tendon changing and marrow/brain washing chi kung: The secret of youth*. Jamaica Plain, MA: YMAA Publication Center.

Yang, J. (1989). *The root of Chinese chi kung: The secrets of chi kung training*. Jamaica Plain, MA: YMAA Publication Center.

· 6 ·

Aikido Kokyu-nage: The Sublime & the Practical
by Roy Suenaka & Christopher Watson, B.A.

Suenaka Sensei demonstrating aikido's *irimi-nage* (entering throw).
All photographs courtesy of R. Suenaka & C. Watson.

One of the most common and dynamic techniques in aikido is the *kokyu-nage*. Kokyu-nage encompasses a broad category of aikido techniques, all of which can generally be defined as a throw of some kind. Yet when one deconstructs the term, *kokyu-nage* reveals itself to mean more than just physically hurling your attacker across the mat or pavement.

Nage

Those who study judo are intimately familiar with the term *nage*. *Nage* essentially means a throw, or to throw (although in aikido it also means the defender, one who performs the technique). Perhaps the most common example of this in judo is the category of techniques that fall beneath the umbrella of *koshi-nage*, or hip throws. Likewise in aikido, almost all throw designations end with the term *nage*, for example *irimi-nage* (entering throw), *sayu-nage* (sideways throw) and *shiho-nage* (four directions throw). Still, all of these throws, and even those that do not end with the *nage* designation, such as *sumi-otoshi* (corner drop), are *kokyu-nage*. It is apparent that the key to a better understanding of *kokyu-nage* rests within the definition of *kokyu*.

Kokyu

The most often encountered definition of *kokyu* is breath, or to breathe. Indeed, many martial disciplines, including aikido, pay great attention to the meditative discipline of *kokyu-ho*, the way of proper breathing. Yet still, *kokyu*, even in this sense, means much more than simple respiration. Though the literal translation of kokyu-nage is "breath throw," *kokyu* in the context of aikido technique refers to the unimpeded flow of ki through oneself and so through one's technique.

Ki

One of the greatest ironies that exists within the world aikido community is the ongoing heated debate concerning the definition and even the existence of ki and its place, if any, in aikido study and execution of technique (*waza*). Indeed, it is arguably this frequently profound difference of opinion that most often differentiates aikido styles. The irony is that the debate exists at all.

Ki is the heart of aikido. The very designation *aikido* clearly demonstrates this: *ai*, meaning harmony or blending; *ki*, meaning vital life energy, the energy of the universe; and *do*, the way. Thus, aikido is most-commonly translated as "the way of universal harmony." This admittedly sublime definition is interpreted by some *aikidoka* to mean there should be zero conflict and resistance when engaged in aikido training, and that in this way they are demonstrating universal love for all things in accordance with aikido founder Morihei Ueshiba's guiding doctrine, while simultaneously fostering *ki* development. On the other side of the debate are those who firmly believe that such an apparently passive philosophy has no place in martial study and that if this philosophy is the result of incorporating awareness and development of *ki* as part of their training, then *ki* has no place in a martial system; and so, they train without this awareness.

This dichotomy can be at least partially resolved by removing the definition of *ki* from its lofty, esoteric shelf and bringing it down to a more practical, accessible level. Mind you, more esoteric definitions of *ki* are valid: an earnest discussion with a quantum physicist concerning the increasingly accepted theories of universal "superstrings" and the immutable, intricate vibrations of space-time will set even the most ardent *ki* skeptic's mind reeling with previously unexplored explanations of what *ki* might be. But for purposes of this discussion, let us focus on the more practical aspects of *ki*; let us define *ki* as it relates to the successful execution of aikido techniques, and therefore its relationship to *kokyu*.

Ki: A Practical Definition

For practical defense purposes, one may define *ki* as the energy of intent—*ki* is focus and concentration, the total unification and commitment of body, mind and spirit when executing technique (*kime*), so that everything at that moment suddenly becomes clear, relaxed and natural. Rather than being a mystical force few can ever hope to even understand, let alone make manifest within themselves and their technique, practical ki awareness and control is born of diligent training with an eye towards its conscious development. This development may be accomplished through exercises specifically designed to nourish the intrinsic and instinctive sense of *ki* born within us all, as well as through sincere and consistent *waza* training. The point to be made is that no matter what one's vocation, as mastery grows, so too does development and awareness of *ki*, no matter how they define it or the degree of their conscious awareness of it. A professional athlete may call it "being in the zone," or say they were "seeing the ball really well," so that they could do nothing wrong. For purposes of this discussion, this is ki and what it means to be aware of it and use it.

Ki and Kokyu

As noted earlier, kokyu, in the context of aikido technique, refers to the unimpeded flow of ki through oneself and so through one's technique. Thus, *kokyu-nage* means to use this unimpeded flow of ki to effect the throw. However, this does not mean one throws one's attacker without touching him, using only the power of ki. Although Ueshiba's was often observed doing just that (with several instances recorded on film), this ability is arguably beyond all but the most gifted and utterly dedicated martial artists. Rather, using ki to effect kokyu-nage means unifying body, mind and spirit through *kime* at the moment the technique is executed, so that there is no conflict or clashing with the attacker's own physical movement and ki. In order to achieve this, one must also capture and lead the attacker's ki.

Capturing and leading an attacker's ki depends on several variables. Again, let us focus on the more practical ones. There are the mechanics of technique, including but not limited to proper distance from the attacker (*ma-ai*), proper timing (*ri-ai*), and body movement/position (*tai-sabaki*). By observing proper mechanics of technique, coupled with a conscious awareness and extension of one's own ki, one may effectively capture and subsequently lead the attacker's *kime*, his own focus and energy of intent, his commitment to his attack. Through so doing, one brings about *kuzushi*, the physical and mental off-balancing of the attacker. When one correctly incorporates all of these variables into one's technique, then *seigyo* is achieved: total control of the situation. One's own ki is flowing, the attacker's ki is captured, blended with one's own and redirected, the mechanics of the technique click, and the attacker is thrown. There is no conflict or resistance because there is no physical or mental clash between defender and attacker. Rather, both are in harmony; their ki is linked (*ki-musubi*) and flowing (*ki-no-nagare*) in one dynamic moment, which both culminates in and defines kokyu-nage.

What follows are four examples of aikido kokyu-nage, demonstrated by Roy Suenaka. Study these examples to observe not only the proper mechanics of each technique, but how the successful execution of each technique depends on the variables discussed above.

SIDE BAR: Tenkan Versus Irimi

When one executes aikido waza, the technique is performed either *tenkan* (turning away) or *irimi* (entering). This also holds true for kokyu-nage. While the decision to move either tenkan or irimi very much defines the kokyu-nage, both movements share the same goal: to lead the attacker's ki and simultaneously effect *kuzushi* (breaking the attacker's balance). The primary difference between tenkan and irimi, for practical purposes, is directional.

Tenkan

Tenkan means to turn. It is the circular, blending movement that is perhaps the hallmark of aikido waza. When one turns away (*tenkan*), one is accomplishing the dual purpose of removing oneself from the attacker's offensive sphere—moving off the attacking line—while capturing and leading the attacker's body and ki, breaking his balance in the process. Once the attacker's ki is captured and full control is attained (*kuzushi*), this captured energy is re-directed and used to effect the throw. (Refer to the photo series depicting *katate-tori kokyu-nage hantai tenkan*.)

Irimi

Irimi means to enter. Irimi is to move into the attacker's offensive sphere. This may appear to fly in the face of aikido convention, to clash and conflict rather than harmonize, but it does not. While tenkan depends on waiting until an attacker has fully committed to his strike, irimi is to move into the heart of the attack at the moment of commitment but before the attack has the chance to fully manifest itself. One still captures and blends with an attacker's ki and attains full control (*kuzushi*), only much earlier, and re-directs his ki to effect the throw. (Refer to the photo series depicting *yokomen-uchi sumi-otoshi irimi*.)

• • •

A simple analogy illustrating the primary difference between tenkan and irimi can be found in striking a match and holding one's hand above the flame. Tenkan is to remove one's hand from the stream of heat and extinguish the match by, say, blowing it out. Irimi is to cover the match with your hand at the moment it first flares, extinguishing it before it has the opportunity to fully ignite.

**Special thanks go to uke
David Isgett and Chad Taylor
for their help in illustrating
the technical section.**

Technical Section

KATATE-TORI KOKYU-NAGE TENKAN
(wrist grab attack, breath throw defense, turning)

A-1 As the attacker grabs Suenaka's wrist (*katate-tori*), Suenaka moves to the attacker's right, taking the attacker off-balance.

A-2 Suenaka continues moving to the side out of range of any possible counter strike and further off-balancing the attacker. He simultaneously captures the attacker's head with his left hand and brings it into his right shoulder securing control. Note how the attacker's grasp on Suenaka's right hand is broken as Suenaka has full control (*kuzushi*), blending the attacker's ki with his own.

A-3 Having led the attacker off-balance, Suenaka reverses direction, moving forward on his right foot as he begins rotating his right shoulder forward, re-directing the attacker's balance and ki to the attacker's rear. At this point, it is the attacker's head, rather than his body, that is being thrown.

A-4 Suenaka completes his move forward on his right foot, dropping his hips and directing his ki downward **A-5** thus completing the throw.

YOKOMEN-UCHI SUMI-OTOSHI TENKAN (side of the head strike attack, corner drop defense, turning)

B-1 The attacker strikes toward Suenaka's head (*yoko-men-uchi*). Suenaka begins moving rearward on his left foot, turning away (*tenkan*) as he raises his hands **B-2** and captures the attacker's striking hand with his left while striking (*atemi*) with his right to the attacker's head. Note that this capture is not a block, but a blend. Simultaneously, he continues turning while initiating control of the attacker (*kuzushi*) and directing his ki downward **A-5** thus completing the throw. **B-3** Suenaka continues turning, further capturing and blending with the attacker's ki as he lays his right hand to the side of the attacker's head and cuts downward **B-4** propelling the attacker off his feet **B-5** and onto the mat, completing the throw. Note how Suenaka keeps his grip on the attacker's lead hand, so that a submission may be employed.

YEOMEN-UCHI IRIMI-NAGE (side of the head strike attack, entering throw)

C-1 The attacker intends to strike toward Suenaka's head (*yoko-men-uchi*), moving his right hand backwards, chambering for the strike. Suenaka moves in (*irimi*), sliding with his left foot.

C-2 and cutting down and back with his left hand on the attacker's striking wrist. Simultaneously, he slides his right hand up the attacker's chest and

C-3 over his shoulder, close to the attacker's head, while continuing the downward/rearward cut with his right arm. Note how Suenaka continues moving in (*irimi*). At this point, he has blended with the attacker's ki and re-directed it rearward.

C-4 Suenaka continues the downward cut, dropping his hips. The attacker is thrown.

KATATE-TORI SAYU-NAGE IRIMI (wrist grab attack, sideways throw)

D-1 The attacker grabs Suenaka's wrist (*katate-tori*) and prepares to move in to strike with his left hand.

D-2 Suenaka moves to the attacker's right side, simultaneously turning his body to the left, leading (not pulling) the attacker off-balance and blending with the attacker's ki. This also removes Suenaka from the attacker's offensive sphere. As he does so, Suenaka strikes, further destroying the attacker's focus (*kime*).

D-3 Suenaka continues to move in, extending his left hand into the center of the attacker's sphere/center of balance, until his left shoulder is beneath the attacker's chin. At this point, Suenaka has blended completely with the attacker's ki and has re-directed it, leading the attacker even further off-balance.

D-4 Suenaka rotates his left shoulder rearward while dropping his hips and bringing his right hand down atop the attacker's chest. The attacker is thrown. It is the hip drop and shoulder rotation that effects the throw. Without this, the additional strike to the chest has less impact.

TENKAN VERSUS IRIMI

The following examples illustrate the difference between *tenkan* (turning away) and *irimi* (entering), using the same technique. Refer to the sidebar **Tenkan Versus Irimi** for further explanation.

YOKOMEN-UCHI KATA-OTOSHI TENKAN
(Side of the head strike attack, shoulder drop defense, turning)

E-1 The attacker strikes toward Suenaka's head (*yoko-men-uchi*). Suenaka begins moving into proper stance to respond to the attack.

E-2 As the attacker strikes, Suenaka turns away (*tenkan*), moving to his rear on his left foot at an oblique angle, taking himself off of the attacking line. He simultaneously captures the attacker's striking hand and places his right on the attacker's shoulder, capturing and blending with the attacker's ki and leading him off-balance.

E-3 Suenaka continues moving away (*tenkan*), cutting the striking arm downward with both hands. At this point, his ki is completely blended with the attacker's, further off-balancing him.

E-4 and propelling him off his feet, completing the throw.

YOKOMEN-UCHI KATA-OTOSHI IRIMI

(Side of the head strike attack, shoulder drop defense, entering)

F-1 The attacker strikes toward Suenaka's head, as shown before. This time, however, instead of waiting for the attacker to strike, **F-2** Suenaka immediately moves in, cutting down and rearward on the striking hand as it is still being chambered, re-directing it and the attacker's ki rearward (see *yokomen-uchi irimi-nage*). Suenaka simultaneously places his right hand on the attacker's shoulder and cuts downward and rearward on it as well. **F-3** Suenaka continues moving inward and cutting downward, moving forward on his right foot, dropping his hips and completing the throw.

· 7 ·

Energy Projection in Aikido Wrist Techniques
by Bob Ward, B.A.

All photographs & calligraphy courtesy of Dave Champ.

As with all higher martial arts based on universal principles, aikido can be practiced and understood on many different levels. Over the years, an aikidoka will experience the same technique being performed in a myriad of ways, ranging from very athletic to extremely subtle. Of course, your perception of the technique will depend on your own athletic ability, maturity, and the level of your teachers. The first time I felt a *shihan* (master or "root" teacher), who was twenty-five years my senior, move me easily and with no apparent strength or speed, I was amazed and extremely excited. From that moment on, my focus shifted: my only desire was to direct my training and study toward the development of that energy.

> Ultimately, you must forget about technique.
> The further you progress, the fewer techniques there are.
> The Great Path is really No Path.
> – Morihei Ueshiba, founder of aikido

On a mechanical level, the fundamental aikido techniques of *nikyo* (second principle), *shihonage* (four directions throw), and *kotegaeshi* (wrist turn) all seem to be based on the principle of applying enough pressure (felt as pain) to your opponents' wrists to convince them to compromise their balance to avoid further pain. Because of aikido's nonviolent ideals, any refinement of technique that allows you to take your opponent's balance with less pain or risk of injury elevates the art to a higher level.

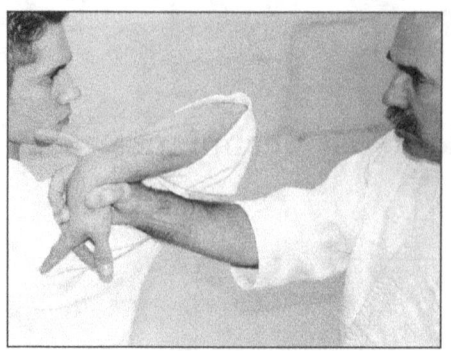

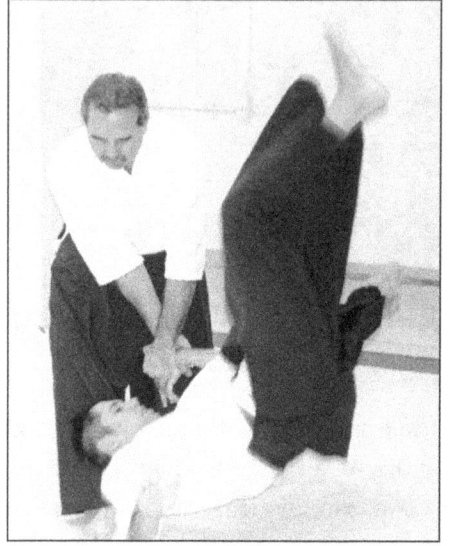

As an internal martial art, aikido teaches its practitioners to use intention rather than strength or speed. Unfortunately, all too often this idea is expressed in theory, and although long-term practitioners eventually experience it, it is not usually explained with respect to specific basic techniques. Through the development of awareness and visualization, energy (*ki*) is projected beyond the physical limits of your body, and beyond and through a clearly defined target in your opponent's body. Your energy becomes unified and extended. To defend himself, your partner may attempt to relax and separate his joints so that this energy does not effect his center. You can overcome this by exploiting the limitation of his flexibility. In wrist techniques, this involves using a wrist lock simply to connect the wrist and forearm energetically to the elbow, then projecting your energy from the elbow to the shoulder and beyond so that when the technique is applied the target of the pressure is your opponent's spine and center of balance rather than their wrist.

This can be accomplished by "tightening the links." Imagine a chain composed of half a dozen large links with lots of slack between each link. If you push on a link on one end of the chain, the other end may not even move because the looseness of the links allows them to separate and move outward in all directions. Now, if you hold the chain at one end and twist the entire chain from the other end until the links are unified, then pressure on either end creates movement at the opposite end.

The classic example of the application of this idea in aikido is a technique that Morihei Ueshiba performed in the 1935 film, "Budo." As an attacker grabbed his lapel (*munedori*), master Ueshiba instantaneously aligned himself so that forward energy would lock his opponent's elbow. Then, by projecting his whole body forward from his center, he drove the now rigid arm directly into the attacker's shoulder and spine, knocking him completely off balance.

By experiencing the hand, wrist, forearm, arm, and shoulder as links in a chain, you can modify your approach to nikyo, shihonage, and kotegaeshi, three of the mainstays of aikido training. Not only the bones, but the muscles, tendons, and other connective tissue can be used to link up the elements. To be completely successful, your hands must be relaxed and sensitive. Too much tension in the grip will not only stop the flow of energy, but also distract you from the awareness needed to sense the pathway to your opponent's center. In general, become aware of the amount of strength you normally use and try to forego its use altogether for the best result.

For the examples, we will focus on the actual execution of each technique, as that is the aspect that distinguishes the technique's individuality, and the preliminary movements vary with different attacks. The main thing to remember about body position is to keep your center lined up with your opponent's center. This requires a stable but moveable stance, in case your opponent should attempt to move outside of your center alignment to thwart your technique and counter with his own. This is essential if he wishes to perform *kaeshiwaza* (reverse techniques). At first, however, is it best to practice with someone who will remain still while you explore the sensations of extension and connection. Later, when you feel comfortable with this awareness, ask your *uke* (person receiving the technique) to attempt to move out of alignment and use your whole body movement to reestablish the energetic pathway.

Technical Section

Nikyo 二教技

Let's begin with *nikyo* (second principle). Although there are several versions of nikyo that can all make use of this idea, let's concentrate on the shoulder-assisted version of the technique. Use your left thumb in combination with your left little finger and ring finger to twist your partner's left hand until their left *tegatana* (hand blade) is pointing upward and twisted toward their face. Then rest the back of your left thumb on your right shoulder as in figure 1. Reach around with the fingers as far as necessary and tighten the wrist until you feel that you have connected the wrist to the forearm. Now, reach over the top of your partner's wrist with your right hand and press down and forward until you feel the forearm connecting to the elbow. If done properly, the uke will feel the connection immediately. Now, to connect the elbow into the shoulder, you have to keep a subtle but constant forward pressure on the linked structure leading to the shoulder. Nikyo is invariably taught with this forward pressure, but usually to keep the elbow bent. Also, for the correct alignment, the uke's little finger must be aimed directly at their center. When the correct connection of the links is felt and alignment is correct, apply downward and forward pressure at the wrist, visualizing a continuous pathway to the uke's center (see figure 2). Take your time and experiment with different partners. Those with more flexible joints will require somewhat more tension and more accurate alignment.

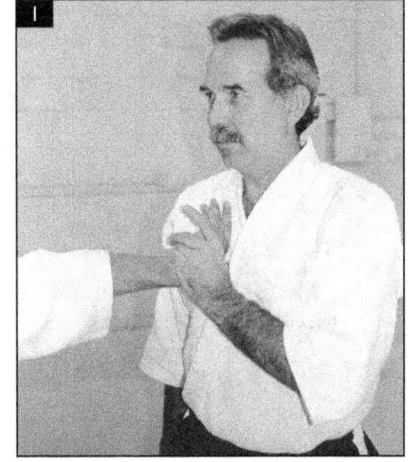

Shihonage

四方投げ

For shihonage, the links are tightened not by lining them up, but rather by bending them around in concentric circles until one end of the structure clearly affects the other end. With your right hand, grasp your partner's right hand at the wrist with the back of your hand facing away from you as shown in figure 3. Now gradually strike forward and downward as if striking with a sword. As with nikyo, your hand must be an instrument of sensory input as well as an instrument of energy output. So, relax and feel the tight circle created by the hand as it connects to the forearm. It is very important that the trajectory of the strike be toward the uke's back, in the line created by the natural bend of the arm, to avoid outward pressure on the elbow (see figure 4). As the forearm connects to the elbow, feel and visualize the elbow as the tip of the sword, which you are holding as one unit and striking forward and down. As you continue downward, the upper arm will tighten and the shoulder will be connected to your strike, thoroughly taking your partner's balance, both to their back and downward. As with nikyo, performing shihonage with this awareness of alignment and energy projection will be more effective and less painful or potentially harmful to your partner.

Kotegaeshi

小手返し

Finally, let's look at *kotegaeshi*. Nikyo tightened the links by turning and compressing them, shihonage by directing them in a spiral. Kotegaeshi tightens the links by turning and extending them. Take your partner's left hand in your right, with your thumb on the back of the hand just below and between the middle and ring finger knuckles, and your little and ring finger wrapped around the base of the wrist as shown in figures 5a-b. Visualize

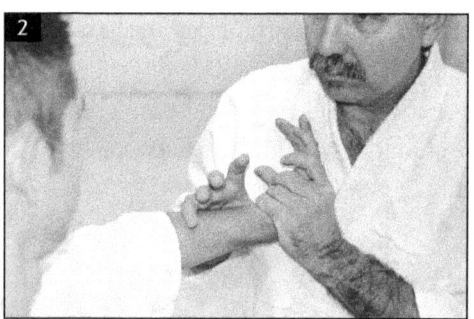

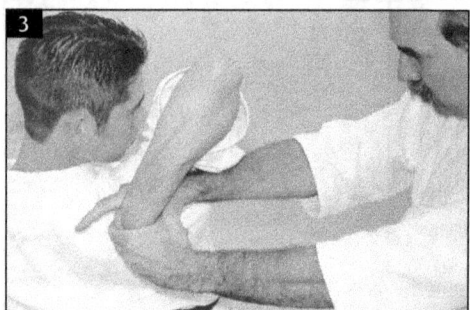

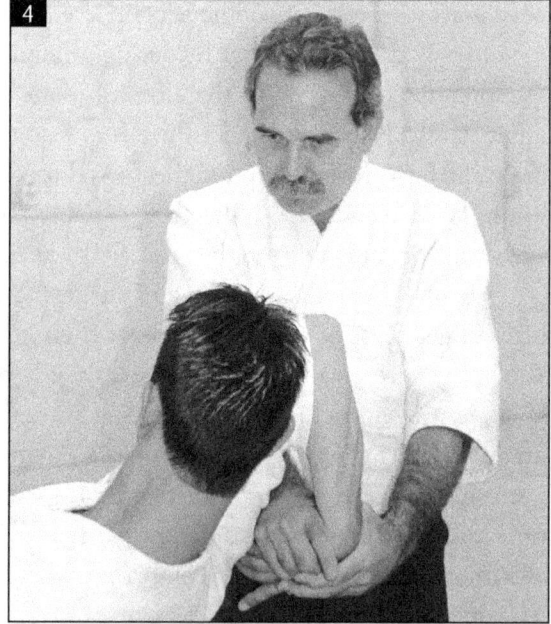

the pathway up the arm. Then, while pulling with the fingers, apply pressure with the thumb in the direction that causes the hand and wrist to tighten and link to the elbow. Feel the connection to the elbow. Experiment: turn the wrist in different directions until you find the clearest link. Now the extending part. Continuing the forward pressure on the wrist that energetically links it all the way to the elbow, direct that whole structure down and away from your partner's body, keeping your hand in front of your center and turn from your waist, until the elbow is linked to the shoulder and the shoulder drops down to an unbalanced position (figures 6a-b). Using your left hand to assist by pressing with your left palm on your right thumb, turn from your center, directing downward with your hands until you completely take your partner's balance and force them to take a fall.

It is essential to the execution of all three of these techniques that you establish an initial imbalance in the wrist and maintain that feeling while sequentially establishing further imbalance in the forearm, elbow, shoulder, and spine. Eventually, this projection will become second nature, and the entire process will be intuitive and immediate. Then you can reevaluate all of your techniques with respect to finding the most direct pathway to unbalancing your partner's center.

As the taijiquan classics say, there are three levels of practice: hands, torso, and mind. When we begin our aikido journey, we tend to see the techniques as hands and arms manipulating hands and arms. Eventually, we connect our hands and arms to our center and move as one whirling unit from the center of our *hara* (lower abdomen). If we can also connect our center to our opponent's center through the correct use of visualization (mind), then hands, arms, and torsos become but instruments of our true center, and our practice becomes effortless, safer, and infinitely more enjoyable.

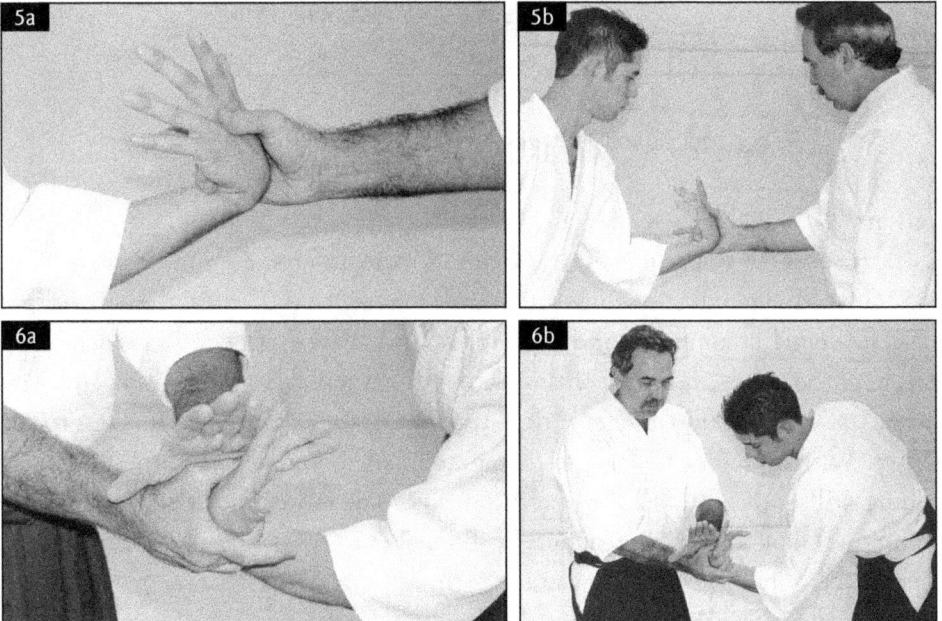

· 8 ·

Aikido's Armlock (*ude-gatame*) Technique: What Tissues are Affected?

by Gregory Olson, M.Sc., Morgan Cook, B.S., & Lisa Brooks, Ph.D.

All photographs and illustrations courtesy of Gregory Olson.

Introduction

As each successive year passes, the Oriental martial arts seem to be growing in popularity. With this popularity comes a gradual recognition of the validity of these arts by the academic community and the media, and there has been some academic investigation of the myths and the realities surrounding these martial arts and ways. The Japanese martial way of aikido and its various techniques are of particular interest to the investigators. With an understanding of the anatomical consequences of these fighting and subduing skills, not only will the practitioner become more efficient in the various *waza* (technique), but the *sensei* (teachers) will be able to teach the skills with a more thorough appreciation of the efficiency of the technique and with greater considerations of safety for the practitioners.

The researchers are interested in understanding the various subduing skills, as taught by the founder of aikido, such as *ikkyo* (first-teaching), *nikyo* (second-teaching), *sankyo* (third-teaching), *yonkyo* (fourth-teaching), and *gokyo* (fifth-teaching), as well as the other subduing techniques of the art. The investigators have completed several anatomical studies examining selected techniques in aikido's technical curriculum (Olson & Seitz, 1990, 1993, 1994; Seitz, Olson, & Stenzel, 1991; Olson, Seitz, & Guldbrandsen, 1994, 1996). The authors have chosen the vocabulary of *ude-gatame* (arm-lock) believing this to be the most common terminology used to describe this technique (H. Ikeda, personal communication, May 16, 1998). In aikido, this technique has been referred to by other terms. Ueshiba (1985: 139) refers to the technique as *ude-hishigi* (arm-smashing). It is interesting to note that he sees this technique as a variation of aikido's nikyo. This waza is also referred to as *hiji-jime* (elbow-strangulation) by Gozo Shioda (1997: 114; 1996: 166). D'Onofrio and Goto (1998: 37) refer to the technique as *rokkyo* (sixth-teaching). While primarily affecting the elbow, this type of extension lock is the same technique as found in judo and jujutsu. This technique is known in Dr. K. Kana's judo as *ude-hishigijuji-gatame* (arm-smashing cross-armlock) as seen in the *Bulletin of the Association for the Scientific Studies on Judo* (1963: 59–66). Whether in judo, aikido, or jujutsu, the technique's fundamental purpose remains the same; to hold the *uke* (receiver of the technique) in a compromised and secured position with a minimal amount of effort.

The objective of this study is to investigate the physical mechanism underlying ude-gatame. The investigators are aware of the complexities related to evaluating pain perception and prefer to focus the discussion on the tissues affected for this preliminary analysis of ude-gatame. Future work will expand to include pain perception, primarily in relation to training.

Ude-gatame is traditionally applied as an unarmed defense to an armed attack. By securing the joints of the elbow and wrist, the *tori* (doer of the technique) is able to maintain control of the uke and the uke ". . . will drop the stick [weapon] and become unable to move as a result" (Ueshiba, 1985: 139).

Anatomical Description of the Elbow

The elbow joint is where the humerus articulates with the radius and ulna bones. The motion of the elbow is a result of the hinging action of the ulna with the humerus reinforced by the medial (*ulna*) and lateral (*radial*) collateral ligaments (Eppright & Wilkins, 1975: 487). Since these ligaments are located on either side of the joint, they act as two stays that have a dual function: 1) to stabilize the joint itself and, 2) to prevent all lateral movement. The strength of the elbow joint depends on these ligaments.

Flexion and extension are the primary movements of the elbow. The elbow is most stable in the flexed position. During flexion, the posterior fibers of the medial collateral ligament are taut; during extension, the anterior fibers are taut (Eppright & Wilkins, 1975: 492).

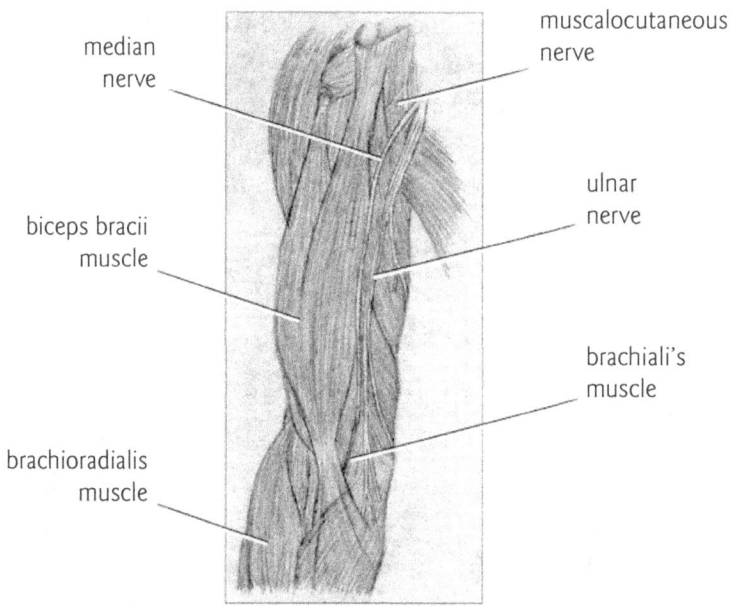

Technical Application

At the beginning of this report, it must be stated and emphasized that the investigators were not looking at hyper-extension of the elbow joint, nor was the investigation concerned with over rotation of the arm. These two phenomenon are commonly seen in beginners and intermediate practitioners of aikido and related arts. In the opinion of the authors, these variations are not the technique being studied.

The advanced application of ude-gatame can be described as the raising of the arm perpendicular to the side of the body and pulling along the axis of the humerus, extending the arm while the hand is held in a pronated and flexed position. With the hand held this way, the humerus can be rotated to its maximum extent. In conjunction with this, two parallel, but opposing forces are applied rotationally in the medial plane at the wrist and laterally at the elbow.

For the effective application of these forces, several conditions should be met:

1. The arm is raised to the side of the body.
2. Longitudinal tension is applied along the axis of the humerus. This tension stretches both of the ligaments and begins to separate the head of the ulna from the end of the humerus. The result is an initial destabilization of the elbow joint.
3. The hand is held in full pronation and is flexed while the humerus is rotated in the medial plane to the maximum extent. The flexed and pronated hand becomes the lever arm on which torque is exerted to further rotate the humerus to its maximum extent, an action which assists in securing the arm. With the arm secured, the torque on the arm further destabilizes the elbow joint by applying strain to the posterior part of the anterior band of the medial ligament. It should be noted that steps 2 and 3 occur simultaneously.

The purpose of these conditions is to "create a situation where the joint is least stable in the medial or lateral planes" (D. Phillips, personal communication, May, 1998). Once the joint has been destabilized in the lateral (side-to-side) plane, force is applied perpendicular to the axis of the arm. At this stage of ude-gatame, these parallel, but opposing forces are applied 90 degrees to the normal range of motion of the elbow joint, rotationally at the wrist and laterally at the elbow. By viewing the arm as a lever, it is easily seen that the fulcrum can be placed in two separate positions along the arm, with force applied at two different points to achieve the same general effect with three combinations of fulcrum and force application.

1. With the arm secured (the fulcrum is at the elbow),
   rotational force is applied to the forearm.
2. With the forearm secured (the fulcrum is at the wrist),
   lateral force is applied to the forearm.
3. With the forearm secured (the fulcrum is at the wrist),
   lateral force is applied to the elbow.

Two anatomy professors[1] with the WWAMI (Washington, Wyoming, Alaska, Montana, Idaho) medical program at Montana State University examined a cadaver as part of the project. Detailed observations were made on the elbow of the cadaver to determine tissues affected. It should be noted that the professors of anatomy had no training in aikido and therefore had no preconceived expectations as to where the applied technique would be felt. The experience of the researchers was taken into consideration when applying the technique to each other.[2]

Discussion

The researchers found that when the technique was applied, the arm was affected in three separate locations:

1. The distal end of the humerus, where tori had secured uke's arm.
2. The posterior portion of the anterior band of the medial ligament.
3. The site of the dislocation of the radius and ulna in relationship to the distal end of the humerus.

While most of the subjects felt the first indication of the technique at the distal end of the humerus, where tori had secured uke's arm, only one of the subjects felt that the technique had become unbearable at this stage of the technique.

Kobayashi and Sharp (1956: 95) state that pressure should be applied "by pulling his arm back," and making "sure his thumb is up." Fukuda (1983: 62) states that "the [finishing] position in which the little finger side of Uke's hand is uppermost" further collaborates the application of the applied pressure in a direction of 90 degrees to the natural bend of the elbow or, to "create a situation where the joint is least stable in the side-to-side plane" (D. Phillips, personal communication, May, 1998).

With regards to anatomical effects on uke only one investigator has speculated on the general effects of ude-gatame on the anatomy of the uke. Suzuki states that:

> ... in this experiment stretch pain was felt, at first, in the soft tissue of the region opposite the point acting as the fulcrum, for example, when the forearm was pulled in the radial direction, pain was felt in the ulnar region opposite the head of the radius. During actual performance of the "Kansetsu-waza" both the stretch pain and the pressure pain are felt simultaneously, so the pain is felt in the entire region of the elbow joint.   – Suzuki, 1963: 60

While there was some straining of both the medial and lateral ligaments due to the initial destabilization of the elbow, the tissue primarily affected was the posterior part of the anterior band of the medial ligament. The two researchers with considerable experience in aikido, found that the technique had to be applied to the point of initial dislocation of the elbow before the technique became unbearable. It is possible that at this point in the technique, the medial ligament is on the verge of either tearing or separating from the bone.

Conclusion

Our objective was to investigate the fundamental mechanics that underlie the securing technique, ude-gatame, and, specifically, to understand how the application of the technique affects the soft tissue of the arm. By understanding the anatomy and mechanics of the elbow, tori can easily and securely hold uke in a compromised position.

> **Glossary**
> *Distal*: Remote from the point of attachment or origin, from a point conceived of as central.
> *Proximal*: Next to or nearest the point of attachment or origin, from a point conceived of as central.
> *Anterior*: 1. Situated toward the front. 2. Relating to or situated near or toward the head.
> *Posterior*: 1. Situated toward the back. 2. Situated or toward the hinder end of the body.
> *Medial*: Here, the plane perpendicular to the axis of the humerus in which rotational forces are applied.
> *Pronate*: To rotate (as hand or forearm) at to bring the palm facing downward.
> *Pronation*: A medial rotation of the hand and radius around the ulna so that the palm is facing downward.

Applied by an experienced practitioner of the martial arts in general and aikido or judo in particular, this technique is one of the more effective subduing and grappling techniques in aikido's repertoire. Whether attacked with a lunging movement, with a weapon, or with a fist, this is an effective technique with which tori can, not only control the outcome, but also nullify, control, and subdue uke with a minimum amount of force and with maximum efficiency.

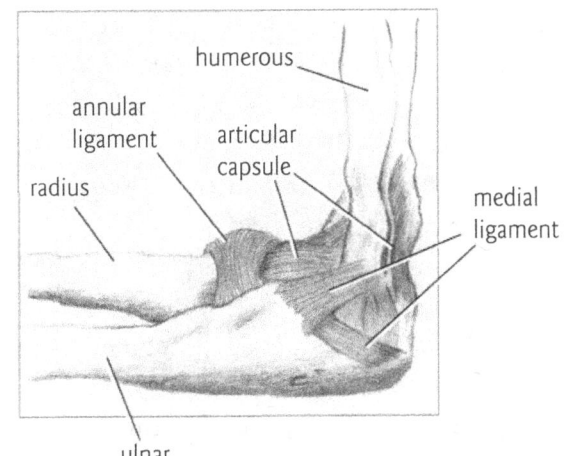

With regard to this technique's limitations, it is the opinion of the researchers that the application of forces here is notably subtle and intricate, and therefore difficult to learn, especially without the direct tutelage by an experienced teacher. Notwithstanding, with the correct instruction and application, this particular technique can be extremely practical and efficient.

Notes

[1] For their anatomical expertise, a special thanks to Dr. Dwight Phillips and Ms. Susan Gibson.

[2] The researchers have a combined total of forty-seven years of training. The first re-

searcher has the rank of godan in aikido and sandan in judo with over thirty-three years of training. The second researcher has the rank of shodan in aikido and has been training for more than twelve years. The third researcher has been training for two years and does not have dan rank.

[3] For her drawings of the elbow, a special thanks to Ms. Kristin Petersen.

Bibliography

D'Onofrio, R., & Goto, H. (1998). Disarming knife attacks (Part 3). *Aikido Journal*, 25(1), 37.

Eppright, R. & Wilkings, E. (1975). Fractures and dislocations of the elbow. In C. Rockwood, Jr., & D. Green (Eds.), *Fractures* (pp. 487–563). Philadelphia: J. B. Lippincott Company.

Fukuda, K. (1973). *Born for the mat: A Kokokan kata textbook for women*. San Francisco: Keiko Fukuda.

Joseph, J. (1982). *A textbook of regional anatomy*. Baltimore: University Park Press.

Kapardji, I. (1970). *The physiology of the joints, vol. 1: Upper limb*. Churchill Livingstone, 78–108.

Kobayashi, K., & Sharp, H. (1956). *The sport of judo*. Rutland, VT: Charles E. Tuttle Co.

Obata, T. (1987). *Samurai aikijutsu*. Thousand Oaks, CA: Dragon Books.

Olson, G. (1996). *Aikido: A beginner's text*. Dubuque, IA: Kendall-Hunt Publishing Company.

Olson, G., & Seitz, E (1990). An examination of aikido's fourth teaching: An anatomical study of the tissues of the forearm. *Perceptual and Motor Skills*, 71, 1059–1066.

Olson, G., & Seitz, E (1993). An anatomical analysis of aikido's second teaching: An investigation of nikyo. *Perceptual and Motor Skills*, 77, 123–131.

Olson, G., & Seitz, E (1994). What's causing the pain?: A re-examination of the aikido nikyo technique. *Perceptual and Motor Skills*, 79, 1585–1586.

Olson, G., Seitz, E, & Guldbrandsen, E. (1994). An anatomical analysis of aikido's third teaching: An investigation of sankyo. *Perceptual and Motor Skills*, 78, 1347–1352.

Olson, G., Seitz, E, & Guldbrandsen, E. (1996). An inquiry into application of gokyo (aikido's fifth teaching) on human anatomy. *Perceptual and Motor Skills*, 82, 1299–1303.

Saotome, M. (1986). *Aikido and the harmony of nature*. Boulogne, France: Serirep.

Saotome, M. (1989). *The principles of aikido*. Boston: Shambhala.

Seitz, E., Olson, G., & Stenzel, T. (1991). A martial arts exploration of elbow anatomy: Ikkyo (aikido's first teaching). *Perceptual and Motor Skills*, 73, 1227–1234.

Shido, G. (1977). *Dynamic aikido*. New York: Kodansha.

Shido, G. (1996). *Total aikido*. New York: Kodansha.

Suzuki, K. (1963). Roentgenographic studies on "kansetsu-waza." *Bulletin of the Association for the Scientific Studies on Judo*, Kodokan, Report No. 2, 59–66.

Ueshiba, K. (1985). *Aikido*. Tokyo: Hozansha.

· 9 ·

Culture, Training, and Perception of the Martial Arts: Aikido's Example
by C. Jeffrey Dykhuizen, Ph.D.

Illustration courtesy of Oscar Ratti. © 2000 Futuro Designs & Publications. All photos courtesy of Akiko O. Dykhuizen.

Introduction

Asian martial arts are now being practiced in cultures other than those within which they originated more than at any other point in history. As the rate of diffusion of these arts increases, specific information concerning how practitioners from different cultures understand them becomes increasingly useful to martial artists and martial arts scholars. This chapter summarizes several of the findings of a two-year cross-cultural investigation into the meaning and perceived training outcomes among aikido practitioners (*aikidoka*) in Japan and the United States. The results are two-fold, having both cross-cultural and developmental implications. In addition to showing how practitioners reported their perceptions of "martial arts" changing as a result of aikido training, the findings reveal similarities and differences in how Japanese and American aikidoka constructed meaning for "aikido," "ki," and the "martial arts."

Donohue (1994) has used the evolution of aikido technique and philosophy in Japan to illustrate that the ideology of budo is malleable and open to reinterpretation across time. He concluded that the "persistence of budo through time, however, has exposed it to social environments (both inside and outside of Japan) that have caused a reinterpretation of the ideology and function of what budo means" (Donohue & Taylor, 1994: 23). To compliment Donohue's historical perspective, this study takes a synchronic, cross-cultural approach to examine how aikidoka training in two distinct cultures structured their understandings of aikido, ki, and the martial arts.

Even a cursory review of the literature concerning outcomes of martial arts training reveals that participants report experiencing psychological as well as physical changes as a result of training (Columbus & Rice, 1991; Fuller, 1988). In addition to being a cross-cultural comparison then, this study investigated how practitioners thought that training in aikido influenced their perceptions of the martial arts. Individuals who have participated in martial arts training know that it can facilitate a process of transforming how one looks at the world, and can change one's perceptions and understandings of the martial arts in particular. This article presents specific examples of how Japanese and American aikidoka reported their perceptions as having changed as a result of training.

Aikido as a Martial Art

As readers of this book are well aware, aikido is a Japanese martial art founded by Morihei Ueshiba. Aikido developed out of Ueshiba's training in aikijutsu, kenjutsu, jujutsu, and other uniquely Japanese martial arts. The art's philosophic underpinnings were influenced by the founder's involvement in the Omoto-kyo religion.

Aikido is frequently translated into English as "the way of harmony" or "the way of harmony with nature." The emphasis upon harmony can be observed during training sessions: instructors frequently encourage practitioners to maintain a dynamic yet calm center and a balanced integration of body, mind, and spirit (Ueshiba, 1984). Aikido is an increasingly popular martial training activity engaged in by persons of both genders and various ages in Japan and throughout the world.

Aikido is often regarded as a martial art with a powerful spiritual component, and the emphasis in aikido techniques is upon turning away an attack (Ueshiba, 1984; Saotome, 1993). Most aikido techniques are initiated by an attempted strike of some form. The primary martial emphasis in aikido is upon attack neutralization, an emphasis that is consistent with the philosophy of harmony and non-aggression that help define aikido as a martial activity. Some form of physical conflict, a chop or punch for example, must be initiated to create a context within which aggression and its neutralization may be studied. Understanding that aikido training involves the study of aggression and its neutralization is crucial for interpreting the results of this study.

Culture as a Research Variable

There are various scholastic approaches to culture that can be used to examine the enormous breadth and depth of forces that influence an individual's thought. In this study, culture is thought of using the cross-cultural researcher Berry's (1992) definition of a "condition" or "context" within which individuals formulate and refine their understandings of particular activities and ideas.

Referring to culture in this manner, the terms "America" (employed to parsimoniously refer to the United States) and "Japan" are used to indicate specific, socially constructed worlds within which aikidoka train, and not to entire nation-states. As Berry pointed out, the contrast between large cultural populations "is rarely of more psychological interest than between the people of two small groups within the two areas" (Berry, et. al., 1992: 228).

Methodology

A variety of methods were used to gather and analyze data for this study. Quantitative data were gathered using semantic differentials and a participant background questionnaire. Qualitative data were gathered using interviews, participant observation, and observation of training sessions at dojo in Japan and America. The various forms of data were integrated using the constant comparative method (Glasser & Strauss, 1967). Because the semantic differential was crucial in discovering how practitioners understood aikido, ki, and the martial arts, this tool is outlined below, along with a short description of the aikidoka who participated in the study.

Semantic Differentials

The semantic differential (Osgood, Suci, & Tannenbaum, 1957) is a tool designed to measure the meaning that a person or group of people have for a concept. The semantic differential utilizes the principles of synesthesia—using descriptors from one sense to describe a sensation experienced through another. For example, when a person says, "That's a hot move!" when referring to someone's new dance step, they are using the principles of synesthesia. Because receiving instruction and training in the martial arts involves various sensory modes—visual, tactile, aural, kinesetic—the semantic differential was appropriate for use in this study.

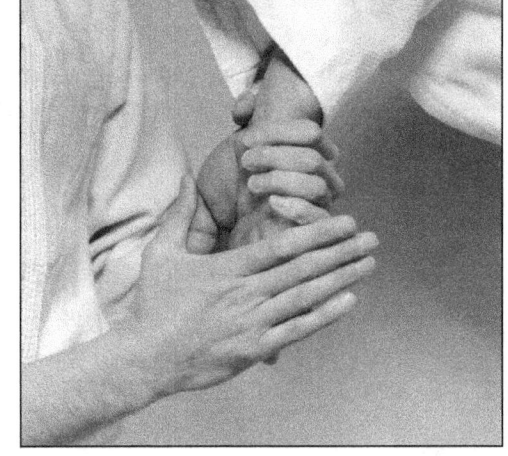

The semantic differential surveys for the concepts measured were constructed using twelve pairs of adjectives, opposite in meaning, arranged on a scale.

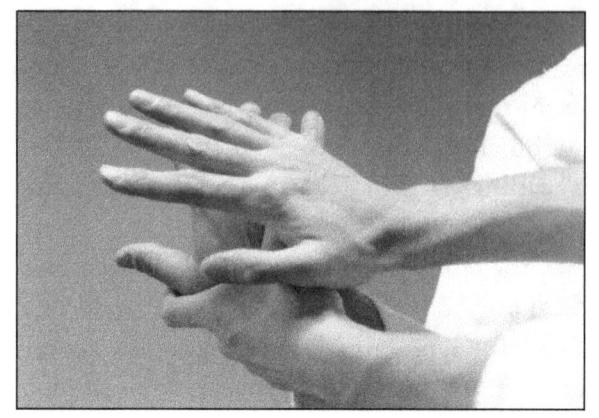

Participants had simply to mark on the scale the degree to which they thought one of the adjectives on the scale was a more accurate descriptor of the concept than the other. For example, the participant might think that the concept "aikido" is much more "rounded" than "angular," and make a mark closer to "rounded" on that particular seven-point scale between the two descriptive words. This was done for each of the twelve scales, referred to as items, for each concept. Each marked item serves as a point to orienteer where in "semantic space" the participants think a particular concept exists—kind of like a Global Tracking System for meaning.

After collecting the completed semantic differentials from all the participants, a factor analysis was run on the data. The data for the Japanese and American participants were analyzed separately. Factor analysis is a procedure that is often used in fields where many variables are part of research; psychology, education, and business are examples. It is a statistical procedure that identifies groups of highly related items that cluster together to represent an underlying factor or property. The procedure is useful because it allows researchers to condense many variables into a few factors that succinctly reveal the primary characteristics of what is being researched, in this case, the primary dimensions of meaning of the concepts. Using factor analysis in this study provided a way to examine how participants structured their understandings of aikido-related ideas in a sophisticated, but not unnecessarily complex, manner. Examining the factors that emerged from the analysis facilitated the interpretation and comparison of data gathered within the two groups.

It should be noted that the number of factors for a concept indicates the complexity of meaning that participants have for that concept: more factors extracted from the data indicates greater complexity of meaning.

In this study, the following concepts were measured using semantic differentials:

❶ "Aikido is…";
❷ "Ki is…";
❸ "Before I began training in aikido, I thought martial arts were…"; and
❹ "My aikido training has helped me understand that martial arts are…".

The factors depicted in the tables represent how participants structured their understandings of these concepts.

Back-Translation

Language is a means by which thought and meaning are generated and expressed. From a linguistic perspective, this study made inquiry into how understandings of an activity indigenous to one culture were generated and expressed in a culture with a different linguistic system. To ensure that the meanings collected among Japanese and the American practitioners would be comparable—that the meaning of "apples" would be compared with the meaning of "apples" and not that of "oranges"—the semantic differentials and interview questions were back-translated (Brislin, 1980).

The back-translation process consisted of a bilingual person translating the material from one language (English) to another (Japanese), after which another bilingual person independently translated the tool back to the original language. The first and third versions of the documents were then compared for consistency. The back-translation process helps ensure the comparability of data in cross-cultural/cross-linguistic studies and the result of the process "means that the research project is not centered around any one culture or language" (Brislin, 1980: 433).

Participants

All participants in the study were adult aikido practitioners training in dojo in Japan and the United States. In each culture, data was gathered only from participants who were "native" to that culture; data was gathered only among Japanese aikido practitioners in Japan, and only from Americans in the United States.

In the United States, 128 aikido practitioners training at nine dojos completed these mantic differential packets. Six of the nine dojos in the United States were affiliated with Aikikai, while three were affiliated with Aikido Schools of Ueshiba. All were located within a three-state area in the Midwest. In the Japanese research setting, 120 aikido practitioners training at twelve Aikikai-affiliated dojos in the Kanto area completed the semantic differentials.

Aikido practitioners were also interviewed. The interviews were conducted in English in America and in Japanese in Japan. The interviews were audio taped, translated in the case of the Japanese interviews, and transcribed to text for analysis. The ages of the Japanese interviewees ranged from 20 to 55 years, training time from one to over forty years, and participants had aikido rankings ranging from fourth *kyu* to eighth *dan* (eight-degree black belt). Two of the ten participants were female, and three of the males were instructors. In the United States, seven participants,

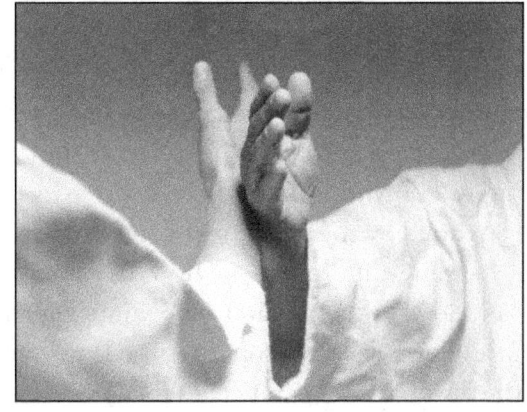

one of whom was female, were interviewed. Their ages ranged from twenty to fifty. Their aikido experience ranged from one year to more than 25, and they had ranks ranging from fifth kyu to fourth dan. Three of the participants in the United States were instructors.

RESULTS

The semantic differential findings provide a basic structure of participants' understandings of aikido, ki, and the martial arts. In addition to serving as an accuracy check for the semantic differential findings, the interviewees' comments helped generate a fuller, more detailed description of participants' personal understandings of aikido and the martial arts. The integrated findings are presented below.

CONCEPT 1: AIKIDO IS...

Of all of the concepts investigated in this study, the greatest similarity between Japanese and American participants was found for "Aikido is...". For both groups, three factors emerged from the semantic differential data during analysis. For the concept "Aikido is...," there were no significant differences in the complexity of understandings between practitioners in Japan and America.

Although the meaning of the concept "aikido" had equivalent complexity for each cultural group, an examination of the items making up each factor revealed slight differences. Items that loaded above .60 during analysis form the connotative value or "meaning" of the factor. The first factor extracted from the Japanese data contained the five items "beautiful," "kind," "graceful," "peaceful," and "rounded." These items connote a sense of ethical fluidity, characterizing harmony. The first factor extracted from the American data contained the items "beautiful," "graceful," and "strong," connoting a similar sense of aesthetic movement, but without an ethical component. However, the first factors extracted from the data of both cultural groups similarly connoted an aesthetic, fluid quality.

An examination of the second factors for the concept "Aikido is..." reveals more obvious meaning differences between the two groups. The second factor for the Japanese contained the items "heavy," "strong," and "active," connoting a quality of strength and assertion. The second factor extracted from the American data contained "cruel," "ferocious," "tenacious," and "active." These items connote a sense of wildness and aggression—a very different quality of meaning than that generated by their Japanese counterparts.

The differences in how the two cultural groups constructed meaning for "aikido" become clearer by examining the interview data. During analysis of the interviews, several properties used to define aikido emerged for each group. Among the distinguishing properties that Japanese participants consistently used to describe aikido were: harmony, ki, an emphasis on non-competition, and recognition of aikido as a means of personal development. These properties coincide with the semantic differential findings.

The properties consistently used by American interview participants to describe their understandings of aikido were: recognition of aikido as a martial art, aikido as a traditional activity, technique as philosophy manifest, and aikido as a means of personal development. While there are similarities among the properties used by the two groups, an emphasis upon recognizing aikido as a martial art was central to American participants' descriptions of their understandings. William, an American instructor, was very straightforward in describing his conception of the nature of aikido:

> I think that ... first, aikido is a martial art, and I want there to be no confusion. It is a martial art, and when you're starting to learn it, you need to learn it as a martial art (CG, transcribed interview, November 1995).

William further stated that he understood the nature of aikido training to be very practical, that the practice of aikido is grounded in issues of physical defense against attack. Tom, another American instructor, shared the same perspective, stating that martial aikido needs to be practiced for defense purposes, "... otherwise, you're just dancing around feeling good" (BK, transcribed interview, December 1995). An emphasis upon martial applicability was commonly observed and experienced during training sessions at aikido dojo within the American research setting.

While there were differences in meaning for the concept "aikido" between the two groups, both Japanese and American practitioners structured their understandings of aikido around a factor that connotes aesthetic fluidity, a sense of "harmony." For the Japanese data, the factor also included an ethical component. The use of a "harmony" factor for the concept "aikido" for both cultural groups may be accounted for by aikido's universal representation as a means of martial training emphasizing personal development and harmony; again, "aikido" is typically translated into English as "the way of harmony."

CONCEPT 2: KI IS...

Ki has been translated into English as "spirit," "mind," "will," and "intrinsic or inner energy" (O'Neill, 1973; Ratti & Westbrook, 1973). "Ki" is a complex term, yet because various Asian martial arts assert its existence and contain training methods designed to enhance ki generation and control (Yuasa, 1993), it is important to investigate how practitioners understand it. This is especially true of aikido: one stated goal of practice in aikido is to develop the centralization and extension of ki, and to coordinate it with the surrounding circumstances in the creation of a "way of harmony" (Ratti & Westbrook, 1973: 59). In addition, "ki" is quite literally central to aikido—the Japanese character occupies the central position in the word.

The first factor extracted from the Japanese data consisted of the five items: "kind," "graceful," "peaceful," "soft," and "rounded." These items connote a very similar sense of ethical, fluid harmony that characterized the first factor for the Japanese understanding of "aikido." The first factor extracted from the American data was very different: it consisted of "cruel," "ferocious," "hard," and "tenacious." The connotative quality of these items is aggressive and wild. No factor that carried a similar quality of meaning was extracted from the Japanese data for any concept.

The second factor extracted from the Japanese data consisted of the items "strong," "deep," and "active"; and the third factor, "heavy" and "tenacious." The second factor extracted from the American data contained "beautiful," "graceful," "strong," "deep," "tenacious," and "active."

As can be seen in Table 2, three distinct factors for the ki concept emerged from the Japanese data, while only two emerged from the American data. This indicates that Japanese practitioners structured their understanding of ki with greater complexity than their American counterparts. This is not surprising, as ki is not an integral part of American participants' linguistic system. Although English-speaking Americans training in aikido have more opportunities to refine their understanding of ki than do Americans who do not train in Japanese martial arts, their understanding of the concept was still represented in a less complex manner than that of Japanese practitioners. Japanese practitioners encounter the ki concept daily; for example, the character "ki" is used to comprise such commonly used words as air (*kuki*), sick (*byoki*), and temperature (*kion*). The character for ki is also contained in the Japanese equivalent of the greeting "How are you?" (*Ogenki desu ka?*); literally, "How is the source of ki?" For English speakers, however, ki is a foreign concept. The lack of complexity in the meaning constructed for the concept ki among Americans suggests that people have difficulty constructing meaning for foreign, abstract, and initially unfamiliar concepts. Hence, it is not surprising that American aikidoka's understandings of ki were less complex than their Japanese counterparts'.

The Japanese interview data also revealed that ki played an important role in their conceptions of aikido. One interview participant described the importance of ki and its relation to harmony in aikido: "If you do not have harmonious ki, you can not do aikido" (HK, transcribed interview, June 1995). Not only does this practitioner's statement illuminate the central importance of harmony to aikido, it also contextualizes this idea within the concept of ki.

While American interview participants were eager to discuss the nature of ki and its role in aikido philosophy and technique, they rarely did so without prompting, and sometimes qualified their explanations by stating that ki was "a foreign concept."

TABLE 1 "Aikido is . . ."

Results of the principle component analysis of the semantic differential data by culture.

JAPAN	Factors 1 Loadings	2	3
beautiful/ugly	.69	.27	.02
kind/cruel	.80	-.05	-.02
graceful/awkward	.79	.14	.10
peaceful/ferocious	.78	-.13	-.13
hard/soft	-.56	-.33	.22
heavy/light	-.01	.61	.06
strong/weak	.13	.79	-.10
deep/shallow	.51	.47	.03
tenacious/yielding	-.13	-.07	.89
active/passive	.19	.74	-.02
complex/simple	.02	.47	.44
angular/rounded	-.78	-.20	.22

USA	Factors 1 Loadings	2	3
beautiful/ugly	.77	-.16	.21
kind/cruel	.32	-.62	.001
graceful/awkward	.79	-.03	-.10
peaceful/ferocious	.16	-.74	-.17
hard/soft	-.15	.32	.65
heavy/light	-.17	.48	.29
strong/weak	.74	.22	-.02
deep/shallow	.57	-.18	-.04
tenacious/yielding	.07	.64	.37
active/passive	.29	.62	-.23
complex/simple	.07	-.02	.80
angular/rounded	-.51	.20	.30

TABLE 2 "Ki is . . ."

Results of the principle component analysis of the semantic differential data by culture.

JAPAN	Factors 1 Loadings	2	3
beautiful/ugly	.43	.59	-.35
kind/cruel	.74	.20	-.18
graceful/awkward	.81	.25	-.20
peaceful/ferocious	.80	.14	-.01
hard/soft	-.85	-.23	-.01
heavy/light	.08	.05	.78
strong/weak	.40	.63	.15
deep/shallow	.16	.85	-.06
tenacious/yielding	-.12	-.09	.69
active/passive	.22	.74	.14
complex/simple	-.14	.39	.50
angular/rounded	-.81	-.13	-.04

USA	Factors 1 Loadings	2
beautiful/ugly	-.35	.72
kind/cruel	-.76	.37
graceful/awkward	-.26	.72
peaceful/ferocious	-.72	.26
hard/soft	.72	-.20
heavy/light	.53	-.05
strong/weak	-.25	.64
deep/shallow	-.15	.73
tenacious/yielding	.69	.03
active/passive	.19	.67
complex/simple	.56	-.07
angular/rounded	-.55	-.36

CONCEPT 3:
Before I began training in aikido, I thought martial arts were...

Two factors were extracted from the Japanese data for concept 3. The first was comprised of the six items "beautiful," "kind," "graceful," "peaceful," "soft," and "rounded." These again connote harmony with an ethical component. The second factor contained the items "heavy," "strong," "active," and "complex."

Three factors were extracted from the American data. The first factor contained the items "cruel," "ferocious," "hard," "heavy," and "tenacious," connoting aggressiveness. The second factor was comprised of "beautiful," "graceful," "deep," and "complex"; and the third factor contained the items "strong" and "active."

A comparison of the two groups' understandings of concept 3 revealed that meaning for "martial arts" was more complexly structured by American aikidoka than Japanese aikidoka. This is a relatively surprising finding, as the "martial arts" (the term "budo" was used in the Japanese semantic differentials) have been an integral part of Japanese culture for hundreds of years, while they have only been introduced and practiced in American on a large scale in the past fifty or sixty years.

One possible explanation for this finding may be that, because the concept "martial arts" is such an integral part of Japanese culture, it was taken as an implicitly understood cultural given, while American aikidoka actively attempted to better understand the nature of the martial arts. For example, American interview participants reported reading and studying about the martial arts to a greater degree than did their Japanese counterparts, and many boasted of having "libraries" of martial arts literature.

Participants' education level is another finding that may help explain between-group differences in the complexity of pre-aikido training perceptions of martial arts. The participant background questionnaire revealed that the mean level of education for the two groups differed: 21% of American participants held degrees at the Master's level or above, while less than 2% of the Japanese participants held degrees at an equivalent level. The difference in mean level of education and the reported amount of martial arts literature studied both probably played a role in the generation of the differences in meaning complexity for the concept "martial arts."

CONCEPT 4:
My aikido training has helped me understand that martial arts are...

Three factors were extracted from the Japanese data for this concept. The first contained the items "beautiful," "graceful," "soft," and "rounded." These items connote a sense of gentle harmony. The second contained "heavy" and "complex"; and the third contained "kind" and "peaceful," connoting a sense of ethics.

Four factors were extracted from the data collected among aikido practitioners in the United States. Factor one contained "kind," "peaceful," and "strong." The second contained "beautiful," "graceful," "deep," and "rounded"; and the third factor contained the items "heavy" and "tenacious." These factors can be characterized, respectively, as ethical fortitude, aesthetic fluidity, and perseverance. The final factor contained the single item "active."

A factor connoting a sense of ethic was extracted on this concept for both cultural groups. Interestingly, the "ethic" factor was the first extracted from the American data but third from the Japanese data. For the Americans, this finding was especially surprising given that factor one for the previous concept—their pre-aikido training perceptions of martial arts connoted aggression. Therefore, American representations of their understandings of "martial arts" are dramatically different as a result of having trained in aikido—the meaning has shifted from being centered on aggression to being centered upon a sense of ethics.

A comparison of concepts 3 and 4 indicates that both Japanese and American aikido practitioners represented themselves as having gained a more complex understanding of martial arts as a result of training in aikido. Therefore, it seems that regardless of the cultural context within which practitioners train, aikido training resulted in changes in both the complexity of understanding and connotative value of perceptions of the martial arts. These findings are examined in greater detail below.

Discussion

The discussion is divided into three sections addressing the most pervasive and compelling findings of this investigation. The first section discusses the finding that practitioners reported their understandings of "martial arts" as having changed as a result of training in aikido. The second section addresses the differences in how the two cultural groups represented their understandings for aikido, ki, and martial arts. The final section briefly discusses several prominent aspects of culture that help account for the differences in meaning found between the two groups.

Aikido Training and Changing Perceptions of the Martial Arts

Before engaging in a fuller discussion of these findings, it should be noted that participants were recalling their perceptions of marital arts before they began training in aikido. It is possible that these recollections were not exact replications of their actual pre-aikido training perceptions. In studies that use data of a self-reported nature, however, it is necessary to take participants responses at face value. While this is not an ideal situation, it is assumed that they have reported their pre-aikido training perceptions of martial arts with relative accuracy, and that they have not attempted to deliberately misrepresent their impressions.

The comparison of concepts 3 and 4 shows that, for both groups, there was an increase in the number of factors extracted from the data—an increase from two to three factors for the Japanese, and from three to four factors for the Americans. This is an important finding. It indicates aikidoka represented themselves as having more complex understandings of the "martial arts" as a result of aikido training. The findings from the analysis of the interview data reinforce this. As one Japanese instructor stated during an interview: "If you do aikido, the way you think of the martial arts will change. Most people, regular people, think they [the martial arts] are for killing, for fighting, for becoming strong, and things like that. If you do aikido, I think your understanding of martial arts changes" (YA, transcribed interview, July 1995).

The reported changes in perception of the martial arts can be explained as a process of "reinterpretation." Participants reinterpreted their understandings of "martial arts" from within the context of the knowledge and experience that they gained as a result of training in aikido. Their experiential knowledge of aikido served as a sort of lens through which they came to refocus and express their understandings of the martial arts. The expanded perspective that their aikido training provided resulted in the generation of more complex understandings of the martial arts.

Some participants in this study had not trained in other martial arts prior to training in aikido. For these practitioners, changes in their perceptions may best be explained as a modification of their non-training-based conceptions of the martial arts: the new physical experiences they acquired from aikido training provided a means to reshape and reinterpret how and what they thought about the martial arts.

A similar process probably also occurred for individuals who had received training in other martial arts prior to initiating training in aikido. Over one half of American and nearly half of the Japanese interview participants reported switching from "harder" arts to train in aikido. For these practitioners, exposure to aikido principles, techniques, training styles, and ritual activities would provide a new dimension to the manner in which they were able to represent their understandings of the martial arts. Steve, an American participant who had trained in aikido for four years at the time of the interview, described his reasons for switching to aikido from karate:

> I just liked the idea of it. It was softer, it was more flowing. Or appeared to be anyway. And once I started reading the philosophy. . . it put enough interest there to check into it further. And, the techniques themselves and the idea that you do as little possible harm to the person. To begin with, the karate I had been studying was more the idea, "One punch, one kill." That was it. Which may have its place and it's cool too, but in my profession—I'm a police man—I don't want to do that. . . And it makes a difference because you can't go around one-punch killing people. Especially, you know, you never know who has a cannon up their. . . you know.
> – Transcribed interview, December 1995

In addition to increases in the complexity of the understandings for American participants, there were also significant changes in the nuance of meaning. To use Maliszweski's (1992) classification system, practitioners' perceptions of the "martial

TABLE 3

"Before I began training in aikido, I thought martial arts were..."

Results of the principle component analysis of the semantic differential data by culture.

JAPAN	Factors 1 Loadings	2
beautiful/ugly	.79	.15
kind/cruel	.82	-.09
graceful/awkward	.78	.25
peaceful/ferocious	.81	-.09
hard/soft	-.76	.23
heavy/light	-.24	.70
strong/weak	-.13	.63
deep/shallow	.44	.59
tenacious/yielding	-.57	.48
active/passive	-.11	.67
complex/simple	.19	.64
angular/rounded	-.76	.18

USA	Factors 1 Loadings	2	3
beautiful/ugly	-.23	.80	.01
kind/cruel	-.75	.19	.02
graceful/awkward	-.23	.79	.22
peaceful/ferocious	-.74	.06	-.17
hard/soft	-.75	.05	.20
heavy/light	.63	.07	-.08
strong/weak	.14	.38	.75
deep/shallow	-.01	.63	.30
tenacious/yielding	.64	-.13	.33
active/passive	.17	.09	.87
complex/simple	.41	.66	.09
angular/rounded	.49	-.40	.12

TABLE 4
"My aikido training has helped me understand that martial arts are . . ."
Results of the principle component analysis of the semantic differential data by culture.

JAPAN	Factors 1 Loadings	2	3
beautiful/ugly	.72	.21	.27
kind/cruel	.21	.00	.89
graceful/awkward	.66	.32	.36
peaceful/ferocious	.22	.11	.83
hard/soft	-.68	-.06	-.41
heavy/light	.05	.66	-.02
strong/weak	.41	.52	.05
deep/shallow	.48	.57	-.08
tenacious/yielding	-.53	.52	.21
active/passive	.25	.56	.24
complex/simple	.06	.68	.07
angular/rounded	-.61	-.19	-.44

USA	Factors 1 Loadings	2	3	4
beautiful/ugly	-.48	.68	.10	.11
kind/cruel	.82	.16	-.22	-.10
graceful/awkward	.39	.65	-.09	.02
peaceful/ferocious	.82	.15	-.18	-.14
hard/soft	-.36	.01	.54	.45
heavy/light	.03	-.16	.81	.14
strong/weak	-.68	.28	.02	.35
deep/shallow	.10	.64	-.02	.49
tenacious/yielding	-.19	-.06	.72	.00
active/passive	-.01	.04	.08	.78
complex/simple	-.15	.52	.52	-.27
angular/rounded	-.12	-.68	.35	.02

arts" became less descriptive of "fighting arts" and more descriptive of "martial ways." Training in aikido could be depicted as resulting in the generation of a perception of the martial arts that emphasizes the "artistic" aspect over the martial. The first two factors extracted from the American data for concept 4 together indicate a sense of ethical, harmonious fluidity. This is a dramatic shift in meaning from the "aggressive" first factor extracted from concept.[3]

Therefore, the data for the American participants indicate that aikido training experiences resulted in a profound change in their understandings of the martial arts—from activities within which "aggression" was prominent, to ones in which harmony and ethical fluidity played a central role. This particular point is discussed in greater detail in the next section.

These findings suggest that training in a particular martial art can have a pervasive and powerful influence upon how martial activities are perceived. The factors structuring the pre- and post-aikido training meaning of the martial arts for the Americans in particular was dramatically altered—the nuance was qualitatively reversed. Generalizing these robust findings to the larger domain of martial training experience supports the contention that training in any specific martial art can profoundly influence how practitioners come to perceive and interpret martial arts, as well as actions and activities in the larger environment.

Harmony and Aggression: Cross-cultural Differences in Meaning Structure

For Japanese practitioners, a factor connoting "harmony" consistently emerged from the data as the central and defining property for all concepts. Analysis of the interview data reinforced this finding: "harmony" was often used to describe understandings of and experiences in aikido. As one well-known and respected instructor stated: "In aikido, you harmonize with your opponent. There are no unreasonable or excessive movements. You harmonize with your opponent naturally" (Kobayashi, transcribed interview, July 1995). The Japanese participants' consistent use of the "harmony" construct in structuring meaning for all the concepts in this study can be seen as a reflection of larger cultural values, such as adjusting one's behavior to harmoniously fit into the given social situation, and generally "not making waves."

American practitioners were less consistent than their Japanese counterparts in the constructs they used to create meaning for "aikido," "ki," and the "martial arts." Although a factor similar to the Japanese construct "harmony" did occasionally emerge from the data, a factor depicting "aggression" emerged with greater frequently and prominence. No factor connoting a similar sense of "aggression" was extracted from the Japanese data for any concept.

Analysis of the interview data support and expand upon the semantic differential findings. While Americans referred to "aggression" when describing their understandings of martial arts during interviews and informal discussions, their comments indicate that their understandings of how aggression was related to martial activity were far from one-dimensional. For example, one American instructor indicated during an interview that one purpose of training in aikido was to facilitate the practitioner's ability to understand and deal with the aggression that is part of our nature as human beings. He stated: "The instinct is to meet aggression with aggression. And the training, and the study is how to meet aggression and deal with it, but not become aggressive in dealing with it" (BK, transcribed interview, December 1995). This indicates that at least one American practitioner had a multidimensional understanding of aggression as it relates to the martial arts, and highlights the usefulness of understanding the nature of aggression for facilitating personal development.

From a similar perspective, another American instructor emphasized the martial aspect of aikido, stressing that training should result in the ability to practically apply techniques for self-defense:

> I think that, well first, aikido is a martial art... If I'm seeking transcendence through a martial art, I need to apply martial principles. Again, we are talking about confrontation and dealing with physical threat. I need for it to work. I don't need to be in some meditative, spiritual, far out state. I need to be solid, focused, committed. And those are the things that are true in meditation. . . . We need to be protective. Then after that, we learn that while doing those things, there is a state of being that we adapt. So the spirituality refers to our state of being.
> – CG, transcribed interview, 1995

While this instructor's comments stress the necessity of being able to practically apply aikido techniques when violence might arise, it also clearly implies that other training goals exist, including spiritual development. This comment also illuminates American aikidoka's recognition that, while aggression is a powerful and integral aspect of their study, the study is not in aggression, but of aggression, and the final goal, in addition to self-defense, is a deeper understanding of oneself.

Cultural Effects on Meaning Construction: Three Variables

From a cross-cultural perspective, it is hardly surprising that the meaning constructed for these concepts was different for the two cultural groups. As cultural diffusion researchers write: "The process of accepting an element from another society generally involves changes in its meaning" (Hunter & Whitten, 1976: 126). The process of aikido's diffusion to the United States entailed its being recontextualized within a culture quite different than that of its origin. This in turn led to a process of reinterpretation of aikido using the variables—words, symbols, behaviors, images—and the conventional patterns of arranging them available in the American setting.

Many cultural variables have undoubtedly interacted to shape participants'

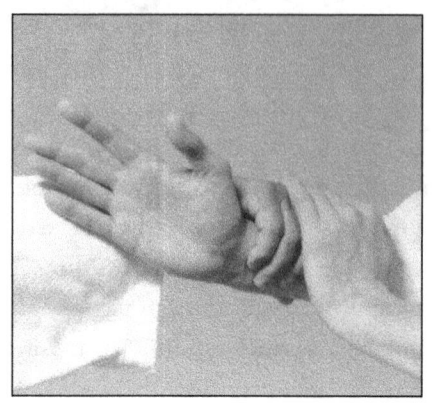

understandings of aikido, ki, and the martial arts, and a discussion of them all is not attempted here. By briefly examining three pervasive features of culture that influence how people create understandings of their world, however, it is hoped that insight may be provided into how the differences in meaning generated by Japanese and American aikidoka arose, particularly, the differences in their usage of "harmony" and "aggression."

Language

The meaning that aikido and the martial arts have for individuals is largely dependent upon the signs available for use in constructing and expressing their understandings. In addition to the symbols available for use, the patterns by which they are conventionally arranged in the particular sign system play a role in the shaping and expression of meaning (Hoopes, 1991; Eco, 1984). In other words, people create meaning for new ideas and activities by using what they already know. Therefore, language is an obviously important means used to create, refine, and express meaning.

The words and grammatical patterns of Japanese and English linguistic systems are quite different. This was alluded to in the earlier example of the Japanese practitioners' daily use of the character "ki." English translations such as "universal energy" and "life force" may provide a relatively accurate "flavor" of the concept, and even approximate the conventional meaning of "ki" in Japanese; however, there is no single word in English that corresponds to and encompasses the same "area" of meaning as the Japanese term. Therefore, English speakers who are not proficient in Japanese are forced to use concepts (and the words that represent them) that are available in their own language to generate understandings for foreign concepts such as "ki." While there may be correspondence between the meanings generated by the two groups, because the meanings were created using different elements and arranged according to different systems, each group "bounded" the meaning for each particular concept differently. The differences that exist between the English and Japanese linguistic systems, or more specifically, the manner in which the differences permit meaning to be represented, is an underlying, yet potent variable influencing how meaning is generated and expressed.

Socialization

Historically, martial arts practice has been highly integrated into Japanese society, and it continues to be a prominent feature of Japanese culture. For example, Japanese public school systems have extracurricular martial arts clubs like judo and kendo clubs. In addition, judo and kendo are integrated into the physical education curriculum, so most students who have participated in physical education within the Japanese public school system have had exposure to or have even participated in martial arts. In addition, harmony is a quality that is valued and often emphasized in Japanese social interactions, and one frequently depicted in cultural activities, art forms, and artifacts. It is likely that exposure to martial arts during the time of primary socialization and schooling in Japan predisposed Japanese aikido practitioners' understanding of martial arts to include and reflect the sense of harmony emphasized around them.

On the other hand, Americans are not typically given formal exposure to and/or training in martial arts during primary socialization. The "martial arts" are "foreign." Hershey (1994: 53) has written that: "The Western mind typically thinks of martial arts as a kind of Asian version of such fighting sports as boxing or wrestling." There is generally a high-level of competition in these sporting activities, and aggression in the images they invoke. Boxing in particular is a violent, bloody sport. If Hershey's statement is accepted, it is likely that individuals socialized in a context with such influences would utilize these images of aggression and violence in formulating understandings of the martial arts.

Danger, Aggression, and Social Context

The meaning and utility that an activity such as aikido comes to have for a practitioner is a function of how it is viewed within the pattern of the larger social context. It can easily be argued that America is a more dangerous social context than Japan. Indeed, Japan has been depicted as perhaps the safest industrialized nation in the world, a fact that may explain why all of the ten Japanese interviewees cited improving health and personal development, as opposed to learning self-defense, as reasons for initiating aikido training.

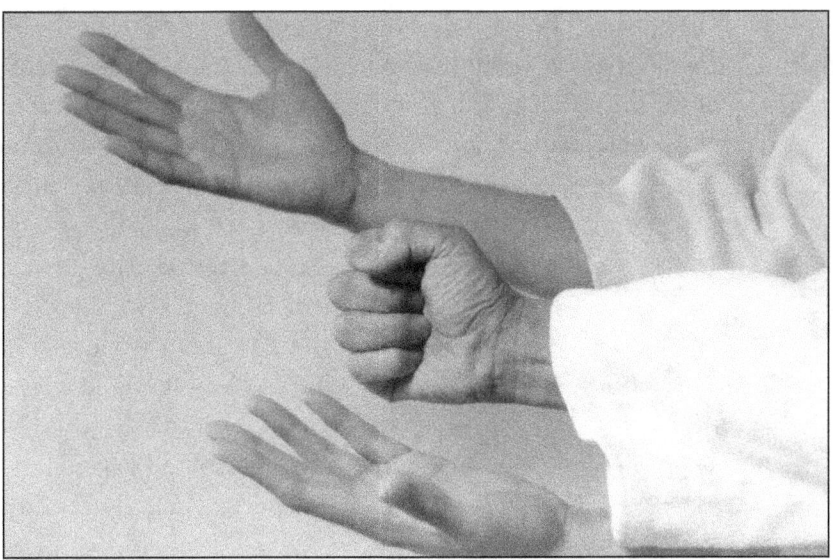

On the other hand, the United States is rarely, if ever, depicted as being a "safe" society. This fact is reflected in the finding that the majority of American interview participants stated self-defense among their reasons for initiating training. Steve's comment presented in an earlier section indicates an awareness of the social context of the United States being dangerous: "You never know who has a cannon up their... you know."

Hollywood representations of the martial arts aside, daily news reports of local and national events in the United States provide vivid reminders of the very real violence that occurs within American society. Frequent exposure to images of aggression is likely to predispose Americans to use such constructs to describe their environment and to make meaning of their world. Daily exposure to images of violence and aggression makes them familiar with these traits, if not comfortable with them, and plays a part in how they understand the world. Hence, individuals living within the United States are likely predisposed to recognize and express "aggression" when explaining events and activities, particularly martial activities. So it is not surprising that factors connoting "aggression" emerged from the American data.

Back & Kim (1984: 12) asserted that "a martial art has two goals: proficiency in combat and artistic accomplishment." Within the relatively safe social environment of Japan, developing the skill needed to defend oneself from violence is likely to be a less emphasized goal of martial training than one of personal development and discipline. However, the above stated two goals do coincide with how Americans represented their understandings of martial arts and training. American aikidoka depicted qualities of both aggression and harmony as being integral components of martial arts training. Donohue has addressed this issue, stating that the martial arts "speak powerfully to American fears and needs" (1991: 90). Among those needs were the need to defend oneself in a violent environment, a need for a spiritual "center," and the need for discipline. The harmony-like factors extracted from the American data correspond to practitioners' desires to engage in training for purposes of personal development, whether artistic or spiritual. Interview comments reinforced this: participants reported developmental outcomes including increased self-awareness, con-

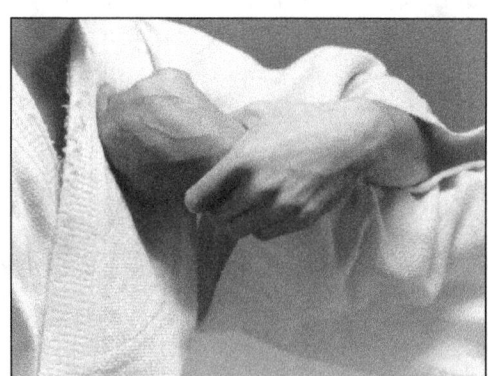

fidence, social flexibility, and spiritual openness.

Nonetheless, the fact that the "aggression" factor frequently emerged from the American semantic differential findings, and that it was entirely absent in the Japanese data, suggests American aikidoka understand aggression to be an integral part of martial training. The interpretive anthropologist Geertz spoke to this, stating: "Art forms can be thoroughly understood only if their wider contexts are taken into consideration" (Rice, 1980: 191). That Americans used "aggression" to shape their understandings of the martial arts indicates that it is a commonly encountered construct in the United States, and one that is important to Americans in constructing understandings of the world.

Conclusion

The study shows that Japanese aikido practitioners training in Japan and Americans training in the United States had different understandings of aikido, ki, and the martial arts. They also reveal a relationship between cultural context and how understandings of martial activities are formed. This finding has apparent and obvious implications for martial artists, scholars, and other individuals working in cross-cultural settings. The meaning that individuals in a given culture generate for an activity can be seen as a reflection of how the ideas and values prominently displayed within that culture are patterned and arranged. In this instance, constructs of harmony and aggression were employed differently among Japanese and American aikido practitioners to generate meaning for the concepts "aikido," "ki," and "the martial arts."

The results also revealed that practitioners represented their perceptions of the martial arts as having changed as a result of aikido training, regardless of the culture within which they trained. This change was most compelling among American participants – results indicate that due to aikido training, the group's understanding of "martial arts" shifted from being centered on a factor of "aggression" opposed to one connoting a sense of ethics.

Not only did participants' perceptions change, but also these perceptions became more complex. This finding increases our understandings of the positive developmental outcomes of aikido training. While we must be cautious in generalizing these results of "aikido training" to training outcomes in other martial arts, it is highly plausible that training in any martial art increases the complexity with which practitioners perceive "martial arts" by simultaneously widening and refining the lenses through which they can interpret martial activity.

These results indicate that regular participation in a particular system of movement and dispositional training strongly influences how people shape their understandings of the activity, and, by extension, their understandings of the world. As martial artists, we must be aware of the powerful influence that training in the art of our choice will have upon our perceptions of other martial arts.

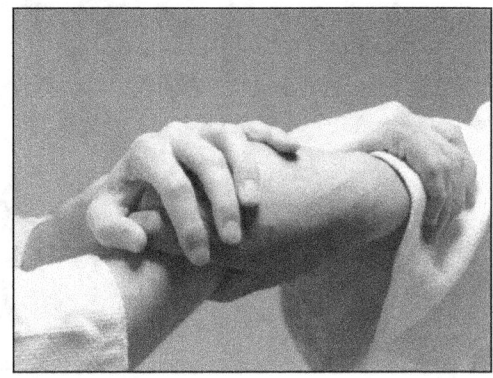

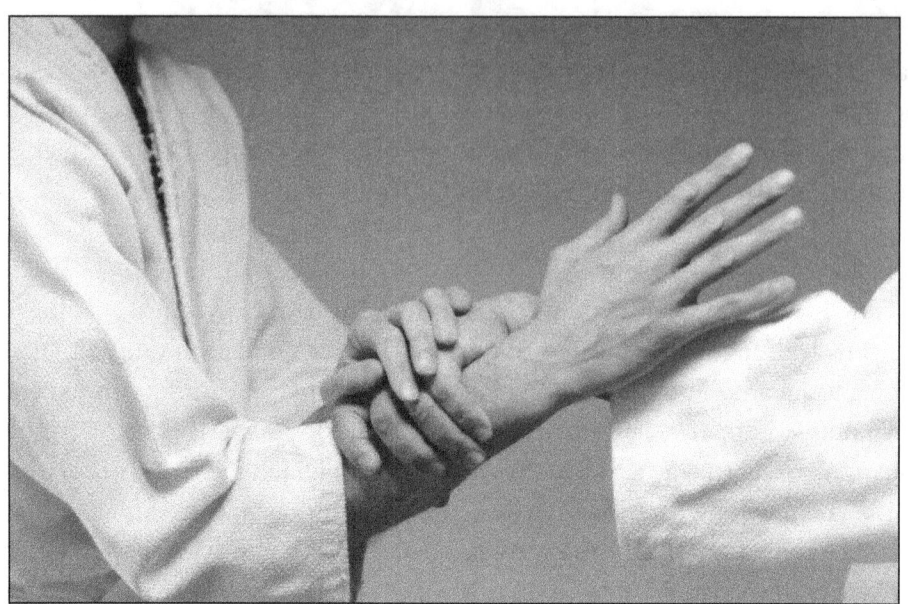

And there is a further implication: if participation in martial arts training results in changes in an individuals' perceptions of their world, it follows that the understandings generated or "reinterpreted" as a result of this training would dramatically influence how the individual comes to act in and interact with the world as perceived. We are all constantly reshaping our understandings of the world as we continue training in and studying about our respective arts. Awareness of the various factors influencing the manner in which we create meaning for ourselves can enable us to play an increasingly conscious and active role in the multidimensionality of our personal development.

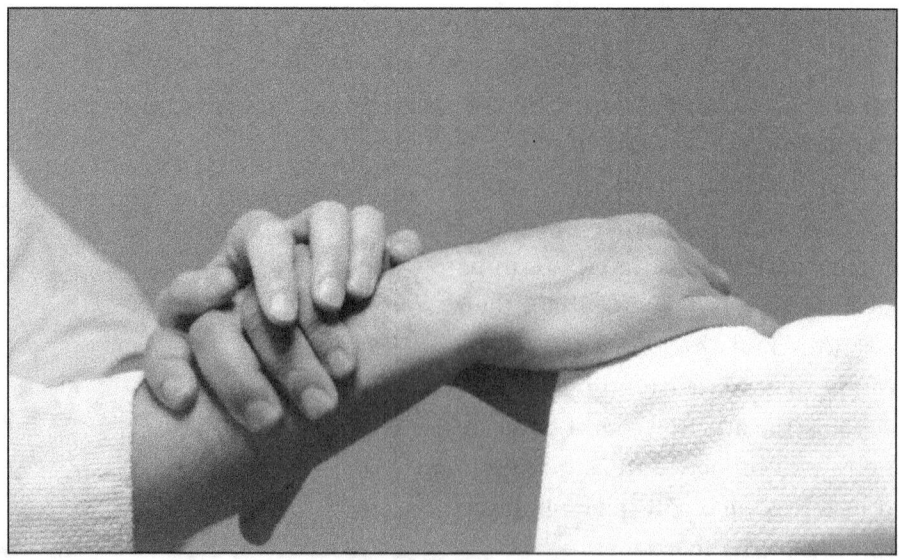

The complexities of how we come to create understandings for activities and concepts 'received' from other cultures can serve as a reminder that, whatever culture(s) we train within, we must use all means available to continually refine our conceptions of our activities, as well as ourselves as performers. The degree to which we reflect upon our training is the degree to which we fulfill our capacity to develop increasingly accurate and sophisticated understandings of the principles that guide our actions as martial artists and human beings. There is never a point at which we are finished. Commenting upon the nature of martial arts training, Yonetani, a Japanese instructor with over 35 years of aikido training experience, stated: "Like a well, no matter how much water you draw from it, there is still more to take" (YA, transcribed interview, July 1995).

Bibliography

Amdur, E. (1994). Atemi: Striking to the heart of the matter. *Aiki News, 21* (2), 22–24.

Back, A., & Kim, D. (1984). The future course of the Eastern martial arts. *Quest, 36,* 7–14.

Berry, J., Poortinga, Y., Segal, M., & Dasne, P. (1992). *Cross-cultural psychology: Research and applications.* Cambridge: Cambridge University Press.

Berry, J. (1980). Introduction to methodology. In Triandis & Berry (Eds.), *Handbook of cross-cultural psychology: Vol. 2. Methodology* (pp. 1–28). Boston: Allyn and Bacon, Inc.

Brislin, R. (1980). Translation and content analysis of oral and written materials. In Triandis and Berry (Eds.), *Handbook of cross-cultural psychology: Vol. 2, Methodology* (pp. 389–443). Boston: Allyn and Bacon, Inc.

Columbus, P. & Rice, D. (1991). Psychological research on the martial arts: An addendum to Fuller's review. *British Journal of Medical Psychology, 64,* 127–135.

Crawford, A. (1992). The martial yen: American participation in the aikido tradition. *Journal of Asian Martial Arts, 1*(4), 28–43.

Donohue, J. (1992). Dancing in the danger zone: The martial arts in America. *Journal of Asian Martial Arts, 1*(1), 86–99.

Donohue, J. (1994). *Warrior dreams: The martial arts and the American imagination.* Westport, CT: Bergin & Garvey.

Donohue, J. & Taylor, K. (1994). The classification of the fighting arts. *Journal of Asian Martial Arts, 3*(4), 10–37.

Eco, E. (1984). *Semiotics and the philosophy of language.* Bloomington: Indiana University Press.

Fuller, J. (1988). Martial arts and psychological health. *British Journal of Medical Psychology, 61,* 317–328.

Geertz, C. (1983). *Local knowledge: Further essays in interpretive anthropology.* New York: Basic Books, Inc.

Geertz, C. (1973). *The interpretation of culture.* New York: Basic Books, Inc.

Glasser, B. & Strauss, A. (1967). *The discovery of grounded theory: Strategies for qualitative research.* New York: Aldine de Gruyter.

Glesne, C. & Peshkin, A. (1992). *Becoming qualitative researchers: An introduction.* London: Longman Publishing Group.

Hershey, L. (1994). Shotokan karate as non-discursive intercultural exchange. *Journal of Asian Martial Arts, 3*(3), 53–61.

Hoopes, J., (Ed). (1991). *Peirce on signs: Writings on semiotics by Charles Sanders Peirce.* Chapel Hill: The University of North Carolina Press.

Hunter, D. & Whitten, P. (1976). *Encyclopedia of anthropology.* New York: Harper and Row.

LeCompte, M., & Preissle, J. (1993). *Ethnography and qualitative design in educational research* (2nd ed.). New York: Academic Press, Inc.

Levine, D. (1984). The liberal arts and the martial arts. *Liberal Education, 70*(3), 235–251.

Maliszewski, M. (1992). Meditative-religious traditions of fighting arts and martial ways. *Journal of Asian Martial Arts, 1*(3), 1–104.

Min, K. (1979). Martial arts in the American educational setting. *Quest, 31*(1), 97–106.

Nosanchuk, T., & MacNeil, C. (1989). Examination of the effects of traditional and modern martial arts training on aggressiveness. *Aggressive Behavior, 15,* 153–159.

O'Neill, P. (1973). *Essential kanji.* New York: Weatherhill.

Osgood, C., Suci, G., & Tannenbaum, P. (1957). *The measurement of meaning.* Chicago: University of Illinois Press.

Pranin, S. (1991). *The aiki news encyclopedia of aikido.* Tokyo, Japan: Aiki News.

Ratti, O. & Westbrook, A. (1973). *Secrets of the samurai: The martial arts of feudal Japan.* Rutland, Vermont: Charles E. Tuttle Co.

Rice, K. (1980). *Geertz and culture.* Ann Arbor, MI: University of Michigan Press.

Ryan, B. (1969). *Social and cultural change.* New York: The Ronald Press.

Rogers, E. (1983). *The diffusion of innovations.* (3rd ed.). New York: The Free Press.

Ueshiba, K. (1984). *The spirit of aikido.* Tokyo: Kodansha International.

Westbook, A. & Ratti, O. (1970). *Aikido and the dynamic sphere: An illustrated introduction.* Rutland, Vermont: Charles E. Tuttle Co.

Yin, R. (1984). *Case study research.* Beverly Hills: Sage Publications.

Yuasa, Y. (1993). *The body, self-cultivation, and ki-energy.* New York: State University of New York.

· 10 ·

Ukemiwaza: The Art of Attacking in Aikido
by Kimberley Taylor, M.Sc.

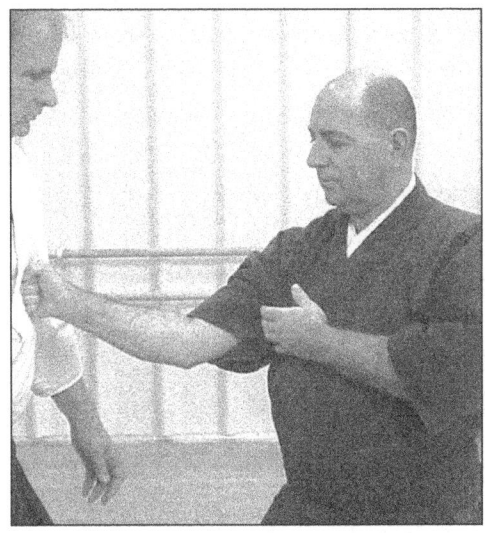

All photos courtesy of K. Taylor.

Introduction

To be a good attacking partner (*uke*), one must realize that the attacking part of aikido practice is just as important as the defending partner's part (*nage*). The success of a technique and how much the defender learns depends to a large extent on the attacker's skill. The attacker must learn to strike or grab with effectiveness and control but without guiding the defender through the techniques. As they advance in skill, aikido students come to welcome a hard, honest attack for the opportunity it affords to explore the aspects of blending with the force presented. For this reason, the attacker should devote considerable time to an analysis of what constitutes a good attack. The following article lays out the groundwork for an analysis of the art of attacking (*ukemi*) and receiving a technique in aikido.

With regards to terminology, *uke* and *nage* are used somewhat differently in aikido than in judo or other arts. Uke is usually one who receives the technique and nage is the one who "attacks" or applies the technique. However, in aikido, uke is the "initial attacker" and nage is the "final attacker." Since aikido is practiced almost exclusively in a defensive manner, this "change in attacker" occurs. Uke is the one who provides the attack to defend against, and nage is the one who applies an aikido technique to "defend and defeat" uke's attack. This article deals with the attacker and his actions.

Sparring in Aikido?

It has been said that aikido has no contests, but only cooperative practice. This means that the art has no place for sparring. It does not mean that aikido cannot be challenging. Attacks must be direct and clean with no feints. In this way, the defender can apply the techniques in their original forms without danger to the attacker. If both parties know what throw is being performed, there should be little or no chance for beginners to hurt themselves. A point that cannot be stressed too strongly is that injuries will occur in practice if techniques are unexpectedly applied. This would be the case if practice became competitive in a antagonistic manner. The reason fighting sports have rules on what techniques can and cannot be applied is to cut down the risk of injury. Techniques that are modified or restricted can be used in a competitive way, but techniques designed to cripple or kill an opponent cannot.

Highly skilled students who possess good control and have a full grasp of breakfall techniques can practice in an open, fluid manner that often approaches a sparring match. However, this is rarely a sporting contest as both are studying the flow of energy and are unconcerned with who throws whom. A constant awareness of energy movement and intentions keeps both partners protected. If the ego becomes involved (as perhaps, in the case of not wanting to be thrown), it will lead to physical damage much more harmful than a "feeling of losing." Senior students should always be working to the limits of their capabilities, each forcing the other to concentrate. It is imperative that the defender allow the attacker to be the guide in making the practice harder. It is useless to simply throw the attacker as hard as possible at the finish of a technique "so he can work on his breakfalls." In a practice where the attacker is "cooperating" with the defender, the attacker may allow his wrist to be placed into a dangerous position for the sake of the training. If the defender decides to intensify the practice after the attacker has allowed or even placed his wrist into this vulnerable position, the attacker may end up with an injured wrist. This type of practice is not "hard practice," it is "stupid practice." Instead, the defender should throw harder as the attacker strikes harder and slow down as the attacker slows down. This is excellent practice in paying attention to what your partner (or attacker) is doing.

When working with beginners, an attack may be "hard" while not being fast. The object is to carry through the grasp or strike with full intention no matter what the speed. If the will and physical body are both involved in a slow attack, a weak defense will not prevent it from being completed. The attacker's speed should be adjusted to the defender's skill level (or the desired "study level"). The attacker should always keep in mind that a faster attack results in a faster throw and a more difficult breakfall. On the other hand, the attacker must also be careful with beginners if his attack is very powerful but slow. Beginners almost always try to use speed, strength and jerky movements once their smooth opening move fails. This violent reaction may cause loss of control and even injury to the attacker.

An attack must be continuous from the moment of intention, through the attack, to the completion of the breakfall. The defender cannot deal with a non-attack. There must be a force with which to work to perform aikido. An attacker who begins a movement and then goes limp promotes bad habits since the defender may begin to push and pull to provide the required motion for the throw. Another bad habit an attacker may acquire is becoming inattentive once the initial attack has been completed. This inattention often results in the attacker becoming unbalanced and thus unable to perform a good breakfall.

An attacker who does not strike toward the intended target does the defender no favors. A punch that is always aimed to one side will promote a false sense of security in the defender and leads to lazy aikido (Fig. 1). In addition, the lack of attention that develops on both parts, may lead to the defender moving into a strike that the attacker has launched to one side, thinking the defender was moving to the other. A punch should travel toward its target and if it is not stopped, should strike through that target. Always remember that aikido is not movie stunt work but, physically, is the study of the interactions of force during a life or death combat.

One method that helps make a forceful attack is to look at the defender directly. Try to catch and hold his eyes and then attack his center through the eyes as well as physically (Fig. 2). Of course, the defender should not fall into the trap but instead look to the direction of his movement.

The attacker's willingness to strike, to press that attack home, and to protect himself, will allow the defender the freedom to put himself fully into the throw without the need to worry about the attacker. Thus, the defender is pleased and the attacker has no reason to complain about the roughness of the practice. Both throw themselves into the art and thereby both are thrown, releasing the joy of aikido.

Most modern aikido practice begins with learning techniques against grabs or holds. This is usually done because there is less chance of accidental contact from unblocked punches or kicks and because, from a practical standpoint, people are more likely to be attacked by a grab or shove than by a strike. A somewhat unexpected benefit comes from starting your aikido practice with grabbing attacks. The techniques are harder to

learn. It is very difficult for the defender to use momentum and timing in a throw when the attacker initiates with a grab. The lines of force and the directions of unbalance for the attacker are easy to see if he is punching. By learning aikido from a grab, such vital fundamentals as grounding, hip placement, arm motion and breath power (*kokyu*) are learned. After the defender has "learned to walk," the effortless "ki throws" discovered later will be based on a solid understanding of his own body positioning. In this way, aikido is understood and nothing remains mysterious.

To allow proper execution of aikido techniques, the attacker must continue attacking after his initial movements. When the attack stops, "aikido" stops. As a general rule, the attacker should always attempt to move into the defender's center while continuing to face him. One benefit of a continuous attack is that the attacker remains involved in the throw, on balance and alert to any changes in the technique that may occur.

Since almost all techniques in aikido may include a strike to a weak or exposed point, the attacker must be constantly aware of openings for strikes that he presents to the defender as the technique progresses. The attacker should be prepared to block these strikes as they are thrown. Similarly, the attacker should be aware of when he can strike the defender if his technique should allow him to do so. Figure 3 shows a strike to the side of the head by the defender that the attacker has blocked.

During fixed or static practice, the attacker should resist the defender along the lines of the attack; that is, he should attack with intent. The attacker should not resist in a direction that is not consistent with the attack since this will force the defender to change to a technique other than the one being studied. Because both partners know the throw being performed, it is not difficult for the attacker to get ahead of the defender and then resist the throw in another direction. It is not difficult, but it is pointless.

As much as possible, the attacker should attempt to blend his motions with the defender during a throw, but not to anticipate that throw by more than is necessary for protection of his joints. If the defender feels no energy at all from the attacker, he cannot lead his movements, but instead must follow. This will cause the defender to hurry his own movements in an attempt to catch up, which results in the attacker throwing himself even faster to stay ahead. The whole cycle leads to oddly truncated techniques that are not satisfying to anyone. Both partners should proceed to the mat together without racing for it. The mat isn't going anywhere, so enjoy the journey without fear of missing the destination.

Blending with the Throw

To protect the joints during vigorous practice, the attacker must be able to match or occasionally move ahead of the defender's timing during the throw. If the defender gets too far ahead of the attacker in, for instance, a wrist twist (*kote gaeshi*), then the attacker, even if he manages to get airborne, may not be able to rotate his body over the wrist in time to prevent torn ligaments. This is one reason why breakfalls should never include active resistance of the throwing technique. The initial attack may be pressed so that the defender must work against or around resistance to enter the technique. Resisting the throw itself is usually possible only in a direction that would necessitate the defender's changing to a different throw. This defeats the purpose of the resistance and usually results in an aborted throw or damage to the attacker after a brief contest between the partners. Figure 4 shows the result of not blending with a wrist twist. The attacker, on the left, is off balance and risks damage to his wrist. Figure 5 shows the correct amount of blending to maintain balance and fall safely, without getting ahead of the attacker.

Another result of resisting a throw is to encourage beginners to "crank" on the ending of the technique. If one already has a wrist bent into a "Z" shape as in the basic pinning technique (*nikyo*, Fig. 6), it is not difficult to cause pain by twisting it. To train beginners so that they twist as hard as possible on the last movement only creates a situation where other beginners get hurt. It is much more useful to make the defender work hard to get the wrist into the "Z" shape than to resist the pin once it is achieved.

Remaining with the defender during the throw allows the attacker to keep his balance and this allows him to react to changes in direction during the technique. Balance, timing, reaction, and control are all elements of good breakfall. Attacking with control is also important in the event that the defender is unprepared and cannot defend himself at that time. By blending with the defender, the attacker is not "cheating" or "helping" the defender but is practicing the "self-defense" of aikido practice, while the defender is freed to practice the throws fully. Both partners thus improve their understanding of the principles of aikido.

SPECIFIC ATTACKS

What follows are descriptions of specific attack forms that are used in aikido. The forms are by no means exhaustive or even intended to represent all possible attacks. Instead, they provide a set of general categories from which the defender may explore the techniques of aikido. The practice of constantly changing partners, and of practicing in as many different clubs as possible will provide the aikido student with enough variation on these themes that an unexpected attack will be perceived as falling into one of these categories. To understand the principles behind the movements, one must first experience as many different, specific examples of movement as possible.

One-Handed Grasp

One hand grasps the defender's wrist. This grip and all grips are used in preparation to push (Fig. 7), pull (Fig. 8), strike, or otherwise continue the attack. Even if the intent is to immobilize the defender, the grip is in preparation to hold (Fig. 9), which is in itself, a continuation of the attack. A grip that sits on the defender's wrist like a wet towel is best just shaken off as one would shake off water. Figure 10 shows a very poor grip—the attacker has grabbed the defender's wrist outside the line formed by their bodies in relation to one another. In this position there is no way that the attacker can apply strength or control to the defender. In Figure 11 one can draw a line from the attacker's right hip through the grip and directly to the defender's center. This configuration allows the attacker to root the defender to the spot.

The attacker should understand what attack is needed for the technique and be prepared to do it. If, for example, a sidestep is to be performed by the defender from a position where the attacker's left hand grasps the defender's right wrist, then the attacker may want to grab and push into the defender's center (Fig. 12). For an entering motion from a position with the right hand grasping the right wrist, the attacker may wish to pull the defender's hand across his own center and up to expose the defender's ribs to a punch. The defender then enters to redirect the attacker's line of motion, perhaps into a locking technique (*ikkyo*, Fig. 13), to protect his ribs. Both partners should think of these possibilities as they practice.

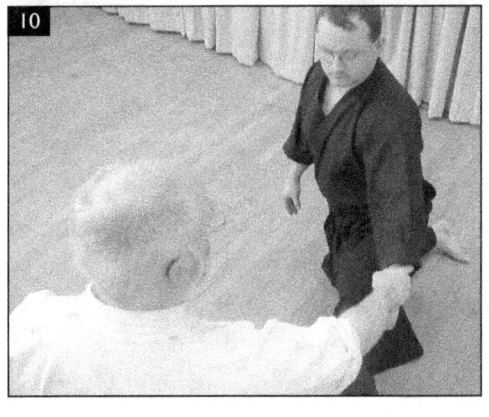

If the attacker intends to immobilize the defender with a one-handed grasp, the key points are as follows: Grip the wrist as if gripping a wooden sword. Please note that grasping the arm and hand at the same time to prevent the defender's wrist movement is "almost cheating," since a grip like this makes it very difficult to move. With beginners, grasp the wrist only (Fig. 14); for seniors, sometimes grasp the base of the hand as well as the wrist to make them work harder (Fig. 15). Use the ring and little fingers to bring the base of your palm firmly into contact with the defender's wrist. Use the base of the thumb to assist the grip but avoid curling the thumb itself under and gripping with the upper part, since this transfers the gripping pressure into the middle and index fingers. When the defender's lower wrist is firmly held, lever your hand down onto the upper wrist, bringing the muscles in the forearm into play to root the defender to the mat through his arm. Think of pressing the defender's elbow down onto the mat between his feet. Always attack the defender's center, pushing toward it, pulling away from it (or across it), and holding through it. Attacks that are off-center are easily dealt with and often may be ignored.

Always remember that aikido involves the whole body at all times. Proper stance must be maintained and the free arm kept in position to stop or deflect any strike from the defender.

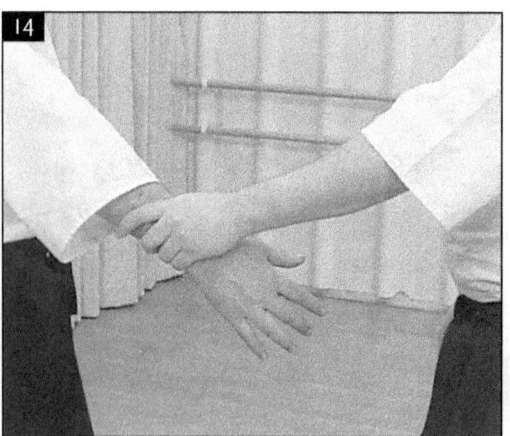 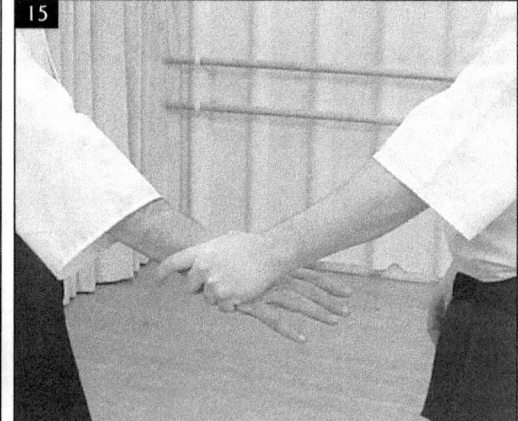

Two Hands Grabbing Two Wrists

Two wrists held with two hands. The grips and attacks are similar to those of the one-hand grip. Neither party has a free hand with which to strike or block, but the knees and feet should be carefully considered. The attacker must be prepared to turn the hips away from a groin kick (Fig. 16) or even an elbow strike to the short ribs (Fig. 17). This form of attack brings up the issue of whether the attacker should hang on to both wrists at all costs or let go of the appropriate wrist to prepare for a breakfall. Since the defender should be able to release his hand from the grip whenever he needs to during the technique, the question of being nice to the defender doesn't arise. If the attacker releases one wrist, the defender can immediately use his newly freed arm to launch a strike or to assist in a throw. If the attacker hangs on to the end, he must do a no-hands breakfall. There is usually a satisfactory midpoint at which to release a hand and, for most throws, it would be at the point when the non-pivot arm begins to rotate around to make contact with the mat. Hanging on until this point helps stop "groping for the mat" and assists in aligning the body for the throw.

Two-Handed Grasp of One Arm

In many ways, this seems the worst attack possible, since the attacker is using both hands to immobilize one of the defender's wrists, leaving him with a free arm with which to launch a strike (Fig. 18). On the other hand, if the object of the attack is to provide a strongly immobilized wrist with which to work, this is a good attack indeed. With this attack, it is easy for the attacker to study the no-hands breakfall and how to breakfall by making partial contact with the elbows first. Figure 19 shows how to grab the defender's left wrist. The forearm should be gripped as if it were a sword, and the elbow directed toward the defender's centerline. The hands and feet are usually reversed if gripping the left arm.

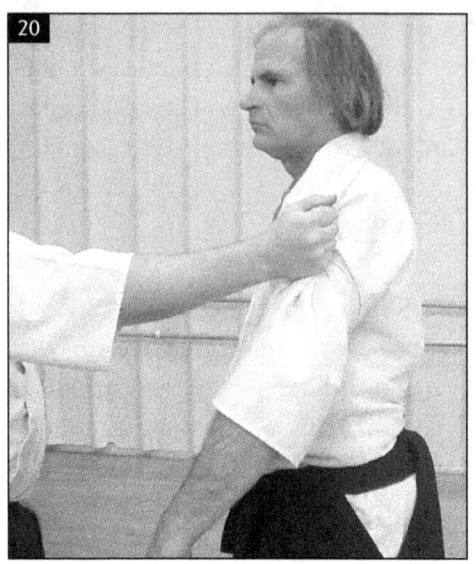

Other Grabs

Grabbing the shoulder (Fig. 20), lapel, collar, and other grabs of the clothing are attacks considered under the same points as those above. The attacker should be aware of the danger to fingers, which may become caught in the defender's practice uniform. When the cloth is gripped, the thumb, if possible, should not oppose the fingers in order to prevent it being jammed as the defender turns (Fig. 21). Similarly, if the clothing is twisted in the grip, the fingers can get caught in the folds and be wrenched as the attacker is thrown.

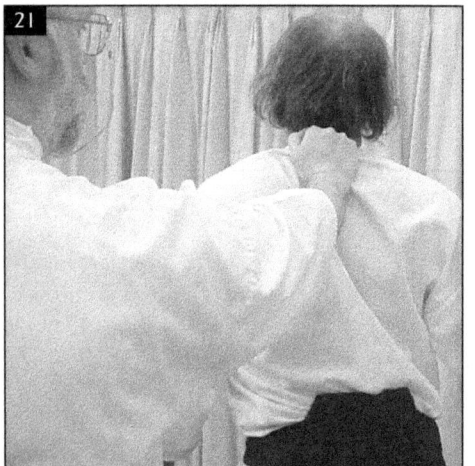

Attack from Behind

Grabs from behind should be done so that they destabilize the defender to his rear, either by pulling his arms backward, or in a close hold, by placing one hip at the small of his back and driving forward and up to lift his center away from the floor. The attacker should be careful of exposing the groin to a kick (Fig. 21) or the face to a strike from the back of the head. All the grips from the front can be made from the rear.

Neck Strangle from Behind

The attacker grasps the defender's right wrist and reaches around his throat to grasp, with the palm down, his right collar under the ear. The defender's right arm is stretched back and the attacker's left hand pulled in the opposite direction to lever the left thumb into his carotid artery (Fig. 22). The attacker's left hip should press into the lower back. It is important to distinguish between a strangle (cutting off the blood) and a choke (cutting off the wind by crushing the windpipe) and to pay close attention to the defender as unconsciousness may occur unexpectedly. Being made unconscious is never a harmless experience and should definitely be avoided.

Unusual Grasps

Exotic grasps (of the hair, with unusual hand positions, etc.) should be done with extra care as sudden unexpected twists of the attacker's wrist may occur during the technique (Fig. A). In some cases, modesty or embarrassment may prevent the attacker from properly grabbing the defender (Fig. B).

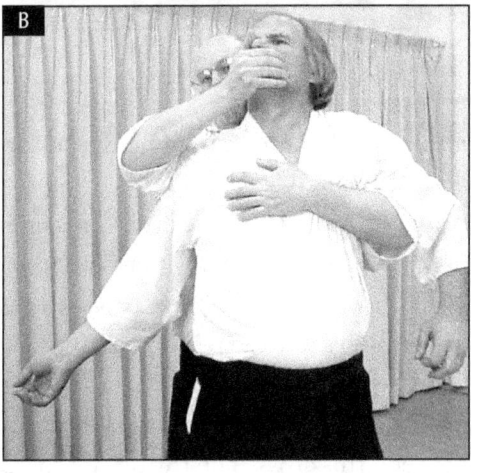

The attacker should not be shy, since a proper attack will help the defender overcome the shock of being grabbed in that manner and to learn to respond without hesitation. This is critical if self-defense is a consideration.

Strikes

All attacks can be broken down to grabs, strikes, and a combination of the two. A grab is usually more difficult to work against, since the attacker has a high degree of control over what movements the defender can perform. Strikes are dangerous mainly due to their greater speed of application, uncertainty of the direction of attack, and of course, their impact.

To achieve speed in a strike, the attacker must use a relaxed motion until just before the moment of impact. If the muscles become tense, control of motion is achieved through using an opposing set of muscles to direct the arms or legs. Since two opposing sets of muscles are working against each other, speed is reduced. If only as much extraneous work

is done as is needed to overcome inertia and gravity, opposing muscles will be used minimally and the limb can move at the maximum possible speed.

Since aikido is practiced in set forms, the angle of a strike should present no surprises; however, if the attacker is unaware of the attack's proper mechanics, the strike may travel in an erratic path toward the defender. Figure 23 shows the attacker punching with a hooked arm that has bypassed the defender's defensive movement, the strike will not be hard since the position of the arm is incorrect, but it will be annoying. The attacker will be expected to deliver attacks from eight basic angles and thrusts from two levels. The angles are horizontal and vertical to the attacker's center and the 45-degree angles between this cross. The thrusts are toward the head and the body. Strikes below the hips are rarely encountered outside of weapons practice, being confined largely to kicks and sweeps to the legs.

Power in a strike is generated as a product of speed and strength: the greater the strength exerted and the greater the speed of the strike, the more force generated at the point of impact. Delivered at the point of impact, this force creates pressure on the target. The greater the pressure the more damage generated. Since speed is generated by muscle and force is also generated by muscle, it makes sense for the attacker to be as strong as possible for good defense, either in the attack or the breakfall, where power is also needed.

All strikes will have an optimum power range—that position where maximum force is exerted for the speed generated. The position of maximum force in a strike is usually that point at which the major muscle groups can assist the motion. In a punch, this range is when the arm is about three quarters to fully extended, when the muscles of the upper arm are joined by those of the shoulders, hips, and legs (Fig. 24). Before this position, the arm is bent too much for the efficient transfer of force from these groups (Fig. 25). Of

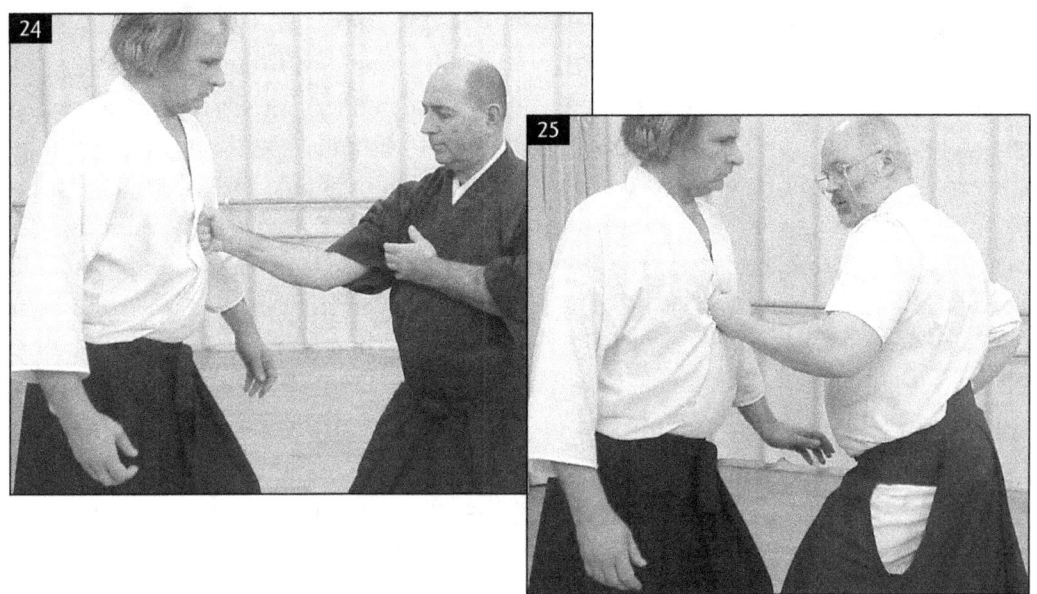

course a punch that doesn't reach the defender isn't of much use to either party (Fig. 26). In a horizontal swing from the side to the attacker's center, the maximum power will be generated as the arm moves to the attacker's front, allowing the muscles of the chest and hips to join the deltoids.

Generally, the maximum power in the arms and legs occurs when they are closest to the centerline in front of the body. The elbows should be kept close to the body at the same time so that the "pecs" and the "lats" can stabilize the shoulder as the hips and legs apply power.

Striking Toward the Forehead

The straight overhand strike travels on the vertical angle of attack in the same strike as that delivered by a sword. The target is usually the defender's forehead, although when striking with the hand a more practical target might be the collarbones, and often includes the exposed neck during a technique. The arms and hands should use the same motions as if striking with a sword. In a right half-forward stance, the right arm is raised above the head in a straight line, protecting the attacker's face as it rises (Fig. 27a). The elbow should be kept in, as when raising a sword. The left hand stops in front of the face as the right reaches maximum height (Fig. 27b). The right hand is then brought down on the same plane to strike with the little finger edge of the palm (*tegatana*) (Fig. 27c). The tegatana is stiffened by pulling the first four fingers back toward the palm while stretching the little finger away from the palm. All fingers remain slightly bent and spread apart to allow easy "ki flow." Since the strike is with the edge of the palm, the fingers do not need to be together. If the hand is stiffened properly, the fingers will not slap each other on impact (Fig. 28). The more usual hand strike position is shown in Figure 29, with the fingers together. Since this strike has the same intent as a sword strike, it should be continued until it reaches the defender's chest or waist level. Stopping at the height of the defender's forehead makes it difficult for the defender to understand and perform the defensive techniques.

It is common to see students raise their arm up at the side of the head with the elbow out to the side (Fig. 30). It is not difficult for the defender to step in and punch the attacker in this case, but often it is difficult to perform the intended kata properly. If the defender intends to perform a throw by first entering on an attacker who has his elbow up and out to the side, he must move a long way to the side to avoid getting hit on the head with the flailing elbow. In the same way, it is rather silly for the attacker to raise the arm and then walk in three or four steps before swinging down. Making a threat and then giving an opponent your face to hit is a little counterproductive. Instead, the attacker must protect himself by swinging up and down in such a way as to force the defender back (if he does not perform the kata properly) and allow him no openings to counterstrike.

When striking, the attacker should strike to the target. If the defender moves while the attack angle can still be changed, then the attacker should follow and strike the target. This is necessary for good practice and is not poor sportsmanship on the attacker's part since missing a target deliberately is simply encouraging bad training habits. On the other hand, the attacker should never anticipate the defender's movement and strike to where he is "going to be," since his actions are known to both partners and the attacker can easily strike him. Again, attacks must be honest and within the limits of the kata. If the defender is good, and sees that the strike is to some future position, the defender will change the technique, which is dangerous for the attacker.

Strike to the Side of the Head

This blow to the side of the head or neck is usually delivered with the same hand position as in striking the forehead. The arms are raised in the same fashion. As the striking arm is brought down, the hips are twisted to tilt the strike 45 degrees to the side for a diagonally downward blow (Fig. 31). Since the strike is also from the sword practice, the attacker should refrain from sweeping the attacking arm out and then back in from the side. The blow would normally start at the defender's neck and finish at the opposite hip. Occasionally the blow is more horizontal and would then stop at the opposite shoulder.

Thrusting

The thrusting attack (*tsuki*) includes all forms of thrust at the defender on various levels. *Jodan tsuki* is a thrust toward the head, usually a punch, while a *chudan tsuki* is a punch or kick to the midsection. A *gedan tsuki* would normally be a kick to the legs. The majority of thrusting attacks in aikido are a straight lunge punch to the middle area.

To make a proper fist for punching, hold the hand up, fingers together. Fold the fingers down into the palm tightly and fold the thumb over the middle sections of the fingers in front of the palm, tucking it out of the way and binding the fingers firmly into the fist. The ring and little fingers are squeezed tightly into the palm to take up any looseness and to make the largest knuckles of the first and middle fingers more prominent. These two knuckles are the striking surface for a punch, allowing a minimum area through which to transmit the force. The thumb must be kept out of the way and the fingers folded tightly into the palm to prevent damage to the fingers or loose bones in the hand. When striking with the knuckles, the arm will be extended to the front, the hand, palm down, in the same vertical plane as the solar plexus. If the attacker looks down the arm, the back of the hand should look like a triangle, with the apex at the striking knuckles and the base on a line between the knuckles of the little finger and the thumb (Fig. 32). The forearm and the back of the hand must be in line or the wrist will flex up or down at the impact.

If the right hand is extended and the attacker is in right half-forward stance, this is a straight or lunge punch. If the attacker is in right half-forward stance, with the left fist extended, it is called a reverse punch (Fig. 33). To perform a straight right "karate" punch, the attacker should begin in left half-forward stance with the left hand in the position described above (Fig. 33); the right hand drawn back, palm up, and resting on the waist. In the usual case, the attacker steps forward toward the defender and just before the right foot steps down to the mat, the punch is snapped out. The right arm travels straight toward the defender's solar plexus, palm up and the elbow close to the side (Fig. 34a). As the elbow clears the attacker's side and the hand is about six to eight inches from full extension, the forearm rotates counterclockwise until the hand is palm down at full extension, just as the weight is transferred to the right foot (Fig. 34b). The left arm is pulled back at the same

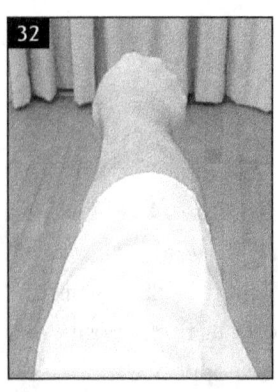

time and in the same manner as the right to finish with the palm up at the side. The punch should land at the moment the weight is shifted to the right foot (with the left leg braced and driving forward), allowing maximum force to be delivered to the hand. Drawing back the left arm at the same time allows the chest to remain open and the hips to twist, giving maximum speed to the strike. The right arm is kept relaxed until just before contact with the target. The target should be struck just after the fist passes from vertical and is beginning to rotate to the horizontal (palm down) position. The little and ring

fingers are squeezed at this point to tighten the fist as it spirals into and through the target. Squeezing the fist and driving to the target in a spiral causes the arm to begin to lock up (and incidentally, to slow down), which allows the legs and hips to deliver force through the contact area. A loose fist or loose arm will collapse under this force and no pressure will be exerted on the defender. Stepping down on the right foot at this moment allows the force built up through the step forward to be transmitted through the punch as well. If the attacker steps down before the punch connects with the target, the forward leg absorbs that forward momentum. If the attacker's elbow comes out away from his body or the shoulder comes up, the punch will be disconnected from the body's center, and the striking force will be from the muscles of the arm up to the shoulder only (Fig. 35).

Another type of punch, often called the "aiki punch", is derived from the basic motion of entering an opponent's space. The attacker stands in left half-forward stance with his left hand at shoulder height in "unbendable arm" (Fig. 36a). As he steps forward into a right half-forward stance, the right hand, which is open and relaxed, moves along with the right hip, palm facing that hip, while the left arm swings down to the left hip (Fig. 36b). As the hips pass the square point and the right leg moves in front of the left, the right arm swings ahead. The right hand is closed into a fist and the arm is made unbendable in a position so that the knuckles will strike the target as the attacker's weight is transferred to the right foot (Fig. 36c). This punch is not linear but travels in an arc up toward the target. The fist is not rotated to a palm down position, but remains vertical to allow a natural curve of the arm movement. There is little arm speed involved in this punch, the power being derived almost exclusively from the hips in a motion that is familiar to aikido students. A major benefit of using this punch is that the attacker's elbow and shoulder both remain down, allowing a breakfall to be performed much more easily than from the straight punch.

In some cases, this punch may be performed by keeping the elbow closer to the right hip with the palm facing upward. This is a straight uppercut and usually involves a greater hip twist than the aiki punch.

When attacking with a punch or thrust, the attacker should not overextend and lose his balance, but should always finish with proper *zanshin* (a lingering awareness of the situation).

Kicks

A snap kick to the midsection will likely be the only kick the attacker is asked to perform (Fig. 37). Standing in left half-forward stance, the attacker raises the right leg up and forward, the foot pointing down, and the toes curled to expose the ball of the foot. When the knee is above the hip, the leg is snapped forward to thrust the ball of the foot at the target. Other, more exotic kicks require specialized training to perform with control and safety for the attacker.

Since all strikes travel along basic angles and finish at the target areas, the strikes described above should provide adequate opportunity to perform aikido against a striking attack. Head butts (Fig. 38), elbow or knee strikes, kicks to the upper-level, and other such strikes place the attacker in a potentially unstable stance, or carry him close to the defender to complete the strike. This allows the defender to throw the attacker much more easily, so the attacker must be prepared to perform a quick breakfall.

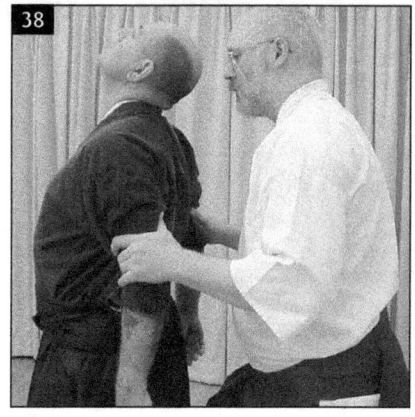

Finally, the attacker should always remember that a strike is not a matter of shoving an arm out for the defender to grab and pull on. If the attacker forgets about the defender as soon as the strike misses the target, aikido will not be practiced fully.

It is hoped that this presentation concerning some of the philosophy and techniques of the "attacker" in aikido will stimulate aikido students, and all other students who practice in a similar way, to pay a bit more attention to the "losing" side. In martial arts that are practiced through kata or set piece exercises, it is very easy to "dance" your way through class. While this may look very good, and while dancing is a worthwhile exercise in itself, the process removes the martial from the art. The attacker's part in aikido is a vital part of the practice and as much time should be devoted to it as to the "real techniques" themselves.

Acknowledgments

The author would like to thank Gary Cole, David Shannon, Ken Morgan, Ed Chart and members of the Sei Do Kai for assistance with the photos and article.

index

aikido, definition, 1-2, 13, 95, 144
Aikikai Hombu (headquarters), 18-24, 26, 147
Aioi-ryu, 14
altar (shomen), 43, 45-46, 48-49, 100-102
armlock, 136-137
atemi, striking technique, 23, 27-31, 73, 90, 92, 117 note 1, 126-127, 129-130, 180-185
bayonet, 14
bokken (wooden-sword), 7, 15, 48
bowing, 42-43, 45-46, 48-49, 61-62, 100
breath throw (kokyunage), 122, 125
breathing techniques, 7-8, 21, 38, 46, 122
center (hara), 4, 7, 135
choke, 73, 82, 177
Daito-ryu, 13-14, 16, 37, 39
Daoism, 2
Deguchi, Nao, 37
Deguchi, Onisaburo, 14, 20, 37
diety (kami), 37, 50
elbow lock, 27, 33, 67, 69-72, 75, 78-82, 87, 137
entering throw (iriminage), 76-77, 83, 85
entry technique (irimi), 14, 16, 33, 73-74, 76-77, 80-83, 85, 87, 92, 109, 121, 124, 127-130
fifth teaching (gokyo), 37, 78, 81, 137
first teaching (ikkyo), 33, 74, 78, 92, 110, 137, 172
four direction throw (shihonage), 75, 78-78, 121, 131-132, 134
four-sided throw (shihonage), 72
hakama, 49, 103
halbred (naginata), 59
hip throw (koshinage), 121
Hozoin-ryu, 14
iaido, 58, 89
International Ki Society, 13, 18, 24
Ishiyama, Ishu, 3, 5
katana sword, 48, 57
kenjutsu, 14-15, 58, 144
Ki no Kenkyukai (Ki Society), 13, 18-19, 22, 24, 26
kiai, 39

kicks, 169, 174-176, 178, 182, 184-185
kokyuho, see breathing exercises
kotodama (universal sounds), 39, 96
life energy (ki; qi), 2, 4, 7-9, 13, 16, 20-25, 38, 50, 95-96, 112, 122-130, 132, 149-150, 152, 160, 170, 180
meditation, 2, 4, 6-7, 14, 21, 36, 38, 43, 45-46, 49, 159
Nakamura, Tempu, 20
Omoto-Kyo, 14, 37-40, 95, 144
pressure-point, 21
rei ceremony, 43, 45-46
reverse technique (kaeshiwaza), 28, 133
Russo-Japanese War, 14
sankyo (third teaching), 68, 71, 92, 137
second teaching (nikyo), 70, 73, 79, 81, 131-134, 137, 171
Sekiguchi-ryu, 58
sixth teaching (rokkyo), 137
Shin-Shin-Toitsu Aikido, 13, 19-20, 22-23
shinai, 48
Shintoism, 2, 14, 95-96
shoto short sword, 55
sideways throw (sayunage), 128
spear, 3, 14, 95
staff (jo), 3, 7, 14, 21, 48, 53, 58, 63, 84-90, 93
tachi long sword, 57
Takeda, Sokaku, 14, 37, 50
takemusu aiki, 16, 20, 24, 26
tanto knife, 7, 53, 55-58, 61-93
Tohei, Koichi, 13, 17-24, 26
turning (tenkan), 14, 124
Ueshima, Kissomaru, 20, 54
Ueshiba, Morihei, 2-3, 10, 12-13, 37-39, 45, 49, 54, 95-96, 116, 122, 132, 144
Ueshiba, Yoroku, 13
wakizashi sword, 57
windmill throw, 108
wrist lock, 79, 132
wrist turn (kotegaeshi), 30, 106-107, 131
yonkyo (fourth teaching), 137
Zen, 1-2, 6-7, 13